THE MIDDLE EAST
IMPERATIVES and CHOICES

THE MIDDLE EAST
IMPERATIVES and CHOICES

Alon Ben-Meir

Decalogue Books
MOUNT VERNON, NEW YORK

Library of Congress Catalog Card Number: 75-26110
ISBN: 0-915474-01-8

Copyright ©1975 by Alon Ben-Meir

All rights reserved under International and Pan-American Copyright Conventions.
Published in the United States
by Decalogue Books, Mount Vernon, New York

Manufactured in the United States of America

Acknowledgments

In the preparation of *Imperatives and Choices*, I have been very fortunate in receiving assistance and good advice from many individuals. I am especially indebted to the following:

To Roger Nye, for his assistance and guidance, as well as his much appreciated collaboration.

To Richard Boyer, for his special interest and encouragement, and to Ira Sharkansky for his in-depth review, which contributed significantly to the improvement of the manuscript.

To Professor Victor LeVine, for his constructive criticism and invaluable suggestions, and particularly for writing the *Foreword* to this book.

To Hal Kosut, for his dedicated and proficient editorial review of the manuscript.

To Ira Hirschmann, for many stimulating conversations and for insightful observations.

To Virginia Teague, for her most helpful editorial assistance.

To Miriam Mehler, who has been a devoted and enormously efficient secretary, without whose cheerful patience in typing and retyping the manuscript this book would have been delayed considerably.

To Shirley Langfeld, for her typing of the final draft and for her exceedingly helpful technical suggestions.

To the personnel of *Decalogue Books*, especially William Brandon, Ronnie Freedman and Jackie Levine who deserve the credit for turning my manuscript into a book.

To my many friends in Israel and other countries for their encouragement and help with the research.

Finally, to my very good friend Dr. Janice Dorn, for providing inspiration and intellectual stimulation during our many conversations.

Although I have been influenced by many writers and thinkers, I accept full responsibility for my analyses and interpretations. Needless to say, any shortcomings in this work are mine as well.

A. Ben-Meir

To my wife Dina

to whom I owe more than I can ever repay.

Foreword
by Professor Victor T. LeVine

A colleague of mine recently wondered about Dr. Kissinger's extraordinary standing in American eyes, about his quite remarkable ability to be heard willingly — and with apparent respect — by the major participants in the Middle East conflict, and about the aura of tense expectancy that seems to surround his every foray into the capitals of the perennial antagonists. My colleague also remarked on an oft-remarked irony of the situation: that it was a German Jew, and an Americanized one at that, who of all his peacemaking predecessors — the Jarrings, the Bunches, the Rogers, the Trigvye Lies, the U Thants — seemed for a time to have the best chance of finding a mutually acceptable *modus vivendi* for the most intractable enemies of recent times. Perhaps, my colleague suggested, Kissinger had something special — perhaps a better sense of timing, perhaps a better ear for the real nuances of both Arab and Israeli rhetoric, or perhaps he was just a great deal smarter than the whole pack of them.

At this writing — the end of August, 1975 — Dr. Kissinger's latest attempt at shuttle diplomacy had been crowned by a new Sinai military disengagement agreement. Happily, the new agreement dispelled the gloom caused by the failure — in May — of Dr. Kissinger's first attempt to negotiate the second accord. For a time, it seemed as if Dr. Kissinger's luster had worn off. The parties blamed each other, for being too intransigent, for making impossible demands, and the Ford administration retired into a period of "reassessment" of its Mideast policies, but not before letting it be known unofficially thta it held the Israelis primarily responsible for the failure of the talks. In any event, the August agreement permitted all concerned to voice cautious optimism about the future. Only the Russians, who absented themselves from the formal signing ceremonies, appeared visibly put out by the new arrangement. But the question of Dr. Kissinger's successes or failures lies apart from an explanation of the Kissinger phenomenon, or from the Secretary of State's considerable talents, or from the disagreements attending any particular set of Kissingerian negotiations.

One suspects that the explanation lies not so much with Dr. Kissinger, but in a strange mixture of frustration, anger, resignation, and hope that appears to have seized almost all those unlucky enough to have been caught up in the Middle East's troubles for the last forty years or so. There may be something at work, perhaps caught only in the unlikely metaphor of Alexander and the Gordian knot.

Possibly then, Dr. Kissinger found himself unconsciously cast in the role of a latter-day diplomatic Alexander, expected by all participants to cut the Gordian knot they had somehow tied, strand by strand, in the passion of their frequent encounters. By the end of the October, 1973 war, it may have become clear to the protagonists that all their hacking and hewing — at the knot and at each other — had only served to tighten the knot still further. For all the rhetoric on both sides, it was clear that the October war brought peace not one step nearer. The revelation shattered what was left of Israel's 1967 arrogance, and cast a pall over the Arabs' "victory" celebrations. It forced some "agonizing reappraisals" in the U.S., and almost certainly persuaded the Russians that Arab romances were usually fruitless in the long run. The stage was thus set for Dr. Kissinger: the knot seemed beyond parting, but not beyond being picked apart by someone with both the patience and skill to try. Enter the new Alexander, armed not with sword, but with a kit bag of almost infinitely adaptable small and large bargains.

As was noted above, the Spring, 1975 Kissinger talks failed, leaving the parties facing a resumption of the multilateral Geneva conference that had met briefly in December, 1974. It is interesting to observe that even at this point, the Egyptians showed little enthusiasm for a return to Geneva, in which they would have to confront not only Israel and the United States, but also the Syrians, Jordanians, Iraqis, the PLO, and last but not least, the Soviet Union, and in which Egyptian concerns would become but one of a set of other larger issues. And even at this point the Kissinger-Alexander image continued to exert some effect: Egypt issued veiled suggestions from its own sources (and through friendly Saudi Arabian intermediaries) that if only the Israelis would make some additional concessions, they might be able to turn to Kissinger again. By August, however, both sides had made sufficient mutual concessions for a new agreement to materialize. And again, Dr. Kissinger's patient picking at the knot — combined with pressure on both sides, to be sure, proved a key factor.

Alon Ben-Meir's book comes along at the right time, for it illuminates the strands of the Middle Eastern Gordian knot, and suggests, calmly and judiciously, what it might take for a Kissinger, or anybody else, to pick it apart. His emphasis is very important. Ben-Meir, unlike many who have written on the subject, neither expects nor even hopes for the right Alexandrian (or Kissingerian) sword to resolve the conflict once and for all. The "true formula" for peace does not exist, if it ever existed at all, except in the fevered imaginings of those who hoped that this *war,* or the next, would finally settle the conflict. Peace, Ben-Meir rightly implies, if it comes at all, will come gradually, painfully, and only after a multitude of the smaller knots yield gradually to compromise and growing good will. It need hardly be pointed out that events of the past few months have certainly proved the correctness of his analysis.

Writers of introductions ought not make their prologues into tables of contents, and I will not do so here. But it is very important to note where Alon Ben-Meir has done something unusual or worthy of special remark. In this light, his first chapter has particular merit. In clear and calm language, he sets out the manner in which the great powers, the Zionists, the Arabs, and then the Israelis tied the psychological strands of the great knot. The story itself is too well known to need retelling here; what is important is the blend of contradictory elements involved: Double-dealing *realpolitik* by the great powers, millennial Jewish hopes of Zion restored, the traumatic horror of the European holocaust, betrayal of Arab hopes and trust, and finally, the seemingly endless cycle of bloody and frustrating confrontation between Israeli and Arab. All served to reinforce and crystallize mutually hateful images, and to increase the inability of each side to recognize what is true and legitimate in the other's position. In the end, it almost seemed that Arabs and Israelis had become incapable of recognizing each other, save as distorted reflections of their own fears and suspicions. The Yom Kippur War, asserts Ben-Meir, had at least the salutary effect of clearing the psychological air, enabling both Arabs and Israelis to face, perhaps for the first time in several decades, the realities of each other's needs and aspirations. I'm not entirely sure that either the Syrians or the Iraqis shared fully in these revelations; undoubtedly Col. al-Qadhafi of Libya did not, and certain Fedayeen elements even less so. Yet the point seems to apply to the Jordanians, the Egyptians, as it certainly does to the Israelis. And even if only the Israelis and the Egyptians were so affected, that might be enough to change the situation.

Let me also comment on a few of Ben-Meir's final arguments (Chapter 8) about "Conditions for Peace in the Middle East." As I suggested earlier, he offers little hope that the Middle Eastern Gordian knot can be severed neatly and decisively by some new diplomatic Alexander. He admires Dr. Kissinger, but has no illusions about the enormous obstacles on the road to peace. Moreover, forces other than those over which Dr. Kissinger has any control now operate in the situation. These include new leaders in Israel and Egypt, less bellicose and certainly less committed to the intransigencies of the past; a rediscovery by the superpowers (the U.S. and the Soviet Union) that Middle East brink was closer than either thought; and a new accounting by Israelis and Egyptians of the enormous economic and social toll taken by their protracted conflict. And then, there has been, Ben-Meir argues, a decline in the Soviet Union's influence in the Middle East relative to that of the United States, which has become — partly through Dr. Kissinger's good offices — the only (temporarily?) indispensable guarantor of whatever agreements the principals will work out. Ben-Meir insists that it is, in the final analysis, only the principals who can do the negotiating, since it is only they who can decide on the territorial adjustments that must be part of any final set of arrangements. One can only hope Ben-Meir is right. A new set of more accommodating leaders in both Israel and Egypt (and perhaps Syria), if they become *too* accommodating, could easily fall prey to their respective domestic hawks; the superpowers, even in the full warmth of detente, continue to pour armaments to their respective clients and to insist (in the face of past experience) on the sanity and responsibility of the recipients; the high cost of suicide has not in the past deterred those bent on self-destruction, and less so those involved in a suicide pact; and finally, the history of the past twenty-five years provides little assurance that *any* great power, much less the United States, could long remain in the good graces of any Mid-East country except Israel. A cynic, after considering the mess left by more than fifty years of almost continuous conflict in the area, might well argue that peace could come in only three possible forms: (1) imposed forcibly by the superpowers, (2) as the result of the absorption of Israel into some sort of new Arab hegemonial system, or (3) through a Carthaginian peace, following another war and the total destruction of Israel by Arab armies. I imagine there are no lack of cruel cynics who could argue the above — and other equally imaginative — final solutions to the Arab-Israeli conflict. Happily, Alon Ben-Meir is no cynic, and if he is right (and I hope he is), neither are the most important decision-makers in the United States, the Soviet Union, Israel, and perhaps, in some of the key Arab states.

Alon Ben-Meir's book was not written for the specialist in Middle Eastern affairs, or for the professional expert in matters Arab or Israeli; it is, in any case, too clear and direct for most of them. For that reason, and for its other considerable merits, I commend it to what I am sure will be a wide and appreciative readership.

VICTOR T. LeVINE
Professor of Political Science
Washington University, St. Louis

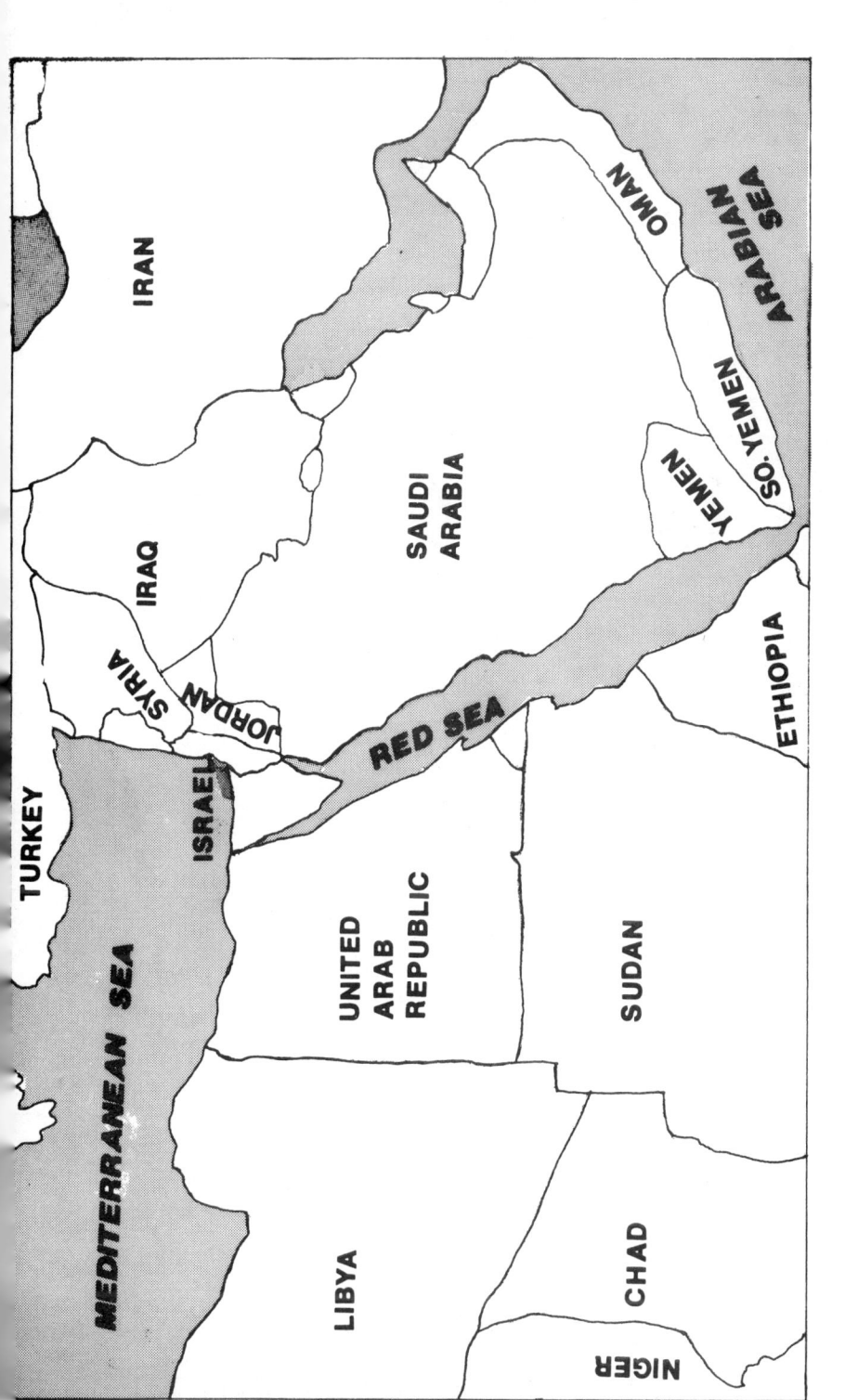

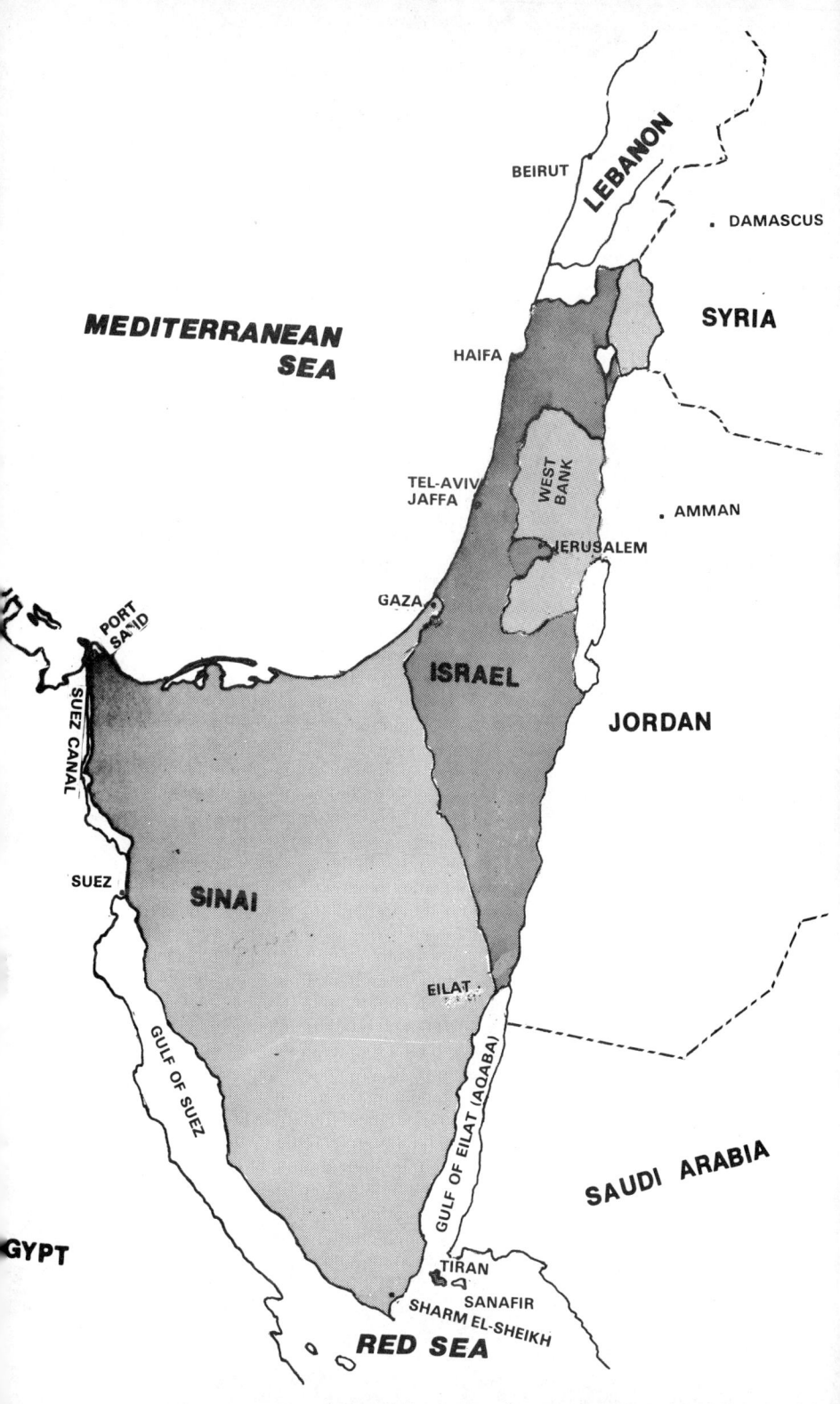

Table of Contents

Acknowledgments

Foreword by Professor Victor LeVine v

Introduction xxii

Chapter I: THE PSYCHOLOGICAL DIMENSIONS OF
THE ARAB-ISRAELI CONFRONTATION ... 3
—The Historical Record
—Exclusionism
—The Partition and the Refugees
—Injured Pride
—Mass Indoctrination
—Myth, Reality, and Disillusionment
—An Opportunity for Negotiation

Chapter II: SOCIO-ECONOMIC DISPARITY 33
—The Arab-Israeli Social Encounter
—The Military Establishment — Objectives and Influence
—Israel's Internal Problems and Social Predicament
—Israel's Class Struggle
—The Privilege of Circumstance
—Political Inhibition
—Shortsightedness
—Israel's Internal Politics
—Israeli Population Growth as a Peace Factor
—Territorial Annexation
—Jewish Birth Rate
—Discouragement of Yordim
—Encouragement of Aliyah
—Oil On Troubled Waters
—Toward Social and Economic Cooperation
—Areas of Potential Cooperation

Chapter III: CONFLICTS AMONG THE ARAB
STATES 67
—The Sources of Arab Internal Instability
—Arab Nationalism
—Ideology of Arab Nationalism
—Arab Socialism
—Arab Unity

Chapter IV: THE PALESTINIAN REFUGEES 95
—The Creation of the Refugee Problem
—Arab States' Attitude Toward the
  Palestinians
—Israeli Attitudes Toward the Palestinians
—The Fedayeen and the Palestinians
—The Role of the United Nations

Chapter V: THE FEDAYEEN
[Arab Palestinian Resistance] 118
—Historical Background
—Ideology and Tactics
—The Alienation of the Arab States
—The Disenchantment of the International
  Community
—The Apathy of the Arab Palestinians
—The Israeli Counter-Measures
—The Ideological Crisis
—The Fedayeen Decline as an Effective
  Terrorist Force
—The Rise of the PLO as a Political Force
—The UN Resolution
—The Rabat Resolution

Chapter VI: THE ROLE OF THE SUPERPOWERS
IN THE MIDDLE EAST CONFLICT 147
—The Regional Importance of the Middle East
—Soviet Penetration
—Russia's Attitude toward Israel

—The New Soviet Tack
—The First Russian Setback
—The Second Russian Setback
—The Third Russian Setback
—U.S. Political Vulnerability in the Middle East
—The Arab Disenchantment with U.S. Policy
—Opposing Objectives
—Conflict of Interests within the Arab States
—The Pursuit of Oil
—American Counter-Measures
—U.S. Interests in the Middle East
—U.S. Psychological Gains Among the Arab States
—Soviet-American Interaction in the Middle East
—Detente and the Middle East: Pros and Cons
—The Arab-Israeli Crisis and Detente
—China and the Middle East

Chapter VII: **ISRAEL'S NATIONAL SECURITY — SECURE BORDERS AND ANNEXATION** . .185

—The Arab States' Contradictory Statements
—Arab Domestic Instability
—Missiles and Nuclear Weapons
—U.S. Defense Treaty with Israel: How Viable?
—Secure Borders and Annexation
—The Golan Heights
—The Gaza Strip
—Sharm el Sheik
—The Sinai Peninsula
—The West Bank

Chapter VIII: **CONDITIONS FOR PEACE IN THE MIDDLE EAST** 202

—Why Peace Must be the Choice
—Peace and Concessions

—Egypt
—Syria
—Jordan
—A Palestinian Entity as a Natural Solution
—Security, Military, Economy, Secure Borders, Self-Determination
—The Fate of the Palestinian Refugees in the Arab States
—Lebanon
—A Word of Caution

Index 219

Introduction

Efforts over the years to negotiate a lasting peace between the Arab nations and Israel have been unsuccessful because until recently the antagonists weren't psychologically ready to enter into meaningful negotiations. Besides, to say the least, political, social and military conditions were most unfavorable. The 1967 and 1973 Arab-Israeli wars, however, have dramatically improved prospects for securing a lasting peace.

As surprising as this might seem at first, the Six-Day War of June, 1967 convinced the defeated Arab nations that Israel was militarily superior. While this made even the acceptance of negotiations with the Israelis far more difficult than ever, it also created a more favorable social, economic and psychological atmosphere as will be documented in this book.

The Yom Kippur War of October, 1973 introduced another important new dimension to the crisis: the Arabs after some initial success on the battlefield, no longer felt militarily inferior and could begin to negotiate with the Israelis more or less as equals. The Yom Kippur War also forced the United States and Russia to reassess their positions in the Middle East and to test their new and fragile detente.

In short, the 1967 and 1973 wars have presented the various factions with a new set of circumstances that compel them to apply more realism and less rhetoric to their pronouncements on peace and war. While the foundation for a durable peace between the Arabs and Israelis had not been securely laid as of September, 1975, it is widely accepted by most scholars and political observers that there is common ground for an accord if the desire for genuine peace prevails, if the will to cooperate can be found, and if the wisdom to make realistic concessions exists. Although such concessions are likely to provoke opposition from hard-line factions on all sides, it appears that the parties to the crisis may now be willing to take limited risks for the sake of establishing a lasting peace.

Several crucial historical trends that enhance the chances for peace in the Middle East have converged to the point where a relative equilibrium (both psychologically and militarily) now exists between the foes. A peace formula could not have been realistically envisioned or formulated without them.

For the last five decades the Jews of Palestine and later on Israel and the neighboring Arab nations, particularly Egypt, Jordan and Syria, have been avowed political and military opponents. The Jews have considered the struggle to be a matter of national survival, while many of the Arabs had long convinced themselves that the total destruction of the state of Israel was imperative. So preoccupied had both sides become with these notions that neither made any significant effort to understand the other's motivations and the psychological needs which lie at the very heart of the controversy.

The outcome of the military confrontations between the Arab nations and Israel in the years 1948, 1956, and 1967 hardened the Arab position even more. Injured pride, sullied honor, and a loss of dignity grew to formidable proportions and outgrew in importance the political-territorial dispute; many Arabs felt that the restoration of their pride and honor could not be accomplished through negotiations, but only through some future military victory over the Jews.

The inherent contradiction between the national aspirations of Arabs and Israelis stemmed mostly from an ignorance of Arab needs on the part of the Israelis, and a lack of understanding of Israeli nationalism on the part of the Arabs. For Israel, and Jews in general, *nationalism* means survival itself in a hostile world. For the Arabs, *nationalism* means Arab unity, Islamic solidarity, economic development, and independence from western colonialism. Israel, understandably, has always refused to compromise her right to exist as a nation; most of the Arabs, on the other hand, have been unable to reconcile their social, political and military misfortunes with the existence of Israel.

The continual confrontation between the Arabs and Israel forced both sides to build military might beyond their economic means. Apart from the effects that such buildup has had on their respective economies, preoccupation with military matters has decisively affected domestic and foreign policies. In short, what one would normally expect to be achieved by sound diplomacy and political realism has often given way to military extremism, with predictable effects on the attitudes and the conduct of the average person in both societies.

Periodic upheavals and political instability in the Arab nations have no doubt further contributed to the prolongation of the crisis between these Arab nations and Israel. Although the Arabs have a common religion, culture and history, until the 1960's the Arab states failed in their efforts to achieve any degree of political unity. They were unable to transcend various geographic, political, sociological, economic and parochial differences, as well as compensate for a general lack of statesmanship. The goal of destroying another sovereign country (Israel) often served as the sole unifying principle among the Arab states.

Therefore, the repeated failures of Arab leaders to produce economic growth, strengthened their need for a scapegoat on which they could put all the blame for the misfortunes they encountered. Israel served that purpose well and diverted the attention of the Arab masses from their more immediate economic problems.

Finally, the promised liquidation of Israel was another Arab hope that was battered again and again. The failure of the Arab countries that surround Israel to accomplish this objective has caused a number of schisms among the Arab states. Jordan, for example, began to accept the facts that Israel was a reality and that coexistence would be inevitable after the 1967 war. The more radical leaders of Libya and Iraq, on the other hand, still insist that the final solution to the Middle East crisis is the liquidation of Israel.

While the Arab nations today cannot claim political unity, they do demonstrate a stronger than ever political, economic and military front. Arab nationalism, an ambiguous concept dating from the turn of the century, has finally developed into a pan-Arab movement which reflects the views of increasing numbers of Arabs. Although many significant political, social and economic differences still divide the Arab states, the revolutionary and the traditional regimes among them seem to be on the threshold of reaching a new era of reconciliation. The conspiracies, uncertainties and fears that marked their relations through the fifties and sixties have given way to dialogue, better understanding and more cooperation. The reasons for this include the transition in Egypt to a "postrevolutionary" leadership (less bombastic and more pragmatic) and the recent Arab achievement of a large degree of military "parity" with Israel. Until now, no Arab leader could even suggest negotiating an agreement with Israel and hope to survive politically.

The increasing political consciousness of the Arabs (particularly those living in the countries surrounding Israel) seems to have produced a new set of values as a byproduct. They realize that internal stability as well as tranquil relations among the Arab nations is a prequisite to making peace with Israel. The Arab nations, by and large, have also come to the conclusion that the status of "no war — no peace" with Israel has not been serving the cause of stability. The social and the economic needs of most Arab nations have become so urgent, particularly in Egypt since 1967, that a new war with Israel is viewed as undesirable and futile. The years of constant confrontation between Arab and Israeli may at best have contributed to political maturation and internal stability on both sides, certainly pre-conditions for the start of meaningful negotiations. The repercussions of the October war on both the Arab nations and Israel have set the stage for testing this political maturity.

The Palestinian refugee situation is another crucial aspect of the Middle East problem which must be resolved before an enduring peace can be achieved. While the Arab states have frequently assumed the task of representing the refugees, they have usually subordinated the interests of the Palestinians to their own. The Arab countries on the one hand have perpetuated the dilemma of the Palestinians by using the refugees as pawns in order to extract maximum concessions from Israel and the international community. Israel, on the other, has generally exempted herself from any responsibility, apart from offering a certain amount of compensation to the refugees willing to settle permanently in one of the Arab nations.

An important factor in the struggle of Palestinians was the growth in popularity and strength of the *fedayeen* (The Palestinian resistance movement). The history of the fedayeen is explored in detail in this book in order to provide the basis for appreciating the events of the fall of 1974, which brought the PLO again to the fore.

American-Soviet relations in the Middle East have decisive implications for war and peace and this topic is also analyzed. The position of the two big powers with regard to their "clients" in the Middle East may ultimately dictate how meaningful and durable an Arab-Israeli peace will be. The Middle East has become an extension of the United States' struggle with the Soviet Union for new spheres of influence and domination, and is an integral consideration in their global policies. Such being the case, the Middle East may be amenable to what U.S. Secretary of State Henry A. Kissinger terms "a new world order, based on the concept of detente as a prerequisite."

Although the Soviet understanding of detente or relaxation of international tension differs from that of the American, both sides still seem extremely anxious to preserve it. However, since the Soviets have generally adopted foreign policy positions with the intention of retaining a degree of flexibility, the question must be posed about the extent to which the Soviets would be willing to compromise their stakes in the Middle East for the sake of detente. The same question may be asked about the People's Republic of China, although China's involvement in the Middle East is relatively negligible at this point.

In view of recent American peace efforts in the Middle East, will the Soviets continue their support of the extremist Arab revolutionary regimes? By the same token, one might ask whether the American reconciliation with some of the Arab nations (Egypt, Syria, Algeria) will affect her commitment to Israel, and if so, to what degree? And finally, what factors are involved in the American commitment to Israel?

In addition to the impact of the United States and the Soviet Union on Middle Eastern affairs, there are other broader considerations to examine. What effect, if any, does NATO have on the Middle East? Will the reopening of the Suez Canal make the Persian Gulf a new site of military buildup similar to that in the Mediterranean? What spill-over effects does the Chinese-Soviet rivalry have in the Middle East? The answers to these questions are of great significance and will be dealt with at length in the text.

The Arabs and the Israelis are beginning to realize that today's global power structure, i.e., an "equilibrium of invulnerability" between the United States and the Soviet Union, makes the use of force between nations or the threat of force a much less effective and determining factor in solving ideological or territorial differences, for the U.S. and the Soviet Union can intervene in one form or another to bring about the kind of resolution they want. The Arabs and the Israeli leaders recognize that their overdependence on the United States and the Soviet Union for arms impedes their freedom of action; they tend to lose control of their own affairs, even when their national survival is at stake.

From the point of view of Israel, its national security depends upon secure, defensible borders. Israel's leaders believe, contrary to the Arab position, that peace with the Arabs is not by itself a guarantee of security. Rather, Israel contends that her security would be jeopardized even after a peace treaty has been signed. Two considerations warrant this contention: first, the instability of the Arab regimes with their constant internal turmoil, rivalry for power, and the presence of conspiratorial groups arising out of the lack of a habituated system for the orderly transfer of power; second, the credibility gap that present and past leadership has created with Israel through its half-hearted peace negotiations, accompanied by unrelenting war against Israel.

America's consistent support of Israel gave rise to some speculation late in 1973 that a permanent defense treaty between the United States and Israel might be a vital contribution to Middle Eastern political stability as well as a substitute for Israel's demand for secure borders. However, the U.S. experience in Vietnam and the outcome of that involvement have made the Israelis somewhat skeptical about this kind of guarantee. Israel's leaders also do not feel that the stationing of Soviet troops on a permanent basis between Israel and her Arab opponents (as has been suggested by Russia) would serve either Israel's interests or those of the United States. Such an arrangement might result in taking away from the Israelis as well as from the Americans the flexibility to react appropriately to any given situation. It would also make the Soviets a permanent factor in the preservation of peace. Israeli leaders usually consider three measures indispensable and pertinent to their nation's security: a formal peace, secure borders, and a strong military posture. Without the inclusion of all three factors, it is doubtful whether a durable peace can be achieved.

Despite all the difficulties which shouldn't be underestimated, peace between Israel and the Arab states, particularly those that surround Israel, seems likely in the foreseeable future. Israel realizes that its ultimate survival is contingent on a durable peace with the Arab states. Besides, it would bring economic advantages to both sides. For this reason, the governments of Egypt, Jordan and Syria have begun to adopt a more realistic approach to the Israeli problem. Besides, the use of force by itself has proven ineffective in resolving the confrontation.

While the Six-Day War of 1967 seemingly widened the gap between the national objectives of the Arabs and the Israelis, it is my belief that the war also put an end to the Arab delusion that it could eliminate Israel. They have come to the realization that although the United States may reasses periodically its policies toward the

Middle East it will not abdicate its commitment to Israel's survival. I suspect that for the Arab leaders — President Nasser and King Hussein particularly — to adjust pyschologically to this harsh reality was a vital step that made the tacit acceptance of peace negotiations with Israel possible. The decision of President Anwar Sadat of Egypt and President Hafez Assad of Syria, with the possible collaboration of the Soviet Union, to go to war in 1973, was made in order to salvage a degree of national pride and prestige without which Egypt, Jordan, and Syria could not have taken the second step, namely to speak overtly about peace with Israel.

There is no doubt that each of the countries involved in the Middle East crisis wants a peace that serves its interests, at least for the immediate future. And there is no guarantee, of course, that an Israeli peace treaty with the Arab states would last several generations. The Middle East region has been, is, and will continue to be, a region rife with rivalries. However, present conditions are such that at least a temporary peace must be reached if a new regional, or possibly global, calamity is to be avoided.

The timely American peace initiatives in the Middle East since late 1973 are of historic importance. Not only have Israel and the Arab nations that are in direct conflict with her come to accept the notion that peace is the only recourse, but also the Soviets, due to their economic difficulties and their increasing fear of China's intentions in the Far East, have been induced to cooperate with the United States in the peace effort. That is not to say that the Soviet Union will not shift her policy when it suits her interests to do so. Yet the U.S. remains at a political and economic advantage, while the Israelis and the Arabs directly involved in the crisis are at a comparative disadvantage due to their dependence on the United States and the Soviet Union respectively for modern armaments and financial help.

The Palestinian refugees, whose status must be resolved before peace can come to the Middle East, have also concluded that their interests will best be served by reaching an accord with Israel. After visiting the West Bank and the Gaza Strip in 1967, 1969, 1973 and 1975, and meeting scores of Arabs from various countries, I have come to the conclusion that the only permanent and just solution is a Palestinian entity within the limits of the West Bank and probably the Gaza Strip. Although Israel and Jordan will reject this idea in principle, both countries will sooner or later have to come to grips with the heart of the issue; that is, that no peace agreement between the Arabs and Israelis can endure without some kind of Palestinian autonomy. I maintain that such a solution is the only practical one that no party to the Middle East crisis can reject on moral, legal, or territorial grounds. The last twenty-seven years of Arab-Israeli confrontation have introduced psychological, social, economic, political, and military changes in the region. A new equilibrium has been shaped, based not necessarily on military forces, but rather on mutual needs and mutual vulnerability. It offers an opportunity which none of the antagonists can afford to pass by.

ALON BEN-MEIR
Saint Louis, Missouri

THE MIDDLE EAST
IMPERATIVES and CHOICES

Chapter I

THE PSYCHOLOGICAL DIMENSIONS OF THE ARAB-ISRAELI CONFRONTATION

A most important aspect of the Middle East dispute that has not received adequate attention by either Arabs or Israelis has been each side's lack of understanding of the other's emotional and psychological needs. The political and territorial disputes that have characterized the Arab-Israeli conflict since 1948 resulted in part from basic psychological differences. Each side's misapprehensions of the other's motives and actions have prolonged the hostility, impaired diplomatic efforts and made the dispute appear irreconcilable.

To begin to understand the respective psychological make up of the Israelis and Arabs it is necessary to study how each developed historically. This will help provide an explanation as to why the two opponents have not been able to "reconcile" or "satisfy" their psychological needs. Hence, the events that have largely contributed to the continuing conflict between Arab and Jew in the Middle East must be examined, particularly those that occurred before and during the Six-Day War of 1967. Since that time, a greater awareness on the part of each antagonist of the other's psychological needs has begun to develop. And the period from 1967 to 1973 must be carefully analyzed to understand why some of the mutual psychological misapprehensions that are crucial stumbling blocks to negotiating a settlement, let alone real peace, have been partially removed.

THE HISTORICAL RECORD

Two thousand years of pogroms and persecutions culminating in the Nazi holocaust contributed immeasurably to Jewish thinking and behavior after World War II. A generation motivated not only by long held religious ideals but also by a newly reasserted national pride directed its energies toward building a Jewish state that would finally put an end to the persecution of Jews.

> *In the eyes of the younger, post-Zionist generation, the holocaust has thus come to confirm the basic tenets of classical nineteenth century Zionism: without a country of your own, you are the scum of the earth, the inevitable prey of beasts.**

The Israeli perspective is provided in the following excerpts from the State of Israel's Proclamation of Independence (published by the Provisional State Council in May 14, 1948), which explicitly asserts the psychological motivation behind the creation of Israel. In the first place, the Proclamation speaks of the relationship between *Eretz Yisrael* (Palestine) and the Jews:

> The land of Israel was the birthplace of the Jewish people. Here their spiritual, religious, and national identity was formed. Here they achieved independence and created a culture of national and universal significance. Here they wrote and gave the Bible to the world.

The Proclamation then deals with the Jewish people who occupied that land and with their fate — a destiny that bound them psychologically and emotionally to the land.

> *Exiled from the land of Israel, the Jewish people remained faithful to it in all the countries of their dispersion, never ceasing to pray and hope for their return and the restoration of their national freedom. Impelled by this historic association, Jews strove throughout the centuries to go back to the land of their fathers and regain their statehood. In recent decades they returned in masses. They reclaimed the wilderness, revived their language, built cities and villages, and established a vigorous and ever-growing community with its own economic and cultural life . . . and looked forward to sovereign independence.*

---

*Amos Elon, *The Israelis: Founders and Sons*, (New York, Holt, Rinehart & Winston, Inc. 1971), p. 267.

After establishing this historical relationship between the land and the people, the Proclamation of Independence reasserted the right of the Jews to a home in Palestine by pointing out the moral obligation of Britain, which was then politically responsible for most of the Middle East region.

> In the year 1897, the first Zionist Congress, inspired by Theodor Herzl's vision of the Jewish state, proclaimed the right of the Jewish people to national revival in their own country. This right was acknowledged by the Balfour Declaration of November 2, 1917, and reaffirmed by the Mandate of the League of Nations, which gave explicit international recognition to the historic connection of the Jewish people with Palestine and their right to reconstitute their National Home . . . The recent holocaust, which engulfed millions of Jews in Europe, proved anew the need to solve the problem of the homelessness and lack of independence by means of re-establishment of the Jewish state which would open the gates to all Jews and endow the Jewish people with equality of status among the family of nations.

Finally, the Proclamation set the tone for the future:

> The state of Israel will be open to the immigration of Jews from all countries of their dispersion, will promote the development of the country for the benefit of all its inhabitants, will be based on the principles of liberty, justice, and peace and conceived by the prophets of Israel, will uphold full social and political equality of all its citizens without distinction of religion, conscience, education, and culture, will safeguard the holy places of all religions and will loyally uphold the principles of the UN charter . . . We extend our hand in peace and neighbourliness to the neighbouring states and their people, and invite them to cooperate with the independent Jewish nation for the common good of all. The state of Israel is prepared to make its contribution to the progress of the Middle East as a whole.

The creation of Israel was thus based on several fundamental principles that Israelis deemed non-negotiable. Palestinian territory alone could provide a site that would be historically, culturally, and religiously meaningful to the Jews. Palestine, or Zion, was the source, the birthplace of Jewish culture and faith, the land where God first appeared to the Jews, the land where the first and second temples were erected.* No other land, it was felt, could offer them the same kind of haven from harassment and the recovery of a lost heritage.

Although the Arabs do not deny in principle the historical, cultural, and religious relationship between the Jews and Palestine, they maintain nonetheless that the founding of Israel was based on the Western guilt feeling for the persecuted Jews, especially after the Nazi experience, and The Western Powers' desire to implant an "imperialistic tool" in the midst of the Arab nations for long-run political expediency. Whether it was a guilt feeling on the part of the Western countries or a Jewish "historical right," or otherwise, the existence of a growing, thriving Jewish community in Palestine could not be denied. Observers wrote:

> *We know of no country to which the great majority can go in the immediate future other than Palestine. Furthermore, that is where almost all of them want to go. There they are sure that they will receive a welcome denied them elsewhere.***

> *During the last two or three generations, the Jews have recreated in Palestine a community, now numbering 80,000 ... This community with its town and country population, its political, religious, and social organization, its own language, its own customs, its own life, has in fact "national" characteristics. When it is asked what is meant by the development of the Jewish national home in Palestine, it may be answered that it is not the imposition of*

---

*The first and second temples are considered by the Jews to be the holiest of the holy temples. Both were located where today's Wailing Wall stands in Jerusalem. The Wailing Wall is actually one of the external walls of the second temple. The first temple was destroyed by the Babylonians in 586 B.C.E. The second temple, built 70 years later, was destroyed by the Romans in the year 70 A.D. For Jews everywhere, the Wailing Wall, which came under Israeli control in 1967, is as holy as the temples themselves.

**Excerpts from Document 21 of the Anglo-American Committee of Inquiry that was published on May 1, 1945.

> *a Jewish nationality upon the inhabitants of Palestine as a whole, but further development of the existing Jewish community, with the assistance of the Jews in other parts of the world in order that it may become a center, which the Jewish people as a whole may take on grounds of religion and race and interest and pride.* *

Since 1948, when the state of Israel was born, Israelis, natives as well as immigrants, have felt themselves living in a state of political and geographical isolation. During this period, Israel has been mobilized as if for a permanent state of war. The heavy loss of lives and resources as a result of the four wars (1948, 1956, 1967, and 1973) and other intermittent military operations, deepened the psychological and socio-economic gap between Israel and the Arab states that surround her to the point where Israel's sense of isolation became deeply rooted. Against the background of the Nazi holocaust, this sense of isolation intensified and gave rise to a pessimistic solitary philosophy which is a chief characteristic of the Israeli mind set.**

> *When the images cast upon the dark mirrors of the mind at a very crucial early stage were those of a veritable Dantean hell, it was a hell that included extermination of one-third of the Jewish people. The Nazi holocaust caused the destruction of the very same Eastern European world against which the early pioneers had staged their original rebellion, but to which, nevertheless, Israel became both outpost and heir. There is a latent hysteria in Israeli life that stems directly from this source. It accounts for the prevailing sense of loneliness, a main characteristic of the Israeli temper since independence. It explains the obsessive suspicions, the towering urge for disaster to happen. It explains the fears and prejudices, passion, pain and pride that spin the plot of public life and will likely affect the nation for a long time to come.* ***

---

*Excerpts from Document #12, statement of British policy in Palestine, issued by Winston Churchill in June 1922. (The Churchill White Paper of 1922.)

**Elon, *op. cit.* p. 278

****Ibid.*, pp. 259-260.

These psychological and emotional factors gave a tenacity to Israel's stand in its more than a quarter-century of confrontation with the Arab nations. "How can we be expected to negotiate away our past?" the Israeli leaders inquired. Our future cannot be envisioned from a vacuum; our entire existence began in Palestine and proceeded from there; then there can be no future for Jewish life without the past which is the foundation of our religious and cultural heritage.

This concept was expressed long before the establishment of the state of Israel. Ahad Ha-am, one of the most influential philosopher-writers advocating the return of the Jews to Palestine, in one of his philosophical essays, observed:

What one means when one says "I" is not hair or fingernails that might be here today and end up in the trash tomorrow. "I" is the unification of one's memories with his wants; in other words, the combination of one's past with his future ... The concept "I" is a spirit blended with inner strength and unified in some mysterious way with the memories and the impressions of the past. *

Jewish nationalism, then, is based on the fulfillment of religious, psychological and emotional needs. The creation of the state of Israel was the concrete political expression of that nationalism.

Most of the Arab leaders, on the other hand, seemed unable to comprehend or accept the emergence of this Jewish nationalism. Until the early 1920's, the Arabs had generally treated the Jews kindly and tolerated their religious differences. As to the Jews in Palestine, however, most Arabs tended to view them as an inferior racial minority with no political thrust or ambition.

For close to fourteen hundred years, the Middle East has been preeminently the spiritual center of the Islamic world, the birthplace of the Muslim faith where the civilization of Islam reached its classical formulation. Although the political and administrative unity of the Arab empire was destroyed over the centuries through repeated invasions and internal dissent, the religious and cultural unity of the Arab world has been maintained. The Arab domination

---

*Ahad Ha-am: *The Writings of Ahad Ha-am*. (Jerusalem: The Jewish Publishing House, Ltd., 1956) p. 81. Ahad Ha-am is the pen name of Asher Ginsberg, born in Skovina, Russia, in 1856 and died in Tel Aviv in 1927.

of the Middle East has, in effect, never ceased, and Arabs as well as Jews can and do claim historical, moral, and legal rights to Palestine. As early as 1908, the Arabs were voicing their objection to a Jewish home in Palestine. The following excerpts from evidence submitted by the Arab Office in Jerusalem to the Anglo-American Committee of Inquiry in March 1946, concisely presented the Arab side:

> The Arabs of Palestine are descendants of the indigenous inhabitants of the country, who have been in occupation of it since the beginning of history. They form the majority of the population; as such, they cannot submit to a policy of immigration which, if pursued for long, will turn them from a majority into a minority in an alien state . . .
>
> Geographically, Palestine is part of Syria; its indigenous inhabitants belong to the Syrian branch of the Arab family of nations; all their culture and tradition link them to the other Arab people . . . . It is demoralizing to the population [i.e., Palestinians] to live under a government which has no basis in their consent and to which they can feel no attachment or loyalty . . . . The chasm between the administrative system and the institutions of Palestine and those of the neighboring countries is growing and her traditional Arab character is being weakened. The entry of incessant waves of immigrants prevents normal economic and social development . . . . It [influx of Jews] is bound, moreover, to arouse continuous political unrest and prevent the establishment of the political stability on which the prosperity and wealth of the country depend . . . The superior capital resources at the disposal of the Jews, their greater experience of modern economic technique, and the existence of a deliberate policy of expansion and domination have already gone far toward giving them the economic mastery of Palestine . . . . It should not be forgotten, too, that Palestine contains places holy to Moslems and Christians, and neither Arab Moslems nor Arab Christians would willingly see such places subjected to the ultimate control of a Jewish government.

Sharing similar Semitic origins, Jews and Arabs have by and large existed side by side for generations. Indeed, when the idea of building a Jewish home in Palestine was first seriously contemplated, neither the Jews nor the Arabs envisioned any violent confrontation. The Jews living in the Arab states have undoubtedly experienced occasional anti-Jewish outbursts. For example, the rise of Rashid Ali, who was pro-Nazi, in Baghdad during World War II, gave impetus to the anti-Jewish movement, culminating in 1941 in a massive pogrom against the Jewish community. In that one outbreak, over 150 Jews were killed and many scores injured, while Jewish property was looted or destroyed. Yet despite such sporadic anti-Jewish violence, many Jews who lived in Arab countries viewed the entire Middle East as one Islamic entity, as did the Arabs, and therefore believed that they had the right to live in the place of their choice within the region. They naturally chose the birthplace of their ancestors which is Palestine.

Unlike the Jews, the Arabs were not homeless and landless, and they had not been systematically and methodically persecuted over the centuries as an outcast minority. The Jews had come to the bitter realization that until they had a country of their own, they would always be considered strangers and beggars in their respective host countries. They had neither name nor right nor acceptance as equals among the community of nations. To be blunt, they were the "bastards of humanity."

Vladimir Ze'ev Jabotinsky (1880-1940), a leader of the Zionist-Revisionists, stated the case quite clearly in a statement made in the British House of Lords, February 11, 1937:

> *The Arabs' claims confronted with Jewish claims; I fully understand that any minority would prefer to be a majority; it is quite understandable that the Arabs of Palestine would also prefer Palestine to be the Arab state number 4, number 5 or number 6 — that I quite understand. But when the Arab claim is confronted with our Jewish demands to be saved, it is like the claim of appetite versus the claim of starvation. No tribunal has ever had the luck of trying a case where all the justice was on the side of one party and the other party had no case whatsoever. Usually in human affairs, any tribunal, including this tribunal, in trying two cases, has to concede that both sides have a case on their side, and in order to do justice, they must take into consideration what should constitute the basic justification of*

> all human demands, individual or mass demands — the
> decisive terrible balance of need. I think it is clear.*

Working in an atmosphere of national fanaticism, the Zionist organization did, in fact, promote a Jewish revolution leading to a national home, but did not contemplate that the fulfillment of the Jewish national aspiration would have to be, at least in part, at the expense of other nationals.

> *Hindsight may make this sound unbelievable today. The fact is that Arab nationalism was clandestine before 1908; it came to the surface only after the Young Turks' revolution. Before 1908, a few of the settlers and none of the Zionist leaders in Palestine and abroad ever contemplated the possibility that Arabs and Jews one day would clash in a bloody battle over the stretch of soil, as the Germans and French over Alsace or the Turks and Greeks over Thrace.* **

Showing lack of foresight, the Zionist leadership, headed by Theodor Herzl, ignored what it considered to be the "Arab problem." Zionist leaders were certain that the indigenous Arabs would receive the Jews with open arms. After all, they assumed, Jewish settlement in Palestine could only benefit the Arabs, and that harmony and cooperation would prevail.

> *Zionism was as much a product of the new age of nationalism as was its Arab protagonist. The clash in Palestine was not between native and colonialist in the ordinary sense, but between two nationalist movements. Both were in their own way "right" and "natural." The fault, if there was one, lay less with the men directly involved on both sides than with the new world of ferociously hostile nation-states in which they lived. If men had higher aims, there would have been no Palestine conflict, nor, probably, "Jews" and "Arabs."* ***

---

*A Zionist-Revisionist is a Zionist Jew who maintains that the Jews should not only have a state of their own in Palestine, but also establish such a state within its ancient historical borders, (including the West Bank, the Gaza Strip and what is now Jordan).

**Elon, *op. cit.*, p. 175.

****Ibid.*

Yet the national aspirations of both the Arabs and the Israelis were slowly taking shape; for the Jews, the goal was a national home in Palestine; for the Arabs, the goal was national independence over the same land. Clashes between the growing Jewish settlement and the native Arab community were inevitable.

Minor clashes between the Jews and the Arabs erupted as early as 1910. Violence against Jews in Palestine intensified greatly after the Balfour Declaration in 1917. In April, 1920 in Jerusalem, and in May, 1921 in Jaffa, Jews were murdered in outbreaks of violence. At that time, it became obvious that attempting to fulfill the nationalist demands of both groups would be at the least very difficult and at the most extremely costly, bloody, and painful.

In August, 1929, 133 Jews were killed and 339 injured in the religious centers of Hebron and Safad. In the 1930's, Arabs, encouraged by the Higher Arab Committee, raided Jewish settlements. About 80 Jews were killed and 396 wounded in 1936. Jewish retaliation was limited in the beginning to self-defense, and to trying to achieve coexistence by peaceful means. However, by 1936 Arab attacks were followed by Jewish retaliation. The report published in July, 1937 by the Palestine Commission of Inquiry under Earl Peel clearly stated that the underlying causes of the continuing Arab-Israeli disturbances (most recently the Arab revolt of 1936) were (1) the desire of the Arabs for national independence and (2) their hatred and fear of the establishment of the Jewish national home. The commission found that Arab and Jewish interests could not be reconciled under the British Mandate. The Peel Report suggested, therefore, that Palestine be partitioned.

In his *Memoirs*, David Ben-Gurion, Israel's first prime minister, stated the Jewish case to George Antonius, an historian and leading theoretician of Arabism, on the eve of the Arab rebellion in 1936:

> It is not by caprice that we return to this country. For us it is a question of existence, of life and death. We have come here and shall come here whether there will be or will not be Arab-Jewish understanding. Riots will not stop us. If we have the choice between riots in Germany, Poland, or in any other country, or riots in Palestine, we prefer riots in Palestine. Still I ask, what is better for both our sides — to fight or to help one another?

After the Arab revolt in 1936, both the Jews and the Palestinian Arabs decided to pursue their mutually exclusive objectives by adopting social and economic measures and countermeasures as well as military ones. Thus deepened the conflicting aims of Arabs and Jews and placed the entire Middle East in bloody and constant turbulence that continues right up to today.

EXCLUSIONISM

Arab hostility toward the Jews, intensified after the early 1920's, prompted the latter to concentrate more and more on their own economic and social welfare. The better-educated and the better-skilled Jews put their knowledge into practice; within a few years the old traditional saying from the Diaspora "We have come to Zion to build and be built" — became a reality. The Zionist leadership emphasized what was termed "Hebrew labor," which, *ipso facto*, excluded Arab labor from all Jewish enterprises.

There is deep and tragic irony in the fact that the policy of Avoda Ivrit [Hebrew labor] was in its time seen as a means to avoid or allay conflict between the two nations. In some ways it made the conflict worse. It might have given Jewish colonialists a sense of moral superiority over colonial settlers elsewhere; at the same time, it compounded the future tragedy by causing the deliberate exclusion of the native from the new society. It prevented the establishment of a joint basis upon which, perhaps, in the fullness of time, a binational policy opens to all might have been tried.*

For at least four decades prior to the establishment of the state of Israel in 1948, the Arabs in Palestine, and those Arabs who surrounded Palestine, consistently refused to acknowledge or accept the Jewish right to exist as a separate political entity in Palestine. In response to this uncompromising stance, the Jews began to solidify their position by slowly separating themselves from the Arab community. Educational and social exclusion followed economic exclusion, each of which gave impetus to greater hostility and a deeper sense of distrust between the two communities.

*Elon, *op. cit.*, p. 224.

THE PARTITION AND THE REFUGEES

By 1947, the decades of intensified hostilities had reached a decisive point. The United Nations' decision of November 29, 1947 to partition Palestin, which included most of the Negev, a narrow stretch along the Mediterranean coast, and a number of parcels of land on the northeast along the border of Syria and Jordan, as had been recommended in principle by the Peel Commission ten years earlier, was immediately rejected by the Arabs. The Arab rejection of the partition plan was based primarily on political, nationalistic, and territorial reasons. Psychologically, the partition symbolized another Jewish victory over the Arab "might." Here again, one important factor must be emphasized: the mere idea of creating a Jewish state in Palestine was unacceptable to the Arab leaders. The resulting atmosphere of psychological incomprehension, shock, and disbelief gave rise to the bloodiest confrontation between the Arabs and Jews up to that point.

Despite cease-fires in June and July, 1948, fighting continued until February 24, 1949, when Israel and Egypt signed armistice agreements, and similar pacts were signed with Jordan, Lebanon and Syria. The War of Independence left thousands dead on both sides.

However, the events that followed were to overshadow the immediate bloodshed. A new tragedy with far-reaching consequences was beginning to unfold. Within weeks of the beginning of the war, more than 600,000 Arab refugees fled to Jordan, Syria, Lebanon, Iraq, Egypt, the West Bank, the Gaza Strip, and in much smaller numbers to other Arab countries, adding a new and important dimension to the Arab-Israeli crisis. Whether the mass departure of the Arab Palestinians was prompted by the Jews in order to obtain more territory or secure borders, or whether it was encouraged by the Arabs in order to promote a world reaction, these questions remain without a definitive answer. Nevertheless, the refugee problem added another complication to the Arab psychological posture toward Israel.

As far as Israel was concerned, the mass exodus was a direct result of the Arab states' invasion, without which no refugee problem would have been created. Thus Israel felt morally and legally exempt from any obligation toward the Palestinian refugees.

For the Arabs the refugees were a mark of disgrace and infamy which gave impetus to their consistent refusal to assume any responsibility for the refugees' fate. The refugee problem was to plague all sides in the Middle East maelstrom, providing the momentum for the three wars that followed, and eventually giving birth to the Palestinians' resistance movement (Fedayeen).

INJURED PRIDE

The humiliating defeat in 1948 of the combined Arab armies of Egypt, Syria, Lebanon, Iraq, and Jordan shattered any hope of a psychological reconciliation and understanding between the two camps. Arab suspicion, hatred, and fear of the Israelis were now buttressed by matters of pride, honor, and national dignity.

> *The emergence of Israel in 1948 — or rather the failure of the Arab armies to prevent it — was a climactic event in the history of the Middle East, comparable in many ways to the landing of the Greeks in Izmir in 1917. It was bad enough to be dominated by the Franks, but they were after all the invincible masters of the world, who on both occasions, had just defeated their enemies in a great war. It was a very different matter and an intolerable humiliation, to submit to the Greeks or Jews — to local Dhimmis whom the Muslims had long been accustomed to despise as inferiors. The Franks, moreover, would sooner or later go back where they came from. The Greek great idea — MEGALE IDEA — of a revived Byzantine empire and the Zionist idea of a revived Jewish state were clearly intended to be permanent. The military defeat in Palestine at the hands of the despised Jews was a terrible shock.* *

The Arab attaches much importance to his pride and honor. Arab proverbs express this explicity: "Better die with honor than live with humiliation," and, "The head that has no pride deserves to be cut." Arab pride, of course, is not just individualistic, but extends to the glory of his past and the Arab contribution to civilization as well.

---

*Bernard Lewis, *The Middle East and the West*. (Bloomington: Indiana University Press, 1967) p. 125.

Just as the Arabs failed to understand the psychological motivation behind Jewish nationalism, especially prior to 1948, Israel also failed to appreciate Arab psychological needs, particularly after 1949. Diplomatic efforts to achieve a peaceful settlement between the Arabs and the Israelis through the UN between 1948-1956 were all in vain. The Israelis were clearly unwilling to modify their position in any way through negotiation or otherwise, and the Arabs were similarly unwilling to compromise their pride. That is not to say that the question of pride was the only problem between the Arabs and the Israelis. Political and territorial differences were the main issues, yet at that point in time they were given secondary importance. The crushing defeat in 1948 made questions of pride, national dignity, and honor assume such a formidable role that nothing else seemed to matter to the Arabs.

The internal rivalries, political instability, and turmoil that engulfed the Arab states in the years following 1948 only contributed to their psychological hysteria in regard to Israel. No Arab nation was willing to assume the responsibility for what was termed a "national calamity." The blame and the responsibility for their military defeat and for the creation of the state of Israel altogether were shifted to the Western Powers, mainly Britain and France. Meanwhile the Arab masses were told to prepare themselves for the "day of judgment" when the Israeli state would be liquidated.

Britain and France were cast as the imperialistic powers that had the mandate over most of the Middle Eastern states. England was blamed for the Balfour Declaration of 1917, with France as an accomplice. The immediate recognition of the state of Israel by Britain and France was taken by the Arabs as supporting evidence that Israel was just a tool in the hands of the imperialists. The Soviet Union's immediate recognition of the state of Israel was not viewed by the Arab states as having any special significance because Britain and France were playing the main roles at the time in Middle Eastern political affairs.

The Israelis were jubilant about the outcome of the War of Independence. The keeping of additional territories captured beyond the United Nations partition lines was justified by pointing out that it was the Arab states who declared war in the first place. And the Israelis were unwilling to assume any moral or legal obligations toward the Arab Palestinian refugees.

MASS INDOCTRINATION

The Arabs' national pride compelled a rationalization and justification for the setbacks in terms which would not reflect poorly on the Arab leaders' judgments, policies, and military weakness. Massive propaganda campaigns in Egypt, Syria, Jordan, Iraq, Lebanon, and other Arab countries employed two themes. One discredited Israel's military victory in the war of 1948 and called for its liquidation. The other stimulated Arab nationalism, socialism, and unity.

Both themes required the spreading of false information, which was justified on the grounds of national interest. As S.M. Swemer observed "If a lie is the only way to reach a good result, it is *halâl* (allowable). A lie is lawful when truth leads to unpleasant results; tell the truth only when it leads to good results."* And indeed, lies were common in the official media. The truth was distorted in the "national interest," i.e., to protect the incumbent leaders' reputations, honor, and high political positions.

With regard to the first theme, Israel was labeled as the imperialist tool by which the Western Powers intended to exploit the Arabs. Israel was blamed for all Arab misfortune and disunity. Israel was painted as a monstrous creature that, unless exterminated, would contaminate the Arab world and slowly destroy it from within.

> *The establishment of Israel in 1948 is commonly referred to by the Arabs as a calamity so great that it reflects not only upon their military prowess, but injures in an almost metaphysical sense, the whole human order or being. Israel is an abominable crime; it is a "cancerous growth;" an injection of unspeakable evil.* * *

The only solution to the Israeli problem according to Arab thinking at the time, was therefore to excise the "cancerous growth," until which time the Arabs were resolved not to rest. This strong desire to eliminate the newly-born Jewish state supplied the

---

*S.M. Swemer, *Childhood in the Moslem World*. (New York: Fleming H. Rewell Co., 1915), p. 115.

**Elon, *op. cit.*, p. 286.

thrust for an intensive and unprecedented (by Arab standards) propaganda campaign geared against the sworn enemy.

> *The winds of propaganda blow day in and day out, and after a time, they are deafening. The manipulation of mass feeling, the shrill discourses of Cairo Radio and the lectures of the controlled press are wearing on the spirit of those who have to take them for long. The world seen at a cockeyed angle through the narrow lens of the political propagandist is a depressing and claustrophobic place.* *

With the guidance of East and West German experts, Egypt in particular engaged every conceivable communication medium — newspapers, television, radio, bumper stickers, sign-posts, textbooks, and mass leaflets — and used the most sophisticated equipment available to build a new pan-Arab image and give a new direction to the Arab people. Children born after 1948 heard on the radio, saw on television, and read in the newspapers and school textbooks that their destiny, welfare, dignity, and national pride depended on only one thing — the total destruction of Israel.

However, the psychological warfare and threats of future annihilation, intended to generate momentum among the Arab population, developed among the Israelis greater efforts to achieve unity and solidarity. Whatever small good will and common ground for understanding had existed previously appeared to evaporate at this point. It should be emphasized that the Arab leaders, particularly the late Egyptian President Gamal Abdel Nasser, believed that the elimination of Israel was inevitable, and on that premise Nasser himself, followed by the other Arab leaders, intensified his propaganda campaigns through the years 1952-1968.

The anti-Israel campaign was only one side of the coin. Slogans such as "Democratic-socialist-cooperative society," and "Republicanism, nationalism, and socialism" were the other side, emphasizing unity and cooperation among Arabs, and neutralism toward others.

This theme resulted in an intensified propaganda campaign against the Western powers. They too, with Israel, shared the brunt

---

*Winston Burdett, *Encounter with the Middle East*. (New York: Atheneum, 1969), p. 6.

of the Arabs' antagonism and hatred. The Arab propaganda that was waged vigorously against Israel and the West became a way of life for the average Arab. The propaganda reinforced not only the Arab misapprehension of the Israelis, but also the prejudice Israelis felt toward the Arabs.

> *Arabs often do seem to believe their own propaganda about Israelis, and the Israelis in turn often view the Arab as a simple-minded person who must be treated like either a child, or a wild fanatic who should be handled like a mad dog. The stories one hears about Arabs, of course, are very similar to the tales one hears in America's deep South concerning the Negro.* *

Why did the Arab populace so thoroughly accept the propaganda? Sania Hamady gives us a clue in *Temperament and Character of the Arabs:*

> *The Arab is characterized by an inflated personality. He shows overt self-confidence, challenges and menaces anyone who accuses him of fear, and demonstrates daring and courage. His apparent strength, however, is not commensurate with his real power. Yet his self-praise and strength are, interestingly, sincere. There is no discrepancy between the show of courage and his feelings. Not conscious of any role-playing, the Arab does not know that he is hiding some weakness behind this facade. He believes in himself and is not aware of the internal weakness that may be driving him into such bombastic behavior.* **

MYTH, REALITY, AND DISILLUSIONMENT

The secret arms negotiations between Nasser and the Soviets which culminated in Egypt's purchase of weapons from Czechoslovakia became known on September 27, 1955. This

---

*Ray Vickers, *The Kingdom of Oil.* (New York: Charles Schribner's Sons., 1974), p. 235.

**Sania Hamady, *Temperament and Character of the Arabs.* (New York: Twayne Publishers, 1960), p. 59.

agreement gave Nasser the weapons he needed for the ongoing confrontation with Israel and offered Russia a diplomatic and military foothold in the Middle East. Both parts of the bargain were to have far-reaching political consequences. The arms deal was followed by another slap in the face of the West, namely, the nationalization of the Suez Canal on July 26, 1956. When Anglo-French negotiations with the Egyptians over the operation of the Suez Canal broke down, the military invasion of Egypt by Britain, France, and Israel resulted.

The Sinai Campaign of 1956 was another humiliating shock to the Arabs, especially to Egypt. Continued Israeli military superiority demonstrated the futility of attempting to solve the dispute with Israel by force. Although the Egyptian army was crushed, Egypt did not concede defeat, particularly after Israel, Britain, and France received an ultimatum from the United States and the Soviet Union to immediately cease all military operations. On November 6, 1956 the Sinai War ended, only eight days after it began. For all practical purposes, Egypt emerged triumphantly, for Israel was warned by the U.S. to evacuate the Sinai or face economic sanctions, while Britain and France agreed to abdicate their rights in the Suez Canal. Nasser was thus, in effect, handed a political victory by the U.S. State Department.

The natural Arab reaction in the wake of a military defeat that they had not acknowledged, and of the political victory that was handed to them was to guard and promote national pride more fiercely than ever. More specifically, the propaganda against the Western Powers and Israel was intensified, coupled with accelerated military preparedness.

The cease-fire between Israel and Egypt soon proved its fragility. Although UN troops guarded the truce, Israel continued to exchange fire with the Egyptians in the south, the Jordanians in the east, and the Syrians in the north. Israel's retaliations deep into Egypt, Syria, and Jordan were causing heavy Arab casualties, yet Nasser was still determined ultimately to wipe Israel off the map. The period from 1956 to 1967 were years of psychological warfare accompanied by Arab and Israeli attacks and counterattacks. Both sides, feeling the constant danger, built and trained bigger, better and more sophisticated armies. Egypt, Jordan, Syria, and Iraq, apart from the other Arab states, tripled their military manpower and arsenals.

To a large extent, the Arab and the Israeli economies tended to be "military economies." Billions of dollars were invested in the military buildup, often at the expense of urgently needed social welfare programs. The immediate parties to the conflict, namely, Israel, Jordan, Syria, and Egypt, were not and are still not independent economically; economic aid in terms of hard currency and food supplies were always sought from outside sources. Arab and Israeli political leaders were forced to justify the exorbitant expenditures on the military, and felt it necessary to prove to their respective populations that their military preparedness was not in vain. Thus, military indoctrination of the civilian populace came to prevail in both societies.

After the 1956 Sinai campaign, Israel agreed to return the Sinai and the Gaza Strip to Egypt in return for a U.S. guarantee that international waterways such as the Suez Canal and the Gulf of Aqaba at the Red Sea would be opened to her. Although Nasser adamantly refused to allow any Israeli ships to pass through the Suez Canal, Israel took some consolation from the fact that her ships from Elath were passing through the Strait of Tiran, east of the southern tip of the Sinai Peninsula, providing access to the Arabian Sea and the Far East. This was a factor with inescapable psychological and economic implications. As long as this status quo was maintained, Israel was willing to accept it and to make every effort not to alter the situation by provoking the Arabs, particularly Nasser.

In May of 1967, Nasser found himself challenged by the Syrians and some militant factions within his own country. Syrian leaders told him that the Arab cause was being severely damaged by maintaining a status quo, and that unless new measures were taken to offset the "relative coexistence" with Israel, the right of the Arabs to regain their "homeland" would be in danger of being forgotten.

Nasser, in order to assert his leadership, accepted the Syrian challenge by attempting to show the Arab world that he was not hiding behind the UN truce force. At this juncture events accelerated. On May 16, 1967, Nasser demanded the withdrawal of the United Nations Emergency Force from the Sinai, and his request was immediately granted. Then, not satisfied with this political victory, Nasser eight days later dispatched his troops to close the Gulf of Aqaba to all ships heading to or from Israel.

In his speech at the United Arab Republic Advanced Air Headquarters, May 25, 1967, Nasser declared on Radio Cairo, "The armed forces yesterday occupied Sharm el-Sheik. What does this mean? It is affirmation of our right and our sovereignty over the Gulf of Aqaba. Under no circumstances will we allow the Israeli flag to pass through the Gulf of Aqaba. Our armed forces and our people are ready for war." Indeed, the closure of the Gulf of Aqaba, taken by Israel as an act of war, was fated to change the course of history in the Middle East, psychologically as well as politically.

While Israel criticized the UN decision which accepted Nasser's ultimatum to withdraw the United Nations Emergency Force from the Sinai, Nasser moved rapidly, unimpeded by any international pressure, mobilizing his civilian and military resources to advance and station themselves in the area. All of these measures were taken with the consideration and knowlege that it was now up to Israel to make the move. It appeared to be a clear and open challenge for war.

Whether or not Nasser meant to go to war remains uncertain. One thing, however, is pertinent: the Soviet Union played an important role in the involvement of Nasser in the soon-to-come Six-Day War. The Russians feared the collapse of the Syrian government, which was under growing internal pressure to act in the face of Israeli retaliation. Thus, the Soviets tried to create certain strategic and political conditions which would persuade Nasser to redeploy his army to the Sinai and hence to divert Israel's attention to the danger on its southern border. However, Russia miscalculated, for Israel's and Egypt's actions were contrary to the Soviet's expectations. Nasser was overwhelmed by his own rhetoric and protestations of war and victory, and made a serious mistake by closing the Gulf of Aqaba. Israel, overwhelmed by her sense of danger and isolation, moved swiftly to destroy the armies of Egypt, Syria, and Jordan. Egypt and Russia soon lost control of the swiftly developing events. Russia's expectation of cashing in on a political victory through political shrewdness and military maneuvering ended with a new Arab disaster.

Winston Burdett, in his book, *Encounter with the Middle East*, analyzed the situation in a similar fashion:

> "The Russians had both a problem and an opportunity. Their problem was to rescue their Syrian proteges and their

> opportunity was to parlay a difficult situation into a major political victory. The man who held the key was Nasser, if he could be induced to ensure the survival of the Syrian regime with a dramatic demonstration of his readiness to act . . . They [the Russians] decided to place in his hands [Nasser] the initiative for a diversion. He would demand and secure the withdrawal of the UNEF . . . The purpose of the diversion was to shift the locale and transform the nature of the crisis. The Egyptian mobilization would oblige Israel to concentrate the main body of her forces on the Sinai frontier; it would deter her from any bold retaliatory action elsewhere, and it would save the Syrians . . . Both Nasser and the Russians could expect a handsome political reward, he as the saviour of the Syrians, and they as the sponsors of resounding political victory for the Arab revolutionary states."*

On May 26, 1967 Hassanein Haykal, who acted as spokesman for the Egyptian regime, wrote in his weekly column in the semi-official newspaper *Al Ahram*:

> I believe an armed clash between the United Arab Republic and Israel is inevitable. This armed clash could occur at any moment . . . To Israel this is the most dangerous aspect of the current situation. It is not a matter of the Gulf of Aqaba but of something bigger. It is the whole philosophy on which Israeli existence has pivoted since its birth and on which it will pivot in the future. For many reasons, chiefly psychological, Israel cannot accept or remain indifferent to what has taken place. This means that the next move is up to Israel. Israel has to reply now; it has to deal a blow. It is in the light of the compelling psychological factor that the needs of security or survival itself make acceptance of the challenge of war inevitable.**

Thus Israel was challenged by threats and actions: a psychological challenge with sensitive and overwhelming implications, and an

---

*Burdett, *op. cit.*, pp. 199-203.

**Hassanein Haykal: An Armed Clash with Israel is Inevitable — Why? *Al Ahram*, Cairo, May 26, 1967.

economic one whose implications far exceeded the importance of free navigation and amounted to both an economic siege and an act of war that Israel could not accept under any circumstances. The war itself was stunning, swift, and surprising by any military standards. Israel demonstrated a capability that amazed military observers all over the world, and shocked and humiliated the armies of Egypt, Syria, and Jordan. In less than a week, Israel's military captured territory three times larger than Israel itself. They took thousands of prisoners of war, hundreds of pieces of heavy military equipment, and above all, the Gulf of Aqaba fell under Israeli control. The high point of the war in the view of many Israelis was the "recapturing" of the city of Old Jerusalem. General George Marshall, U.S. military historian, called the Six-Day War "The Four-Hours War." Indeed, four hours after the outbreak of the war, the outcome became clear to any military observer who had access to inside information on the overall military operations. By that time, the air forces of Egypt, Jordan, Syria, and Iraq were practically demolished. Their air fields were destroyed and their ground troops were left at the mercy of the Israeli air force. Egypt, Jordan, and Syria suffered a humiliating defeat at the hands of the Israeli army — a defeat that they publicly acknowledged. For the first time, after twenty years of Arab-Israeli hostilities, the Arab leadership — Nasser and Jordan's King Hussein — assumed the responsibility for this military setback. Egypt lost the entire Sinai Peninsula as well as her control over the Gaza Strip. Jordan lost the West Bank with the City of Old Jerusalem, and Syria lost the strategic stretch of land, the Golan Heights. Apart from the territorial losses and gains, the Six-Day War had very far-reaching psychological ramifications for both sides.

The Sinai Campaign of 1956 taught Israel that battlefield victories are meaningless if followed by political surrender. The Arab leadership, particularly President Nasser and King Hussein, learned that the Arab-Israeli conflict could not be solved by military means alone. It was this humiliation of the Egyptian, Syrian, and Jordanian armies by the Israelis in 1967 that signified, in my view, that a political and military shift in the policies of all concerned would have to take place.

The propaganda campaign gradually shifted after 1967; Arab statements threatening liquidation or annihilation of Israel, so common before the Six-Day War, were replaced by statements that coexistence with Israel would be acceptable if Israel returned all territories captured during the Six-Day War and permitted Arab Palestinians either to return to their homeland or receive proper compensation. In January, 1975, former Israeli Foreign Minister Abba Eban revealed that he had met on several occasions after the Six-Day War with King Hussein of Jordan, to explore ways of finding an amicable solution to the Jordanian-Israeli crisis.

Although the new Arab political posture was not widely circulated, it had now become psychologically possible for the Egyptian and the Jordanian leadership to speak about making some accommodations with Israel. Arab intellectuals generally responded favorably to this new approach. At the same time, in order to retain some flexibility in its options, the Arab leadership continued mouthing its hawkish attitude toward Israel.

Cecil Hourani, for ten years an adviser to President Bourguiba of Tunisia, in an article in the daily *El-Naher*, Beirut, in November, 1967 observed:

> *At this moment when the destiny of the Arab nation is being decided, it is the duty of every Arab thinker to witness the truth as he sees it without fear and without dissimulation. For too long has the field of publicity and expression been left in the hands of professional demagogues, blackmailers, and semi-educated fanatics. Our silence, on the one hand, their vociferation on the other hand, has led the Arab nation not merely to disaster but to the brink of disintegration. Our first effort must surely be to win a victory over ourselves: over defeatism on the one hand, extremism on the other. These two dangers are in fact intimately linked together. The real defeatists are not those who look facts in the face, accept them, and try to remedy the situation which brought them about, but those who refuse to do this, who deny fact, and who are thus preparing for new defeats.*

Two years later, Hassanein Haykal echoed this theme in *Al Ahram*:

> *The Arab world suffers a crisis of deafness, because the Arabs do not know the truth, and a crisis of suspicion because they do not believe the truth when they hear it. There is a crisis of conscience between the governments and*

the people: how can we activate the crisis, this is the big problem. *

For his part, the Arab soldier was once again humiliated. He became more determined to meet the future better prepared militarily, for now he would be fighting for his own honor, not for an abstract cause such as unity or Arab socialism.

The effects of the Six-Day War on Israel were not all salutary, either. From a purely psychological point of view, the victory did not serve Israel well in the events that followed. Despite the occupation of new territory for the avowed purpose of creating more secure boundaries and of providing Israel with an even stronger bargaining position, the 1967 "victory" became merely the prelude to another war six years later. This is not to say that if Israel had not captured more territory, the Yom Kippur War (October, 1973) would not have taken place. It is the psychological repercussions that concern us here. The Israeli soldier started to believe that there must be a special myth about himself, and that he truly might be invincible as well as "invisible" now that the Israeli military had proved its superiority so dramatically. The civilian leadership, too, was affected, as Yuval Elizur and Eliahu Salpeter discuss in *Who Rules Israel?*:

There has been a considerable increase in the prestige and influence of the military elite in Israeli public life since 1967. In part, this is due to their role in the Six-Day War. But it is also due to the role they played in the days before the war when it became evident that the country's civilian heads depended to a great extent on the military elite for their strategic thinking. **

From 1948 until 1967, Israel openly sought to negotiate a peaceful resolution of Arab-Israeli differences. However, the Arabs refused to enter into any meaningful negotiations because until 1967, most Arab nations still believed that the liquidation of the state of Israel was possible and inevitable. The outcome of the 1967 war, however,

---

*Al Ahram, daily, Cairo, June 1969.

**Yuval Elizur and Eliahu Salpeter, *Who Rules Israel?* (New York: Harper and Row, Publishers, 1973), p. 219.

made President Nasser reconsider his position toward Israel, and forced King Hussein of Jordan to declare that the ultimate solution must be found through peaceful negotiations.

After his defeat, Nasser declared himself ready for the first time to negotiate for peace. For Nasser to use the word "negotiate" directly or indirectly in reference to Israel was in itself a major concession. Having gone this far, he refused, however, to make any additional moves that might be interpreted as evidence of weakness and that could jeopardize his own political security.

The war of attrition initiated by Egypt early in 1969 was designed to aggravate the Israeli forces on the east bank of the Suez Canal, rather than as a long-range policy aimed at the final destruction of Israel. Nasser accepted U.S. Secretary of State William Rogers' truce agreement late in 1970, partly because of the heavy damages inflicted by Israel's artillery and air force and partly (probably mainly) because of his growing conviction that a military solution could not resolve the conflict with Israel. Therefore, coexistence became a new option.

Nasser's belief that Israel did not desire a peaceful solution justified any act of belligerency on his part if only for the sake of national prestige. A few months before his sudden death in September, 1970, Nasser confided to some close aides that he wanted to create a *fait accompli* by landing an Egyptian military force on the east bank of the Suez Canal and establishing a solid position there, at whatever cost, in a desperate effort to salvage national pride.

Israel, on the other hand, emerging overwhelmingly victorious in the Six-Day War, did not feel compelled to make any substantive moves toward a peaceful settlement. Although the late Prime Minister Levi Eshkol declared immediately after the war that Israel was ready to negotiate with the Arab states as equals, Israel would, in fact, be negotiating from a position of strength and on her own terms. The Arabs could not consent to Israel's proposal for negotiations, for by doing so would have meant *de facto* recognition of Israel, and that in itself was not politically acceptable. The paradox following the Six-Day War was that while the Arabs refused either to accept Israel between 1948 and 1967 or to accede to any meaningful negotiations during the same period, Israel, after the 1967 war, felt strong enough politically, militarily and economically not to rush into any negotiations that were not predominantly in her favor. Ironically, although the territorial and the political disparity between the Arab states and Israel became greater in the aftermath of the Six-Day War, both sides came to recognize that coexistence had become a viable solution. Still, the psychological acceptance of each other was not enough to overcome the new emotional and political difficulties that the Arab states were faced with in the wake of the Israeli military victory. This development, however, was not at the time fully appreciated by either side.

Ignoring the Arabs' sensitivity in matters of honor and pride. Israel sought to capitalize on their humiliation in 1967. Once the Israeli military had achieved battlefield victory, it perhaps would have been wise for the Israeli government to translate military success into useful and practical diplomacy. The Israeli leaders failed to see that in order for the Arabs to negotiate, a degree of strength in *their* negotiating position also was an absolute necessity.

In the 1962 Cuban missile crisis, for example, diplomacy supported by the threat of military force compelled Soviet Premier Nikita Khrushchev to withdraw the Soviet offensive missiles from Cuba. President John F. Kennedy did not capitalize on the Russian backdown. In order not to humiliate its rival, the U.S. government made no victory statements. In this instance, a policy of quiet diplomacy avoided what might have developed into a nuclear confrontation and World War III.

The stalemate in the Middle East that prevailed between 1967 and 1973 was not working in favor of the Arabs. (Dissension among university students in Egypt was on the rise, and the frustrations of young Egyptian army officers was increasing.) The national stigma of successive defeats had to be removed, Arab leaders felt, if they were to remain in power.

Meanwhile, Israel enjoyed unprecedented economic growth and prosperity during the post-1967 period. But she paid comparatively little attention to the overall explosive Arab situation and displayed little understanding of the precarious Arab position. The failure of the Egyptians and the Israelis to reach an interim settlement sponsored by U.S. Secretary of State William Rogers in mid-1970* merely cleared the way for resorting once more to the use of force.

---

*The interim settlement called on the Israelis to retreat some 15-20 miles from the Suez Canal, to the Mitla and the Gidi passes. Israel's refusal to withdraw her forces was based on her insistence that the Egyptians not station any soldiers on the east side of the canal, and that only civilians be allowed to cross for the purpose of reopening the canal. Egypt's insistence to the countrary brought the negotiations to a deadlock.

Thus the stage was set for the October war of 1973. Although Israel emerged victorious by military standards, her victory was not total, and the Arabs did not suffer total defeat. To the Israelis, partial victory was frustrating, and to a point, humiliating; the Arabs, on the other hand, could survey their own display of initiative and resistance as positive gains, a kind of victory over their previous military record. The Israeli military setback at the outset of the hostilities and her political concessions to the Arabs after the ceasefire with Egypt and Syria provided exactly the psychological boost the Arabs needed to enter into negotiations from what they felt to be a position of strength.

The Arab armies, especially Egypt's, had improved noticeably since 1967 as a result of better training and new equipment. Since the Arabs did not expect to win a total war, they started their offensive with limited objectives, namely, to show some military prowess, an ability to coordinate their armies and to recapture some lost territory — especially the east bank of the Suez Canal. Even if their armies were heavily battered, they could still claim a partial victory by virtue of the heavy damage inflicted on Israel.

As Dr. Hassanein Haykal observed in *Al Ahram* (March 27, 1969):

> *In any future battle, the Israeli army would face Arab armies with different standards of firepower and its use, different command structures benefiting from past experience, and a higher morale, as the Arab forces would be aware of fighting for the heart of their homeland and not only for its borders.*

AN OPPORTUNITY FOR NEGOTIATION

Israel in the last 27 years, and particularly between 1967-1973, has progressed rapidly in her scientific and technological achievements, especially in the areas of economics, defense and education. Everything seemed to be thriving at an accelerated rate.

As Jews world-wide advanced themselves in science, medicine, and the arts, Israel became the natural recipient of their knowledge and experience, in addition to money and military equipment. Consequently, Israeli culture and industry have developed significantly in a relatively short time.

The social, economic, and military steps in the occupied territories were geared to provide better conditions for the Arab Palestinians. By doing so, Israel hoped to reduce the Fedayeen influence as well as demonstrate her willingness to work hand in hand with the Arabs. Coexistence could be shown to be possible.

In addition, the development of good working relations at the personal, business, and governmental levels between Israelis and Arabs on the West Bank and the Gaza Strip made the Arab leaders, particularly President Anwar el Sadat of Egypt, apprehensive of Israel's "true" objectives in those territories. They suspected that Israel's temporary occupation of the areas gained in the 1967 war might lead to permanent annexation.

Israel has never before exercised military dominance in an area where a conflict of interests between the United States and the Soviet Union existed and where its survival directly depended on those powers. Israel's own military strength has guaranteed its success in all four rounds of war between 1948 and 1973 and as a result its military establishment has been able to increase its influence over Israel's policy-making. Thus, especially toward her adversaries, Israeli policies have become flavored by its military so Israel has come to be recognized as a military power that even the U.S. and the Soviet Union must take into consideration in formulating their Middle East policies. Israel, with little experience in exercising military power, failed to make better use of its military strength, especially in the wake of the Six-Day War. It failed to demonstrate a capacity for diplomatic achievement equivalent to its capacity for military action. In other words, Israel pursued a military policy rather than a political policy that was supported by military power.

> *But the most important influence by far of the defense establishment on the country's civilian authorities is exerted by the head of the Intelligence branch of the defense establishment. His evaluation and reports are a basic element in the government's assessment of possible and probable reactions of the enemy to any proposed course of action . . . On the political level, the defense concepts developed by the military elite are translated directly into government policy, such as the policy of retaliation of the*

1950's or the 1968 concept of static defense along the Suez Canal, and thereby have impact on Israel's international relations. *

In order to bring the conflicting parties together; either Israel would have had to suffer some military humiliation by the Arabs, or to have made major territorial and political concessions to them. Either occurrence might have discouraged future hostilities for the sake of national pride, if not for the purpose of recapturing lost territories. This was precisely what the October war of 1973 provided; the national prestige of Egypt and Syria was at least in part salvaged.

Another outcome of the October war was to force Israel to realize that the ultimate guarantee of her national survival is a durable peace with the Arab states. Big power assurances could only be an added measure to her security, not a substitute for peace. Continual warfare would be self-defeating for the Israelis from both an economic and manpower perspective. Israeli troops could never hope to occupy Cairo, Damascus, Amman or Baghdad for any length of time, so a policy of total Israeli military victory would be costly and fruitless.

The Arabs themselves also awoke to a new reality after the last war. While the Six-Day War ostensibly widened the gap between the national aspirations of the Arabs and the Israelis, it also shattered any hope on the Arabs' part of bringing about the liquidation of Israel. The psychological adjustment of the Arab states to the realization that Israel could not be erased from the map was a vital step forward in the eventual acceptance of peace negotiations with Israel. The Arabs decided to go to war in October, 1973 not to reverse the principle of accepting Israel's de facto existence, but to salvage a degree of national pride and prestige without which the Arabs could not have taken the second step, namely, to speak overtly about peace with Israel, while at the same time attempting to gain maximum territorial and political concessions.

Those who criticized Henry A. Kissinger, U.S. Secretary of State, for calling for cessation of hostilities in October, 1973 when Israel was on the verge of consolidating its victory, did not appreciate that only under such circumstances (i.e., when Israel could not have a

---

*Elizur and Salpeter, *op. cit.*, p. 203.

total victory and Egypt could claim partial victory) would Egyptian President Sadat be able to negotiate as an equal, and the Israelis be able to accede to certain concessions because of no other choice (meaning American diplomatic pressure). Total Israeli victory would likely have made disengagement impossible and would have only produced another round of fierce fighting.

Chapter II
SOCIO-ECONOMIC DISPARITY

Some observers of the Middle Eastern scene contend that the Arab-Israeli crisis is basically a confrontation between two different civilizations. Relations between Arabs and Jews have been uneasy since the turn of the century; differing social and economic values have often made their respective political outlooks and life styles appear irreconcilable. While such values have obviously contributed to the present disparity between the two groups, political and military differences as well as cultural and religious tendencies have played an even more important part in bringing this situation about.

Despite the profound differences between the Israeli and Arab societies in terms of social outlook and economic viability, it is possible the social and economic convergence and cooperation might have been achieved had recent political and military considerations not overshadowed more peaceful social and economic pursuits. And as we shall see, cultural and religious differences were an additional obstacle that made any reconciling of the more overt socio-economic differences all the more difficult.

THE ARAB-ISRAELI SOCIAL ENCOUNTER

The Arab-Israeli social confrontation has manifested itself throughout their cultures — in, for example, such a basic commodity as land and the concept of land "ownership." As early as 1900, Jewish immigrants to Palestine felt their relationship to the land was practically sanctified. New arrivals believed that the achievement of Jewish social and economic independence was directly related to the ownership of this land. But more important to these settlers than even land acquisition was the establishment of a relationship between the worker and the land by which he made his livelihood.

In 1903, the Zionist movement assigned land holdings to a special agency — the Jewish National Fund (*Keren Kayemeth Le'Israel or KKL*] — which purchased land from the indigenous Arabs —

mostly absentee owners — to hold for perpetuity in the name of the Jewish people. This ownership structure had far-reaching implications for future land acquisition and especially for subsequent political developments. A Jew, any Jew, who emigrated to Palestine, could obtain a parcel of land from the Jewish National Fund (JNF) for any mutually agreed upon use provided:

(1) the land was actually used for the stated purpose;

(2) the land remained in the possession of the original user or was given as an inheritance to one person;

(3) the land was not for sale but leased for a nominal fee to be renewed every 50 years upon request; and

(4) no absentee ownership was permitted.

This concept of land holdings was and still is unique.

The acquisition of land in Palestine was seen as essential to Jewish national survival; it was considered prerequisite for a sense of security and social coherence. The political implications of this concept were many. Land speculation was reduced to a minimum, making possible long-range planning concerning land development and distribution. Moreover, land holdings continually increased as a result of contributions from Jews throughout the Diaspora for this specific purpose. In 1930, however, acquisition of land, either individually or collectively, was officially banned by the British who controlled Palestine at the time.

The reclamation of desolate land by the JNF had a strategic objective as well. The JNF would reclaim an uninhabited, remote stretch of land for a new settlement to serve as an outpost for protection of the lands to the west. It was primarily on KKL land holdings that the United Nations partitioned Palestine in 1947. From its inception, the KKL was engaged primarily in land reclamation, reforestation, constructing access roads, starting new settlements, and building initial housing when needed. The KKL continued such work even after the establishment of the state of Israel in 1948. And in 1966, the scope of the organization's responsibility was expanded and it became the land-developing authority in Israel. At that time, the Israeli government turned over all its land holdings to the JNF. Today the organization holds and administers approximately 90 percent of the entire land area in Israel, occupied territories not included.

In contrast to this unique movement that provided Jewish immigrants with the basics needed to begin a new life, most of the Arab Palestinians along with the Arab masses in surrounding areas were subjected to a system of absentee land ownership which neither improved the condition of the land nor the efficiency of the occupant, while appropriating more than half the crop. The Arab social structure consisted of two tiers: a small group of wealthy landowners and a dependent, poverty-stricken peasantry. This division produced neither a sense of responsibility for the land nor a concern for the well-being of the farmer.

> *The whole region with the exception of the Jews in Palestine, is included in the groups of population which derive at least 70% of the energy of their diet from cereals and roots. A considerable part of the population probably belongs to the groups deriving 80% of its calories. That is to say, the area is included among the worst-nourished parts of the world. The underlying cause of poverty of the rural masses was thus attributed to the inequitable distribution of land.* *

While the Jews felt a sense of cooperation, security, and social coherence, the Arabs engulfed in perpetual poverty, lived in an atmosphere of misery, lack of solidarity, and insecurity. Although neither society was directly affected by the other's land policies, the unequal land distribution among Arabs along with aggressive KKL land reclamation projects promoted expressions of hatred and envy on the part of the Arabs toward the Jews. And the Jews in turn displayed contempt for the miserable Arabs.

What further complicated the encounters between the two groups was Jewish preference for Jewish labor because many of the immigrant Jews were highly skilled and knowledgeable in educational, technical, and scientific fields. This resulted in a further widening of the economic gap between the Arabs and Jews, and in addition the Jews were able to quickly expand their educational facilities, in particular in the areas of science, business, management, and medicine. The period from 1936 to 1948 was marked by significant scientific and educational advances.

---

*Arthur Mills, *Present Day Economic and Social Conditions* (New York: Frederick A. Praeger, 1959), p. 231.

The Arabs, by contrast, paid little attention to the development of their educational systems; they made no long-range plans for expanding their educational facilities in such vital fields as economics, science, and business. An exploited peasantry, poverty, and preoccupation with interests of the immediate circle — family and tribe — marked an Arab society which had been isolated from western technology for centuries. The European Jews who emigrated to Palestine in increasing numbers from the 1920's onward were psychologically equipped to work hand-in-hand with the indigenous Arabs, but found to their astonishment that their efforts were repulsed. Technical aid and offers of scientific assistance were turned down, not because they weren't needed, but because traditionally the Arab was too proud to accept assistance, particularly from someone whom he had despised and subordinated for generations.

Amos Elon, in his book, *The Israelis: Founders and Sons*, recalls a conversation that David Ben-Gurion, Israel's first prime minister, had with Mussa Alami, a moderate Arab nationalist during which he told Alami that Jews would come and settle in Palestine whether or not there was an agreement, but he would prefer to have one. Ben-Gurion proposed Jewish autonomy within a larger federation of independent Arab states. In return for Arab Palestinian acquiescence, Ben-Gurion offered large scale economic assistance and technical know-how to the Arabs of Palestine. Mussa Alami, according to Ben-Gurion, bluntly dismissed such aid as unacceptable. "I would prefer the country to remain desolate for another one-hundred years until we Arabs are capable of developing it ourselves." Recalling this talk years later, Ben-Gurion admitted that at the time he himself felt, "If I were an Arab, I would say the same."*

Another important factor underlying Arab rejection of Jewish technical aid was a fear that there would be no end to Jewish expansion. The Arab states whose fears were nourished by radical Zionist campaigns developed the notion that the newly-born Jewish state would expand at their expense. It became a matter of strict policy, therefore, not to cooperate with Israel either socially or economically.

---

*Amos Elon, *The Israelis: Founders and Sons* (New York: Holt, Rinehart & Winston, Inc.), pp. 236-237.

The Arab League* advocated a boycott of Israeli businesses, warning Arab enterprises not to deal with any company having economic or other trade relations with Israel. This boycott policy met with only partial success. Many West European and American companies refused to be intimidated and continued to maintain trade relations with Israel even at the risk of losing their Arab markets.

Behind the Arab states use of economic sanctions against Israel lay fears of territorial expansion, economic growth that would be able to subsidize larger and more powerful military forces, and Israeli take-over of Arab markets. Ray Vickers, while a reporter for *The Wall Street Journal,* recounted a part of his conversation with Wasfi Tell, then prime minister of Jordan.

> *Since a country like Jordan needed so much development, why, I asked him, could not the technology and the drive of the Israeli be wedded with the manpower of the Arab to transform the whole region into a prosperous land? He had a sour expression on his face as he answered, "If such a situation like that developed and there was freedom of movement and capital, the Jews would end up by owning Amman.* * **

Mussa Alami and Wasfi Tell were not isolated examples. Such thinking appears to have been based on principle, pride, fear and a strong desire to be both independent and uncompromising. Each side recognized the need for social contact but for different reasons, each tried to exist without depending upon the other. Gradually, any hopes for social cooperation gave way to deep mutual antagonism and eventual hostilities.

Thus the early social encounter between Arabs and Jews evolved into a permanent situation of separation between both societies. The continual hostilities that followed, erupting periodically into total

---

*The Arab League was established in March 1945 at Bludan, Syria and was composed of five kingdoms: Egypt, Saudi Arabia, Iraq, Transjordan, Yemen; and two republics: Syria and Lebanon. Libya joined the Arab League in 1953 and Sudan in 1956.

**Ray Vickers, *The Kingdom of Oil* (New York: Charles Scribner's Sons, 1974), p. 234.

military confrontation, (1948, 1956, 1967, and 1973) transformed a social separatism into a political-military doctrine bent on resolving the Arab-Israeli crisis by force or threat of force.

THE MILITARY ESTABLISHMENT-OBJECTIVES AND INFLUENCE

One of the most striking phenomena in the Middle East, particularly in Israel and those Arab countries in direct confrontation with Israel (Syria, Jordan, Egypt, and Iraq), is the pervasiveness of their military establishments. The uncompromising position that the Arab states developed with regard to Israel's right to exist was met by a vigorous Israeli determination to counterbalance Arab military power in order to ensure her own survival. Both sides eventually found themselves devoting a great deal of attention and money to their military preparedness.

The repercussions, however, of building huge armies loomed more significant than the military expenditures themselves. The steadily growing armies gained increasing influence over civilian political authorities, and in Syria, Egypt, and Iraq the military assumed political office through a military revolution or coup. Historians and political scientists may differ as to the reasons behind the extensiveness of military influence in so many middle Eastern countries, including Israel.* In my view, the following must be considered in any explanation of the dominance of the armed forces in nominally civilian politics: (1) a feeling that the citizens of any country might develop when surrounded by enemies and who have to be under constant siege (Israel); (2) when civilians fail in government and when internal tensions become acute (Egypt); (3) constant internal divisions between political parties or tribes hostile to each other (Syria); (4) hereditary monarchies that abuse power and turn the people into subjects rather than citizens (Libya); (5) regional rivalries resulting in conspiracies and political instability (Sudan, Iraq, Yemen, and Syria).

In many of these instances, the military feels a sense of mission and a duty to prevent what seems to them the threat of a national disaster. The military often prides itself on having the cohesion

---

*Yitzhak Rabin, who assumed the premiership of Israel in June 1974, is a former Chief of Staff.

needed to represent the nation as a whole. Many times, the military may be the only group that can force a change, especially when dealing with a strong monarchy.

Sometimes the reasons behind a military takeover become known through the conduct and the policies of the military regime once it assumes power. In examining the military establishments of the Arab states and Israel, one detects striking differences, particularly with regard to the exercise of power and the formulation of foreign policies.

It should be made clear at this point that no military takeover of a civilian government has ever occurred in Israel. Rather the military establishment's growing influence there may be explained by the important role it has played in protecting the state from external dangers ever since Israel was created. By way of contrast, in most Arab states (Egypt, Syria, Iraq, Libya, Tunisia, Yemen, and Algeria) military revolts were carried out against often corrupt and unstable governments. Civilian governments were then usually replaced forcefully by the military.

In Israel the army has received wide and popular support; there has been, in fact, a mystique about the whole military institution. Army officers have been held in high esteem. This popularity of the Israeli military reached its zenith in the Six-Day War of June 1967. As a result, from 1967 to 1973, the Israeli army was able to exert great influence over the civilian government, private business and large corporations.

The general policy of both the civilian and the military authorities was to promote integration of the army officer into civilian life, both during his tenure and after his retirement. The private business sector was often anxious to bring ex-army officers into their enterprises, for civilian employers believed that ex-army officers would bring efficiency and smoothness of operation to their companies. As a result, large numbers of army officers were automatically transferred to civilian establishments.

> *The considerable influence of generals out of uniform on Israel's civilian life is due to the fairly large number of top officers who have assumed executive jobs in business and public service after retiring. They have introduced organizational methods customary in the Army, leading to more rational and efficient procedures in banks, business*

> *enterprises, and factories throughout the country. They have also pioneered the use of up-to-date technology and larger expenditures on research in industrial enterprises. Such trends, of course, have had an indirect impact on other enterprises in the economy.* *

While the civilian and military authorities in Israel worked harmoniously to benefit the private sector, in most of the Arab "revolutionary" states where an army had replaced a civilian government, little cooperation between the army and the civilian enterprises resulted because in these countries the army officers lacked expertise in those fields. Even in administration and management, most of the military men could not make the transition to civilian decision-making, which they found differed from the decision-making process in a military framework.

Contrary to the popularity and esteem that military personnel enjoyed in Israel, the Arab revolutionary leaders were unable to establish the same relationship with or gain the confidence of their people. The internal and foreign policies of the Arab military leaders were often dictated by personal needs to establish themselves in power. Cecil Hourani, a leading Arab intellectual, observed:

> *Except in Egypt, however, the "progressive" military regimes have not only failed to implement socialist programmes: they have actually lowered gross national products and seriously damaged the economic welfare of some sections of the population without improving that of others. Nor have they been able or willing to take those social and juridical measures which would have given a progressive character to their regimes, at least on paper. Not one of the "progressive" regimes, for example, has abolished polygamy. On the contrary, some of them have been trying to reintroduce a conservative interpretation of Islam into public life* [Libya]. *And certain of the regimes which have been classified as "conservative" or "reactionary"* [Kuwait, Saudi Arabia, Jordan] *have done much*

---

*Yuval Elizur and Eliahu Salpeter, *Who Rules Israel?* (New York: Harper and Row, Publishers, 1973), p. 203.

for their populations in terms of economic progress and social legislation. *

To better understand why the Arab military regimes have been unable to create better relationships with the various civilian business and political factions the following factors should be considered: (1) government censorship and control of the press as well as other media; (2) severe curtailment of freedom of speech; (3) a total ban on all political activities which were not supportive of the government's official policy; (4) sweeping social reforms without preparing the populace or allowing for a period of transition; (5) misuse of natural and human resources that resulted in resentment and disenchantment; (6) emphasis on military build-up (in order to confront the Israelis) at the expense of urgently needed welfare programs. As Hourani explained, "This does not mean that we should disarm; it does mean that we should reappraise our own strength and find a new relationship between the military power on the one hand and our political, economic, and geopolitical assets on the other."**

To a degree, the Egyptian military establishment followed the Israelis' footsteps in their attempt to utilize the military establishment for civilian purposes.

> ... *the army has long been regarded as a "school" in civic virtues. In addition, today the army has also become a school to impart modern skills, a hospital to cure the ills of society and turn out healthier men, and a source of discipline. Each year approximately 20,000 Egyptians are inducted into the army for three-year enlistments; in Syria about the same are called for a two-year period; and in Iraq, about 8,000 are called up for two years. From 1957 to 1963, perhaps as many as 130,000 Egyptians have passed out of the armed forces into civilian life. When one considers that larger scale modern Egyptian industry in 1961 employed*

---

*Excerpt from an article, "The Moment of Truth", *Encounter,* Beirut, November 1967.

**Cecil Hourani, "Toward a Middle East Dialogue," *Encounter,* Beirut, September 1967.

> roughly a quarter of a million workers, the impact of this group of ex-soldiers can be appreciated.*

The Arab states and Israel became captive to their military establishments and allowed military thinking to dominate their political decision-making and diplomatic maneuverings. For Israel, it was a matter of survival; military build-up and expenditure were not a luxury. Its choices were between military superiority at all costs and "liquidation," the Arab goal for Israel. For the Arabs, armed power demonstrated pride and self-esteem. In addition, military build-up and preparedness were excellent pretexts for covering up shortcomings of the revolutionary regimes, which often were unable to fulfill their promises of social and economic progress. Both adversaries were compelled either by circumstance or design to expand their military capacities and to allocate huge sums, far exceeding their economic abilities, for the purchase of armaments.

The Israeli expansion of its military industry was "instinctive" and circumstantial. Israel had the know-how and needed very little assistance in developing small or light armaments. The constant feeling of being threatened and under siege forced Israel to be less dependent on outside sources for weapons — at least the kind of weapons that required no heavy industry. Furthermore, Israel's arms requirements were extensive, local manufacturing was far more economical and a source of employment as well. The state of ongoing hostilities increased the need for ammunition. Israel could not risk depending on other sources for exclusive supply of arms and ammunition. Thus, a large percentage of Israel's industrial expansion was geared to military-related requirements, although Israel depends on the U.S. for such heavy arms as jet fighters and tanks.

On the Arab side, the armaments industry was still in its infancy in the late 1960's. None of the conditions that prevailed in Israel (e.g., high level technology, a sense of isolation) was relevant in the Arab situation. By and large, the Arab states had sufficient income from oil to purchase weapons and to maintain their arsenals. Yet when the need for industrial expansion became acute in Egypt, Syria

---

*William R. Polk, *Social Modernization: The New Men* (New Jersey, Prentice-Hall, Inc.), pp. 50-52.

and Algeria, emphasis was put on the building of military industry almost as a prerequisite to industrial expansion in other fields.

> *As far as science and technology are concerned, we are endeavoring to catch up with what we have missed in all types. We are developing and expanding our war industry. When I speak this way some people may think that I am divulging secrets. Well, I am not divulging secrets. How can we enter the war if we are not trained and if we do not have a command, arms, and armed forces in which we have complete confidence?* *

Military industry, planning, large defense expenditures and military preparedness became a way of life in both societies. This preoccupation with the military resulted in a slow but steady conversion of the Middle East economies to "military economies," meaning not only the expenditure of a high percentage of the national income on military build-up and/or warfare, but also the existence of military-related jobs for a relatively large percentage of the labor force.

The danger in any military economy is twofold: a) by virtue of exorbitant expenditures or military preparedness, social and welfare programs usually suffer; b) the conversion of military industry to, say, the production of household goods is a slow and complicated process. Often a country with a military economy which is committed to keeping unemployment below a certain percentage of the labor force, will find itself indirectly promoting military policies in order to justify military expenditures, and even maintain a certain level of "prosperity" induced by military spending.

There is little doubt that Israel and its immediate adversaries would have suffered total economic collapse were it not for the billions of dollars in foreign aid both sides received. Israel has relied heavily on direct U.S. aid and contributions by world Jewry. Its opponents have been subsidized by the oil-producing Arab countries, particularly Saudi Arabia, Kuwait, and Libya.

The October, 1973 war sounded a very serious alarm that neither side could afford to take lightly. Economically, the war was a

---

*Excerpt from a speech by the late President Gamal Abdel Nasser, at the opening of the second session of the Arab Socialist Union National Congress at Cairo University, March 27, 1969.

disaster for all involved — Egypt, Syria, and Israel. How many more economic blows of this magnitude any of the opponents can take and still survive is questionable. One thing, however, became obvious. Force alone is no longer a viable alternative for policy-makers; is only one factor to be used in conjunction with diplomacy to bring about desired changes. Those who resort to force alone to resolve political problems are usually marking time at best, and at worst are undermining their economies and promulgating the abuse of power.

The October war provided one additional effect; the relationship of Jews and Arabs to their respective military establishments underwent shifts. Previously, Israelis admired and respected their military men, while the Arabs' reactions to theirs were a mixture of shame and disenchantment.

From the inception of the state of Israel till the time of the Sinai Campaign in 1956, the Israeli general public regarded the self-reliant Kibbutznik as a glamorous superman personifying the highest national ideals. From 1956 till the eve of the 1973 war, the public became increasingly impressed by victorious generals and war heroes who captured the imagination of every Israeli as well as Jews everywhere. Concurrently, however, a new professional class of technologists, scientists and management personnel was rising in prestige and importance. This occupational shift is partially explained by the growing need for professional men in all economic and technological fields. Israeli public confidence in its military was then severely shaken by the lack of preparedness for the Yom Kippur War. The Israeli military establishment lost an appreciable degree of public admiration.

In contrast, Arabs have usually held a negative view in regard to their military establishment. The repeated humiliation of the Arab soldier at the hands of his Israeli counterpart was a source of shame, discontent, and frustration. But the October, 1973 War helped replace shame with pride, discontent with jubilation, and frustration with renewal of self-confidence. One result of the October war, then, has been a reconstructed relationship between the Arab masses and their military establishment. Such changes in attitude toward their respective military establishments have probably contributed to a narrowing of the gap between the two societies. The Arab revolutionary regimes may well find it unnecessary for their prestige to initiate new hostilities against Israel. The Israeli authorities, for their part, may find it necessary to begin to assess the side effects of the military's influence over the Israeli public and over the civilian political machinery. The government's over-reliance on the military establishment for political and economic advice, in addition to the usual duties of the military in intelligence-gathering, may have laid the foundation for Israel's lack of preparedness in the October war.

ISRAEL'S INTERNAL PROBLEMS AND SOCIAL PREDICAMENT

As a rule, a country's political and social structures have a direct bearing on the formulation of its governmental policies. The internal struggle for political power on the one hand, and the makeup and diversity of its class system on the other, can contribute to either stability or disruptiveness in the pattern of policies that a government deems necessary to follow. Internal political and class struggles within each Arab state have undoubtedly hindered their efforts to try to achieve a united political front against Israel.* By the same token, Israeli public policy has suffered from a lack of consistency due to her own internal political and social turbulence. To be sure, both sides followed a policy that to some extent reflected the socio-political structure of their respective societies.

In Israel, two major factors have significantly influenced policy-making in the past, and are likely to continue to do so — class struggle and a constitutional framework.

Israel's Class Struggle

After twenty-seven years of statehood, Israel has still to develop social and political mechanisms which insure equitable standards of living and political representations. Despite democratic elections by secret ballot, freedom of speech and press, welfare reforms and significant land distribution, there still exist great economic disparities among Israel's various classes.

Although the Israeli population consists of over seventy different linguistic groups, the population may be divided into two major categories: the "Western Jews," (Ashkenazim) comprising all the Jews who emigrated to Israel from the Western Hemisphere, in-

---

*For an analysis of Arab political and social instability, see Chapter III.

cluding East European Jews and the "Oriental Jews" (Sephardim) who came mainly from Middle Eastern countries and North Africa, and who are physically distinguishable by their relatively darker skin. There are several reasons why class disparities exist in Israel. Some are circumstantial, some cultural, and still others the result of shortsighted policies of the government soon after Israel's independence.

The privilege of circumstance: The vast majority of the early Jewish settlers were from Eastern Europe, especially from Poland and Russia. Being the first settlers, arriving from the turn of the century till the late forties, they laid the foundation of the Jewish state. It was only natural, therefore, that they would hold the highest positions, particularly since there were few Sephardic Jews in Palestine. This situation, of course, could not be condemned if it were not for the fact that those in power from the inception of the state clung to their positions as if each one was totally indispensable.

> *... in the Israeli system, a forty-five or fifty-year old man aspiring to office is still regarded as a "young Turk" and classed among the "ambitious young." What psychologists call "upward mobility" is, in Israel, a difficult and painful process. For example, in the first Israeli parliament [1949] the average age of the members was forty-three. The average age in the sixth parliament [1969] was sixty-three. The intervening twenty years, the average age has risen by exactly 20 years.*
>
> *And of the 277 members of parliament between 1949 and 1970, 74 percent were born in Eastern Europe or in Central Europe of Eastern European parents. Sixty-eight percent would boast of a past in the "heroic age of pioneering or underground activity. Despite the vast changes in the ethnic composition of the Jewish-Israeli population, the predominance of Eastern Europeans in the sixth and seventh Knesset of 1965 and 1969 was almost as marked as it had been in the Knessets elected in 1961, 1959, 1955, 1951, and 1949.* *

---

*Elon, *op. cit.*, p. 399, 401.

Without adequate provisions for periodic turnover in political personnel, governments tend to produce stale leaders and sterile policies.

An economic consideration which helped perpetuate a social class struggle is the fact that the majority of Sephardic Jews came to Israel with limited financial resources. In contrast, by 1950, most of the Ashkenazic Jews in Israel had been able to establish themselves economically, a factor that had a direct bearing not only on their standard of living, but also on their ability to enhance their own education and that of their children. Since the Israeli government's resources were limited, very few Sephardic Jews were able to pursue higher studies beyond the free elementary level.

> *The Oriental-Western schism personifies some of the social cracks that exist. Israel's Oriental Jews are at the low end of the social and economic scale, often living as an inferior minority though this social class now is in the majority. The children of Oriental Jewish parentage comprise 70 per cent of the school classes when children start in school. Only 16 per cent finish high school, and only 3 per cent finish university. In some respects, the Oriental Jew is the "black" of Israel.* *

Political Inhibition: The Sephardic Jews by and large did not participate in government in their respective countries of origin, nor did they experience Western-style democracy. Their lack of political awareness and of a sense of political efficacy have undoubtedly inhibited their active participation in Israeli politics. The politically unsophisticated image, however, which the Sephardic Jews projected upon arrival, masked their capacity to adjust and effectively contribute to the shaping of this heterogeneous society. The error of the political Ashkenazic elite was not in creating a class of politically disoriented citizens, but in acquiescing to the given situation and fearing competiton from the Sephardic Jews who exceeded fifty per cent of the total Israeli population by 1955. There were at least two consequences of this conservative policy of non-action:

1) It made Israel appear to be a totally Western country, in effect strengthening the Arab claim that Israel was a Western entity

---

*Vickers, *op. cit.*, p. 237.

planted in the heart of the Arabs, and that there was nothing Middle Eastern about her. Many Arab politicians and intellectuals repeatedly pointed out that not a single Sephardic Jew held an important governmental post. Arab students note sarcastically that the Israeli government always manages to appoint a Sephardic Jew for the post of police minister. It is not even lip service, they argue; it is an insult to the integrity of the Sephardic Jews.

2) Thousands of Sephardic Jews emigrated from Israel because they felt unable to combat the inertia and what they considered "racism" within the political bureacracy. Many of these were intellectuals who grew weary and disheartened, and then moved to Europe, Canada, or the United States. The Israeli loss in terms of human resources was indeed substantial since many of these "exiled" Jews succeeded in becoming highly-respected citizens in their adopted countries for their contributions in science, medicine, and business.

By 1970, Israeli social class struggle had become a social dilemma that jeopardized the nation's unity. Only the constant border tension prevented open clashes between Jews. Arab hostility was a unifying factor, without which considerable, social disintegration might have long since occurred.

Shortsightedness: There were and still are several spheres where the government could have played a more active ameliorative role but instead opted to ignore its "race problem" by denying its existence, thus perpetuating the rift.

The Israeli army, which is recruited ideally under terms of social equality, has not been fully utilized as a melting pot. Ironically, it maintained the same ratio of Oriental to Western Jews as in the political sphere. There has not been a single officer of Sephardic origin who reached the two top ranks of general. This particular factor was especially disheartening to many young vigorous Sephardic Jews, not because thousands of them aspired to be generals, but because as far as they were concerned high rank was most unlikely. Another disheartening factor was that even those few Sephardic Jews who reached high political positions were not necessarily chosen because of their personal capabilities; rather they were co-opted into office by an establishment anxious to alter its image of Eastern European ethnocentricity without really changing the makeup of the establishment itself.

This chronic class struggle must be tackled and resolved, especially in the event of an eventual peace settlement with the Arab states. Intermarriage between Ashkenazi and Sephardic Jews, which has been increasing during the last decade, is an important development that may lead eventually to better relations between the two classes. Still, long-range plans should be instituted in order to elevate the Sephardic Jew economically since this is a prerequisite to his achieving a measure of social equality.

Israel's Internal Politics

The struggle for political power in Israel is another factor that has affected its prospects for peace in the past and is very likely to influence Israel's position in any peace negotiations that take place.

Unlike the United States or Britain where a two-party system exists, Israel's various interest groups and ideologies have been represented by as many as twenty-five distinct political parties. An explanation for this situation would have to take into account the cultural and historical background that prevented the acceptance of a two or three party system. The Israelis have preferred that their government consist of representatives from several ideological groupings rather than any one particular political philosophy. The government's desire to secure maximum participation and jealousies among the various parties also contribute to the country's political fragmentation.

> *These past quarrels and debates have been so bitterly ferocious, so marked by frequent splits and schisms, so absolute in their respective claims, as to suggest religious sects engaged in argument over secret texts of this or that divine revelation. The word "arachim" [values] has always had an important place in the internal debate. It connotes near absolute ideological and moral fixities. Values are always "basic" — "Jewish" values, "socialist" values, "Zionist" values, "moral" values, "national" values, "pioneering" values, "cooperative" values.**

---

*Elon, *op. cit.*, p. 380.

Although many smaller parties have been absorbed by the larger ones during the last ten years, they have managed to maintain their individual ideologies and have acted almost like separate sects within the larger framework. In the December, 1973 election, there were still more than ten parties campaigning for the 120 seats in the parliament.

Since Israel's independence in 1948, the Labor party (Mapai) has ruled with the cooperation of a number of the smaller parties. Mapai has never had a sufficient number of representatives in the parliament (a minimum of 61) to form a government of its own, but has retained power through the formation of coalitions with several other (mostly religious) parties. A lack of confidence vote in the Knesset (parliament; by 61 or more members forces the prime minister to tender his or her resignation, which in effect brings down the whole government. In such a case, the president has the option of calling on another party — usually the second largest — to form a government. Failure to do so results in a new election. Such a constitutional framework has several weaknesses that are relevant to our discussion:

1) The Israeli voter chooses among parties, not individual representatives. Israel is not divided into constituencies, such as in Britain, where each constituency has its own representative in parliament. In effect, the individual member of parliament in Israel is not accountable to the electorate *per se,* but to the party leaders. Thus, representation in parliament does not necessarily reflect the social and economic make-up of society. By not being able to elect their own representatives, the majority of Israelis, the Sephardic Jews, are not represented in proportion to their numbers.

2) Party discipline in parliament is strong; that is, party members must vote on behalf of the government's policies when their party is part of the government coalition. Hence, very few members of a governing coalition have the audacity to argue against the government, fearing expulsion from the list in the following election.

3) Because no single party has ever been able to muster a majority alone, coalition government has become a way of life. Compromise and give-and-take are an essential exercise for the sake of political stability. But if a party in the coalition finds itself at odds over some proposal, it may result in the resignation of its members, thus forcing the government as a whole to resign.

4) The proportional election in Israel awards a seat to any party winning at least one per cent of the total vote. This has permitted a number of splinter groups to register as independent parties, thereby encouraging political division and weakening the larger parties. To be sure, even the main parties in Israel, namely, the Labor Alignment (Mapai) and the Likud, are themselves combinations of smaller parties. This situation has made the ideological lines of the major parties highly ambiguous. Thus voters in the election of December, 1973, for example, were not able to accurately determine the policies of the parties and how they would perform in the wake of growing dissatisfaction among the voters in general. One additional weakness of the Israeli political system is that the party's prestige rests largely on the individual who heads the party. Such clinging to the leader, however, has created a generation gap, and does not support the grooming of qualified younger successors. Thus, the parties have found themselves compelled to turn to the army for leadership, which has further increased the influence of the military over civilian matters.

A government that does not enjoy a margin of safety of at least four or five Knesset members beyond the 61 member majority is weak. Often, it will be unable to take steps of national magnitude out of fear that one or two members might "defect." A vote on returning the West Bank to Jordan, for example, might well bring down the present government. Such being the case, the Rabin government will have difficulty reaching a consensus on this issue.

Israeli Population Growth as a Peace Factor:

Another factor that may result in bringing the Arabs and Israelis one step closer to peace is the tripling of the Jewish population since the creation of the state of Israel in 1948. A solid and sustainable Jewish majority, say 75% of the total population, will in itself be a considerable deterrent to any Arab extremist plans to eliminate or absorb Israel through force or by other means. Based on the pre-1967 borders, Jews outnumbered Arabs by nearly seven to one. To maintain this proportion, Israel must aim at doubling its present population of approximately three million in the next twenty-five years. This means that certain political, territorial, and demographic measures must be adopted. Although some of these measures are already underway, other new policies should be enacted by the government in order to better coordinate the work of the various existing governmental departments that are directly or indirectly involved with the question of population planning and growth. There are four main interrelated sources of population growth factors to which the Israeli government should apply new political and economic methods and probably a new set of priorities:

Territorial Annexation: One aspect that will largely contribute to the retention of a solid Jewish majority through the next three decades will undoubtedly be the extent and the demographic make-up of any territory that Israel might annex. It would appear that if Israel were to annex any part of the occupied territories, that will result in the absorption of more than three hundred thousand Arabs and the Jewish-Arab ratio of 87/13% will seriously shift in favor of the Arabs If, for example, Israel retains all the occupied territories, the Jewish population in Israel will move toward a clear minority by the year 2,000. Whereas the return of all the occupied territories with the exception of the Golan Heights and East Jerusalem (with a total Arab population of 72,000),* will enable the Jewish population to retain its clear majority through the year 2,000.

Jewish Birth Rate: Although the government encourages large families, most newlywed Israelis find themselves unable to afford many children. And recent austerity programs have further reduced the desirability of large families.

The Israeli government will have to provide new and far-reaching economic and social incentives for young couples to encourage their having larger families. To double the population by the year 2,000, each family must have between three and four children on the average. One approach would be to reduce abortions (which have been estimated at upwards of one million in the last 25 years) to a minimum, so that abortions will be performed only when the mother's health is in danger. These facets of population growth are perhaps the most crucial in the long run, for unless all Israeli social and psychological behavior is geared toward self-multiplication, immigration will not be sufficient to sustain a Jewish majority over the Arab Palestinians, regardless of their present place of residence. The present net birthrate of Jews in Israel stands at 21.5 per 1,000

---

* Source: Central Bureau of Statistics in Israel estimates based on 1967 data.

versus 45.6 per 1,000 among the Arabs in Israel. If these rates are maintained without offsetting Jewish immigration, the Jewish identity of the country will weaken. Since mass Jewish immigration to Israel is subject to so many outside social, economic, and political conditions that are usually beyond Israeli control, Israel must promote internal population growth if it is to maintain its predominately Jewish image.

Discouragement of "Yordim" *

Another serious problem for Israel is the number of Jews who leave the country and settle elsewhere. Among the most common reasons for this are: 1) economic difficulties; 2) social or political disenchantment; 3) personal fear or apprehensiveness about Israel's future; and 4) a desire to search for better career opportunities. To remove these reasons, it becomes obvious that the burden to change the situation falls heavily on the Israeli government. No persuasion by the government will suffice unless accompanied by specific measures to eliminate the causes that encourage "Yerida" from Israel. It is undoubtedly a formidable task, yet absolutely crucial to Israel's future demographic posture. Therefore, far greater resources, human as well as financial, will have to be allocated by the Israeli government to combat the phenomenon of "Yordim" and bring it down to the absolute minimum. While it is undoubtedly impossible to completely eliminate emigration short of imposing severe restrictions on all travel abroad, the rate at which "Yordim" are leaving must be slowed or the effect on Israel could be critical. The problem is especially significant not only because of the estimated 300,000 who have left since the early fifties, but also because of the psychological repercussions such departures have on other Jews both in Israel as well as those living in the diaspora who are thinking of settling in Israel. Thus is would seem likely that reduction in the number of "Yordim" would almost certainly result in an increase in the number of new immigrants.

---

*The word "Yored" signifies either a native Israeli Jew or an emigrant to Israel who subsequently settles in another country. "Yordim" is the plural for "Yored."

Encouragement of Aliyah*

Finally, another potential way of increasing the Jewish population in Israel is through "Aliyah." Because present Jewish birth rates in Israel are substantially lower than those of the Arabs, Jewish immigration to Israel is considered by Israelis as the most important source, for it represents almost "instant" growth. While, of course, massive Jewish immigration to Israel can provide the desired result, it is very unlikely that millions of Jews from North America will settle in Israel or that Russia will grant exit visas to large numbers. The difficulties imposed on the Soviet Jews wanting to leave Russia and the lack of a fanatic ideological motivation on the part of the North American and West European Jews make the prospect of Jewish immigration *en masse* rather doubtful.

To make *aliyah* more popular, there are certain changes in policy that the Israeli government should implement. It should: 1) Further liberalize Israeli trade and industrial laws in order to encourage greater foreign investments and/or transfers of businesses, 2) Aim to attract a realistic number of immigrants from North America and Europe that corresponds with Israel's ability to absorb them, 3) Negotiate with Russia by means of quiet diplomacy to increase Jewish immigration,** 4) Apply equal treatment to all immigrants irrespective of their countries of origin. By not applying the same measures in the past, it has helped, for example, to create a social schism between the Sephardic and the Ashkanazic communities. 5) Finally, the Israeli government should examine its bureaucratic red tape in processing which has been an agonizing problem to many potential North American immigrants.

---

*"Aliyah" is the act of settling in Israel. It comes from the Hebrew verb "La-Alot" which means to go up.

**The Soviet repudiation of the 1972 trade agreement with the United States is only one example from which a lesson should be learned. Whether the Russians' repudiation of the trade bill is truly related to the Jackson amendment, which attached to the bill the right of Russian citizens to emigrate, is irrelevant. The Soviets used the amendment as an excuse to repudiate the agreement. Since January, 1975, the number of Jews emigrating from Russia has definitely been declining. Thus it would appear that excessive publicity regarding the "Russian understanding" as to how many Jews would be allowed to leave Russia once the trade agreement became law did not serve the cause of Russian Jewry.

In sum, Israel's prospect for peace depends in part on what it does internally to improve the size of the Jewish community. In the long run, this might turn out to be the most critical of factors.

Hostilities on the borders, and the constant tension and insecurity have always been and will probably continue to unify the Israelis. Social and political differences are obviously set aside in the wake of a common external danger; in this particular sense, Israel's social cohesion and political unity has resulted from Arab hostility. The removal of this threat from Israel's borders might stir and release dissension that has so far remianed latent for the sake of national security. Political and social fragmentation could be the net result.

The stability of any peace agreement will depend on the degree to which Israel becomes a Middle Eastern country rather than a European one. Israel will not be able to reach a peace of reconciliation* with the Arab states while more than 50 percent of her population is a "neglected minority." Any Israeli government that does not recognize the necessity to fully involve the Sephardic Jews in government, military, and big business will become a victim of its own shortsightedness.

Israel could weaken its Jewish identity even after a peace treaty with the Arab states is signed, if the disenchantment of the Sephardic Jews persists. The Arab states could capitalize on this disenchantment by simply opening their borders to any Jew, particularly when business opportunities are unlimited. Likely candidates would be Sephardic Jews who would be able to communicate and mingle as full-fledged Jewish Arabs.

The growing Jewish community in West Germany is an indicative and vivid example of what might happen to some of the Sephardic Jews in Israel. An estimated number of some six to seven thousand Jews of German origin have left Israel and resettled in West Germany. This would not have been a significant phenomena if it was not for the fact that in comparing the German Jews to the Sephardic Jews, two important differences make the Sephardic case far more compelling: 1) the German Jews who have left Israel have done so for socio-economic reasons far less acute than those faced by the

---

*In the Arabic language there are two words which mean peace, *salam* and *sulch*. The word *salam* means coexistence or cessation of hostilities, while *sulch* means coexistence coupled with reconciliation of differences and exchange in all walks of social encounter.

Sephardic Jews. 2) the Sephardic Jews who lived among the Arab states prior to 1948 had not been subjected to the same severity of pogroms, persecution and slaughter that the German Jewish community has experienced in Germany during World War II.

> *Our greatest victory, Cecil Hourani observed, will be in the day when the Jews in Palestine will prepare to live in an Arab society rather than in an Isreali one. It is up to us to make that possible**

OIL ON TROUBLED WATERS

Oil is the most potent weapon the Arabs can bring to bear in confrontation with Israel. This factor will greatly influence any ultimate settlement and indeed is already playing a significant role in the shaping of Western foreign policy toward the Middle East.

As a political tool to be used *directly* against the Western nations, Arab oil may have lost much of its impact. Many observers of European and Middle Eastern politics may disagree with this proposition. Yet the experience of the October, 1973 war, which brought the Arab oil embargo in its wake, showed that the Arabs were willing to settle for less than they had originally demanded. Total and complete Israeli withdrawal from the occupied territories didn't remain a precondition for removing the embargo. What actually took place was an indication that a policy of blackmail, especially against the United States, will not work, and that an indefinite continuation of the embargo could have damaged, if not destroyed, the economy of the Arab states themselves, along with some of the Western European countries. The Arab oil-producing nations, from a purely economic standpoint, are not interested in destroying their relations with the United States. Such attitudes could end up limiting their own future economic development.

Saudi Arabia, the Persian Gulf Sheikdoms and others, have been motivated in their oil policy by a concern for the safety of the many

---

*Cecil Hourani, "Toward a Middle East Dialogue", *Encounter,* Beirut, September 1967.

billions of dollars invested or contemplated being invested in American business.*

The Arab states, for example, in direct confrontation with Israel could hold to extreme positions (i.e., total Israeli withdrawal from the occupied territories) as long as the oil-producing countries, particularly Saudi Arabia, are willing to support them without endangering themselves economically. Moreover, their political strategy was designed to demand the maximum and then settle for whatever Israeli concessions might be extended through political pressure. In retrospect, it seems likely that the Arab states never expected a total Israeli withdrawal from the occupied territories on the basis of the oil embargo alone. As Ashraf Gorbal, the Egyptian Ambassador to the U.S., put it in November 1973, "Oil was meant only to ring a bell in every door and in the world."

The Arabs, of course, understand that direct retaliation against the U.S. by means of a renewed oil embargo would be futile. The U.S. did not abjectly surrender to the Arabs' demands in the face of the embargo in 1973; and it appears unlikely that the U.S. would ever respond favorably to an embargo. The following may provide supportive arguments:

1) The U.S. would probably view the renewal of an oil embargo as a political weapon to gain Western concessions over Israel (which might have been understandable in the past), but as pure economic blackmail, which the U.S. rejects in principle.

2) The partial Arab success in securing the troop disengagement agreement between Egypt and Israel (January, 1974) and between Syria and Israel (June, 1974) was accomplished primarily by American pressure and influence over Israel and the diplomatic efforts of Secretary of State Henry Kissinger. An oil embargo at this juncture would be shortsighted on the part of the oil-producing states, especially in the wake of the new interim agreement between Israel and Egypt resulting from Kissinger's mediation in August

---

*"Nations of the Middle East earned $7.1 billion from their oil in 1971. That total jumped to over $11 billion in 1972 and to around $15 billion in 1973. In the period from 1972 to 1975 their earnings should exceed $60 billion. By 1980, Middle East nations may be earning as much as $60 billion a year from their oil. Seldom in man's history has there been such a dramatic shift in income. Overnight, developing, have-not countries are joining the ranks of the haves." (Vickers, *op. cit.*, p. 74.)

1975 which is likely to be followed by a second disengagement accord between Israel and Syria.

3) Since an oil embargo against the U.S. *alone* is likely to work against Arab interests, the Arabs might consider using oil pressure once again against Western Europe and Japan in order to exert indirect pressure on the United States. It seems, however, that such a step would also be futile, since an oil embargo against Western Europe and Japan *alone* would not by itself compel the U.S. to shift her policies toward Israel, for a number of reasons: a) the United States did not view favorably the independent dealings of Western Europe and Japan with the Arabs regarding the resumption of the oil supply; b) the U.S. considers Israel to be an indispensable ally in the face of Soviet expansionst policy in the Middle East; c) it believes that European security hinges strongly on a demonstration of solidarity and that submission to economic blackmail will be disastrous in the long run; d) also, the U.S. is aware of the Israelis' sensitivity on the issue of secure borders; and e) excessive American political pressure on Israel might force the Israelis to take desperate action that would further enhance Soviet penetration into the Middle East. Western European influence over Israel has declined measurably since the October war and Europe therefore will probably not be able to influence Israel's policies for sometime. Thus an oil embargo against Western Europe would be nothing less than an act of blackmail.

4) The Arab oil-producing countries have repeatedly declared their interest in participating actively in the U.S. effort to search for new sources of energy. They know quite well that their oil wells will eventually be depleted and that unless they join the U.S. now, they might forego sharing in the development of any new energy sources. American determination to become self-sufficient in terms of energy sometime between 1980 and 1985 will undoubtedly change energy consumption requirements in the United States and eventually affect their foreign sources of oil, i.e., the OPEC group.

5) The Arab states who understand the value and the fragility of their new power, naturally are interested in protecting their interests. The economic stability of the Western world depends largely on the stabilization of the dollar and is likely to continue to do so. Thus, in order for the Arab states to maintain their influence, they may find themselves compelled to cooperate with the United States

more than they have in the past.* International cooperation on a broad scale will be necessary to minimize the disruptive effects of a massive accumulation of foreign reserves by Arab nations in the Middle East. Such thoughts have been voiced by Anwar Ali, governor of the Saudi Monetary Agency who has pointed out that Saudi Arabia is well aware of the inherent economic dangers and is anxious to cooperate. He added, "We realize it is to our advantage to handle our surplus funds in a manner that does not disrupt the system. Stability is as important to us as it is to the western world. You must help us by providing opportunities for us to invest our surplus funds."**

One way, for example, for OPEC and the European nations to cooperate is through the cyclical borrowing process.

> *About 20 billion dollars in balance of payments loans have been made by the commercial banks of Europe and North America since the first of the year [1974]. The resources to make these loans have come from the oil-producing nations which have placed the bulk of their receipts from oil on short term deposit with the banks. If they [the oil-producing states] drain money out of the industrialized nations of the world, and it doesn't go back, they have an impossible investment dilemma, because there is no other place in the world which could absorb sums of money in the magnitude they will have.****

An astute observer of the Middle East scene recently wrote:

> *It is popular today to do some projecting on the basis of current trends. I did this before visiting Ali [Anwar Ali, governor of the Saudi Monetary Agency] and concluded that the cumulative incomes of Arab oil lands between 1973*

---

*Many political observers do not accord a high degree of rationality on the part of the Arab statesmen, particularly in their dispute with Israel. However, while one cannot minimize a degree of Arab emotionalism as a factor in decision-making, Arab political awareness and recent conduct since early 1973 show subtlety and responsibility. The Arab oil-producing countries are fully aware of their new position and are not likely to gamble with their future prosperity for uncertain political gains.

**Vickers, *op. cit*, p. 101.

***David Rockefeller, *U.S. News and World Report*, August 12, 1974, p. 41.

> and 1980 may amount to over $200 billion, nearly twenty times the volume of gold held by the United States and a sum greater than the total volume of liquidity held by International Monetary Fund nations in 1973.*

For these reasons it is not likely that an oil embargo will be renewed for the purpose of producing political pressure. What might become a greater concern to Israel is the steady increase in Arab investments in American and West European fertilizer plants, energy concerns, and real estate where they feel a considerable degree of financial security. The continuation of this trend might in the long run offset the lobbying of American Jews for Israel. Although the United States government has been consistent in its policy toward Israel, Israel views the growing financial power of the Arabs as a menace that may affect U.S. support for her in the absence of peace.

> Now Israel faces a situation where the initiative may lie elsewhere, in the capitals of the Arab world, where immense financial and economic power will be resting in the years ahead. This is a sort of power where Israel's admitted overwhelming military superiority means little, which is an unhappy prospect for Israel.**

The accumulation of enormous sums of money by the oil-producing countries is not likely to level off before the 1990's. Although the inflationary trends that are sweeping Western Europe and the U.S. in the early 1970's make the accumulation of funds unattractive, oil is still likely to be produced in huge quantities. Some of the countries, such as Kuwait, Libya, and Venezuela may reach a point, however, where the limitation rather than the expansion of oil production will appear more economical. Saving oil in the ground for future sale may prove wiser than selling it now for cash which may devalue in the banks. Such limited measures, if adopted, would not have a significant impact, however, on the continued accumulation of vast sums by the oil-producing countries.

*Vickers, *op. cit.*, p. 101

***Ibid.*, p. 241.

TOWARD SOCIAL AND ECONOMIC COOPERATION

Future economic cooperation between Arabs and Israelis depends on a political peace. The viability of such a settlement will depend in turn on the willingness of both sides to strengthen it by improving social relations and taking appropriate economic measures. A secure peace will depend upon Arab recognition of Israel's sovereignty. Then the establishment of a modicum of mutual trust must follow along with the integration of their economies into one that has much more of a Middle Eastern cast. Till now, Israel's economy has been centrifugal, for the most part finding its resources in Western European nations. In a more integrated regional economy, if it could be accomplished, Israel could furnish the technical know-how, while the Arab States could supply the necessary financing and manpower.

Since underdeveloped countries usually seek capital investment and technical aid from the more industrialized nations, they often find themselves unwittingly involved in the ideological conflicts and divisions of these suppliers. The Middle East, however, has all the material, land, capital, human resources, and liquidity that it needs to make the region relatively independent. By intelligently using the region's resources and by planning, the Middle East could become one of the most prosperous regions in the world.

While such a unifying trend may not lead soon to mutual disarmament, huge armies and expensive weaponry would not continue to be as urgently needed. The present arms race between Israel and the Arab states finds both sides wasting their natural and human resources in a futile effort to find "security" because a military build-up and the use of force will never by themselves provide a complete solution. Political stability, on the other hand, could conceivably further encourage the oil-producing countries which are not immediate antagonists of Israel to invest large sums of money in Syria, Jordan, and Egypt. Egypt itself might develop into a boom country, provided it can demonstrate the political stability which the oil-producing countries, especially Saudi Arabia, demand as a safety measure before making significant investments.

Areas of Potential Cooperation

The Arab and the Israeli economies are not built to function alone; outside sources for raw materials and finished products remain a necessity for the smooth functioning of their economies. Israel depends largely on her trade with the Western industrialized countries and leans heavily on grants and loans from the U.S. government and contributions from American Jewry. The Arab states by and large, depend almost entirely on the Eastern and Western European industrialized world and the U.S. for finished products, and, to a lesser degree, for food supply. In return, the Arabs export several kinds of raw materials and agricultural products such as cotton, wool, tobacco, dates, citrus, and most importantly, of course, oil. The climate, the land, and the potential availability of water make the entire Middle Eastern region more or less self-sufficient in cereals, edible oils and fats, vegetables, fruit, and meat. The region as a whole is capable of being totally independent of outside sources, were the Arab states and Israel to cooperate. The extent of Arab-Israeli economic cooperation could be so vast and diversified as to actually make the Middle Eastern region not only self-sufficient, but also a source of industrial and agricultural supplies to many countries.

Joint economic development in the Middle East could combine Israel's know-how and the Arab states' natural resources, and hence could contribute to a lasting peace. A political settlement between the Arabs and Israelis should only be considered as a first step toward a peace of "reconciliation." Arab-Israeli economic, social, and cultural exchanges would be an important safeguard against a renewal of hostilities, even after a political and territorial settlement. It therefore behooves both sides to come to grips with certain very real economic issues. After all, Israel's military might in the long run will not be the decisive factor it has been, given the growing Arab economic thrust.

The Arab states, for their part, may find that affluence will not automatically bring changes in their economic and social structure to meet the immediate needs of the average Arab. The economic and social reforms that most of the revolutionary regimes undertook have so far met with little success, not necessarily because of a lack of funds, but as a result in part of not coordinating a regional effort with Israel. No state in the Middle East, including Israel, can presently claim that it is economically independent, and it is most unlikely that any country in the area will ever be able to reach total economic independence. Let us now examine which areas of development might benefit from joint Arab-Israeli efforts.

1. Land reclamation

There is an abundance of undeveloped land in Egypt, Syria, Iraq, and Jordan which has been neglected for generations and could be reclaimed and converted into fertile land. Israeli pre-eminence in reclamation is unchallenged. During the last twenty-five years, for instance, Israel was able to restore over 250,000 acres; more than half of which has been covered with trees and the rest made suitable for agricultural cultivation of all kinds. Israel is in an excellent position to assist the Arab states in reclaiming up to 20 million acres in less than fifteen years, an undertaking that could dramatically increase the region's food supply. The Arab states have the money and manpower to start up such a project; they lack only the technical guidance Israel can supply. Sufficient food is a pillar of economic stability which in turn helps to secure political and social tranquility. Arab cooperation with Israel in the long run is a matter of self interest for all concerned.

2. Irrigation

In conjunction with land reclamation, an over-all irrigation program could include Jordan, Syria, Egypt, and Iraq, utilizing once again Israeli experience in the field of irrigation. Sources of water in the Middle East are not abundant but are ample if well utilized. The water resources consist mainly of five rivers. In Egypt the Nile, in Iraq and Syria the Tigris and the Euphrates, in Jordan and Israel the Jordan River, plus other local streams such as the Orantes and the Latini in Syria, and the Yarkon in Israel. Rainfall throughout the region is limited although in a few scattered sections it is adequate for certain crops. If its principal rivers were properly harnessed, no less than 12 to 15 million acres of new land could be irrigated. This is the equivalent of more than one-half the present cultivated area. And most of this now unfertile land would produce crops all year long. It has been estimated by the Jewish National Fund that with modern technology and the proper planning of crops based on weather and location, a two-acre plot could be adequate to feed a typical Middle Eastern farmer and his family. The additional land if cultivated could provide enough food for as many as 10 million families or 35 to 50 million people. The effective management of water resources in the Middle East is of vital importance, for apart from the increase in agricultural production, it also improves sanitation and health. As one observer wrote:

> *The boon to the Middle East of an imaginative water program can scarcely be exaggerated. If proof were necessary, one need look no further than Israel, where planning, a systematic program, modern irrigation techniques, and ingenious use of every available drop of water have produced remarkable results in a single decade.*
>
> *But the fact remains that what Israel has done even without Jordan River water can be equalled throughout the Middle East, and indeed, surpassed in countries blessed by greater supplies of water. It is clear that water resources are adequate to assure a sustained and flourishing growth throughout the area. But the availability of these resources hasn't been enough in the past, and it isn't enough now, to do it.* *

Furthermore the Arab states had so far ignored a factor fundamental to river development, namely, that watersheds are not defined by political lines. Instead of sharing the rivers on a regional basis, each country has preferred to go about it alone. The result has been tragic in terms of wasted water.

3. Population growth

The food deficit in the Middle East is growing steadily, and might reach the point of critical shortages in essential commodities in countries like Egypt that could result in mass starvation. In addition to the present inadequate regional irrigation system and the lack of sufficient land suitable for immediate agricultural cultivation, population growth throughout the Middle East is becoming an alarming problem, especially for Egypt. Egypt today has an estimated population of 40 million, and is growing by at least one million a year. By the year 2,000, at the present rate of increase, Egypt will have doubled its population, an alarming prospect in view of Egypt's insufficient resources. The other Arab states are not as yet

---

*Eric Johnson, "A Key to the Future of the Middle East," *The New York Times Magazine*, October 19, 1958.

particularly alarmed about their own population explosions, while in Israel, official policy encourages high birth and immigration rates. However, since what happens in Egypt is critical, anything that causes internal turmoil within Egypt could have serious repercussions on peace throughout the region. Besides government-sponsored birth control programs, Egypt's population explosion could be eased by facilitating population shifts throughout the Arab world. Iraq, Syria and Saudi Arabia could each absorb millions but they are unlikely to do so without first reaching greater internal stability and inter-Arab unity. This in turn presumes peace in the region.

4. Industrial expansion

In the area of industrial expansion within the Arab states, Israel could also play a crucial role. Israel's technology and experience could be put to use to create virtually millions of new jobs. The growing Arab population makes it imperative to find new sources of income. Besides, the continuing modernization of agriculture is releasing more and more farm workers who flock to the towns looking for jobs. Expanded Arab industry could utilize all this manpower once intensive and massive training programs get underway. Industrial expansion should ideally stress the manufacturing of personal commodities and household equipment initially and later on developing heavier industry. The Arab market by itself is large enough to consume all of the output.

What makes industrilization possible in the Arab world on a greater scale than ever before is not only the abundance of manpower, but more importantly, abundance of hard currency from the production of oil.

In addition, the Western industrialized countries, primarily the United States, could be induced to invest in large industrial projects, such as car manufacturing as well as other heavy machinery once the threat of renewed war is removed.

5. Tourism and Trade

The tourist industry in Egypt, Israel, Syria, Jordan, and Lebanon could be further developed through joint ventures. Israel's tourist industry has proved highly successful, due to imaginative programs, modern hotel buildings, beautification of landscapes, and preservation of natural landmarks. Egypt alone could benefit immeasurably by developing its tourist industry, especially by rebuilding the cities and towns around the Delta — Alexandria, Port Said, Ismailia, and others. Increased revenue from tourism, however, depends largely on establishing peace.

The Israeli and the Arab Palestinian experience in trade, agriculture, and other social and welfare programs since 1967 has demonstrated clearly that economic cooperation on these levels *can* transcend political and ideological differences. Israel's experience in the Gaza Strip and on the West Bank argues against those who can only accept a solution by military means. Religious and cultural differences between Arabs and Jews have not been significant causes of social friction between the two sides.

Both sides have a greater number of economic and social common denominators to promote cooperation than they have discrepancies to provoke renewed hostilities.

For the Israelis the task of becoming a full-fledged Middle Eastern country is hard and complex, and although it may take some serious internal sacrifices, a peace of reconciliation with the Arabs warrants it. The acceptance of Israel by the principal belligerent Arab states — Syria, Jordan, and Egypt — would not be a sign of weakness, but rather a sign of strength. For it takes imagination and wisdom to move from confrontation to cooperation, especially when the first *may* lead to disaster and the latter is *bound* to lead to prosperity.

As Henry Kissinger once observed: "States interests are intimately linked to their power, and power is a complex compound consisting, of course, of military capability and economic resources, but depending ultimately on the other crucial element — the quality of the political leadership."*

---

*Stephen R. Graubard, *Kissinger: Portrait of a Mind.* (New York: W. N. Norton & Company, Inc. 1973), p. 12.

Chapter III

CONFLICTS AMONG THE ARAB STATES

The rivalries among the Arabs and the political instability in many of the nations prolong the Middle East crisis. It is still the case that the reins of government are more likely to be transferred as a result of force than by peaceful means. The present regimes in Egypt, Syria, Iraq, Libya, and Algeria, for example, were installed through military coups. Usually, these military takeovers resulted in the abandonment of the existing constitution and the institution of a new one that did not permit general elections. Political succession become the prerogative of a small grouping within the military. Even in some of the Arab countries like Jordan, Saudi Arabia and Morocco, whose governments are not the result of military coups, political power is a personal possession of the king, bestowed upon him in perpetuity.

Neither the monarchies nor the revolutionary regimes among the Arab states, however, can be viewed as permanent. The danger of overthrow is always present. The Egyptian, Iraqi, and Libyan monarchies, for instance, were replaced by revolutionary regimes in 1952, 1953, and 1970 respectively. The revolutionary regimes of Syria and Iraq were overthrown in February, 1963 and March, 1973, respectively, not to mention the numerous abortive attempts by counter-revolutionaries over the years to overthrow the revolutionary regimes in Egypt, Libya, and the Sudan. This political instability among the Arab states has socio-economic, cultural, and political roots.

THE SOURCES OF ARAB INTERNAL INSTABILITY

Several factors contribute directly to the internal instability of many of the Arab states and foster rivalries among them.

1) **Economic Problems:** Two issues have dominated the Arab political scene since the late 1940s: imperialism and Israel. The Arabs' preoccupation with these have been used by their leaders to soothe their own peoples dissatisfaction with chronic internal economic and social problems. This is especially true in Egypt. Economic dislocation can be a major cause of domestic political instability. Such unrest, however, cannot be removed by sporadic and shallow economic and social programs.

Economic development throughout the Arab world could be met by utilizing the revenues of the Arab oil producers. Yet the extent to which this will occur depends largely on two conditions: a) the willingness of the rich Arab oil countries to share their wealth, and b) the sincerity of efforts to implement social reforms as economic development occurs. Arab society is still composed mainly of landlords and peasants, with the commercial and industrial middle class in the hands of ethnic minorities. The new professional calss of teachers, lawyers, and journalists lacks the financial resources and political power to actively promote social and economic reforms.

Political independence by itself after World War II did not provide an instant cure to the economic problems facing the Arab countries.

> *. . . When national destiny was under some measure of foreign control, failures in economic, political, and social progress could always be blamed on "imperialism," which could not be expected to give priority to native development over imperial interest. Although the colonial record of France and Great Britain in the Arab world is much better than Arab nationalists admit, it did not keep pace with the growing demands for economic, educational, social, and political progress, and thus appeared to be the major obstacle to the achievement of modernity. Now that the foreigner has departed and responsibility is in the hands of "our" national leaders, there is a popular expectation that everything will be put right. Although national leaders may still try to blame their country's internal problems on the "neo-colonialists," their public is not so easily misled. Having been told for at least a generation that the departure of the foreigner was the precondition for national progress,*

> the masses gradually tend to hold their own leaders responsible for current failures. *

All of the social and economic ills that existed before political independence — the concentration of wealth, the exploitation of the poor, the poverty and disease that engulf the majority of the people, the corrupt judicial system continued after independence. The Arab states, however, after several decades of experience with political independence, have begun to realize that economic cooperation among themselves is necessary for future political stability.

2) **Parochial loyalties:** The economic and social problems within the independent Arab states were magnified by the Arab's centuries-old tendency to be loyal to his immediate surroundings. Therefore, his understanding of "national" interests was limited, and even if he acknowledged them, they were considered secondary to his more immediate parochial interests.

Arab leaders dealt with these interests by harnessing the loyalties of their citizens, the same method Western society had used centuries earlier: creating a supra-local entity known as the "nation" and fostering allegiance to it through taxation, the charisma of the head of state, education, and military service. Local affiliations cannot be totally erased, so adherence to familial and tribal entities continued to persist, as in all societies. Over the years nationalism has gradually swept up the masses and contributed appreciatively to the development of a larger Arab social cohesiveness. Still, a conflict continues to exist between a loyalty to the smaller, more intimate grouping and the larger, less personal nation.

> The real problem is therefore to help the Arab develop a sense of responsibility toward the public and find enough motivation to give his final loyalty to the larger group, the nation. **

---

* John S. Badeau, *American Approach to the Arab World* (New York: Harper & Row, 1968), pp. 37-38.

** Sania Hamady, *Temperament and Character of the Arabs* (New York: Twayne Publishers, 1960), p. 96.

3) **Psychological Burdens:** In the recent past the Arabs have anguished over the vast difference between their historical contributions to civilization and their present inadequacies. The past glories of Arab civilization contrast markedly with the recent experiences of isolation, ineffectiveness and at times, impotence. Arab self-esteem has naturally suffered and the lack of it has heavily burdened the Arab political and social awakening. This disparity between the grandeur of their past and an awakened awareness of their technological and political underdevelopment provided the initial impetus to their resentment of colonialism.

In order for the Arabs to counterbalance somewhat the resulting psychological sense of inferiority, they placed the blame for their exploited condition not on their own leaders, but on Western imperialism. Since Britain and France were the last colonial powers to have a considerable political mark on the Arab states, for a long time they were singled out as the source of all evil. The centuries of Turkish misrule that preceded Western European domination were underplayed.

The Arab people still bear the psychological scars of their colonial experience. It was for them the experience of cultural defeat. It brought a loss of confidence in themselves and their culture that implanted both with a sense of inferiority and a bitter conviction that the West had not only exploited their material wealth but had somehow stolen away their spiritual possessions and cultural heritage. *

But when the battle was won and independence finally achieved, many leaders of newly independent countries have

---

*Winston Burdett, *Encounter with the Middle East* (New York: Atheneum Press, 1969), pp. 50-51.

As pointed out by Winston Burdett, the period of Western rule was much shorter than that experienced by many other colonial peoples: 70 years of British domination in Egypt, 60 in Sudan, 40 in Iraq, 28 in Palestine, 130 years of French Suzerainty in Algeria, but less than half as many in Morocco and only one generation of French rule in Lebanon and a similar brief span in Syria. The oldest British holding in the world was the port of Aden.

> had to realize. at least subconsciously, that they were inwardly a good deal closer to their former rulers than to their own countrymen. It may be too much to say that they resent the West for having taught them patterns of thinking which make them strangers to their own people: it is clear that they require anticolonialism as a means of achieving a sense of personal identity. Precisely because they are inwardly so close to the West, many of the newly independent states cannot afford to align themselves with it politically.
>
> In these terms, neutralism and anti-colonialism are not so much a policy as a spiritual necessity. The constant reiteration of non-alignment may be the means by which the leaders of newly independent nations reassure themselves; they can be certain of their independence only by acting it out every day and on every issue. This explains why the most strident advocates of neutrality are often the very people who in dress, bearing, and manner of thinking are closest to the West — indeed, who often have spent very little of their lives in their own countries. Individuals with firm roots in their own traditions, on the other hand, seem to feel less compulsive about proclaiming their independence daily and seem more prepared to act jointly with the Western powers when their interests coincide. *

4) **Lack of Leadership:** The lack of responsible, strong, and confident leaders among the Arabs has also contributed to political instability. Political fragmentation, local loyalties, suspicion, and distrust have frequently acted to prevent leaders from emerging and assuming power without alienating this or that faction in the process.

> The countries controlled indirectly, such as most of those in the Middle East, suffered the demoralizing influence of foreign control without a corresponding gain in the training of leadership groups or of administrative cohesion. On the contrary, while in areas governed directly boundaries were

---

*Kissinger, Henry, *Nuclear Weapons and Foreign Power* (New York: W. W. Norton & Co., Inc., 1969). pp. 215-216.

> *drawn with an eye to what constituted a viable unit, in other territories they were often drawn to ensure that the countries would not be viable. For the most part, boundaries in the Middle East reflected neither a common history nor an economic or administrative necessity. They were drawn to guarantee weakness and rivalry.* *

> *... for the most part, the people of these countries [the Arab states] lack any experience in governing themselves. More important, they either lack an elite with experience in this essential business or the existing elite is indifferent to public welfare because of its tradition of family self-interest. Both old and new elites are often grossly inefficient or shockingly corrupt, and this is why in so many developing countries [including many long independent like the Latin American] the military officers corps, constituting either the only relatively effective or the only relatively disinterested elite, has taken over the government. Unfortunately, the temptations of power have often proved too much for them to resist, and the result is military dictatorship.* **

Historically, the Arabs have had several outstanding leaders, such as Ali Abn Abi Tarik and Salaeh Al-Din, who left unique marks on Arab history for their vision, heroism, and valor. Recent Arab history, however, can claim only one leader who came close in stature to Abi Tarik and Al-Din. The late president of Egypt, Gamal Abdel Nasser, during his years in power from 1952-1970, reached the heights that commanded the respect not only of other Arab leaders but also those of many other states, friend and foe alike. Nasser showed insight into the workings of power as soon as he acquired it. He had the skills of a statesman and the powers of the mass leader; he was a brilliant tactician, and a bold and imaginative strategist in the manipulation of power. He understood the needs of the people; he spoke their language; and he conducted himself as if he were one of them. Nasser was by far the most distinguished leader

---

* *Ibid.,* pp. 214-215.

** Charles Yost, *The Conduct and the Misconduct of Foreign Affairs* (New York: Random House, 1972), pp. 113-114.

the Arabs have had in the last hundred years. Yet despite his outstanding leadership qualities, he often fell victim to ambition, ruthlessness, and impatience. He was at once a master of political conspiracies and a slave to his self-grandeur. Even with such shortcomings, Nasser was a political figure who considerably influenced the fate of Egypt and the rest of the Arab world.

Nasser's desire to bring about Arab unity, and his intention to initiate sweeping social reforms were met with resistance both within Egypt and from without. The leaders of Syria, Iraq, Sudan, and Libya, who watched Nasser's revolutionary path closely, lacked both the political experience and ability to translate grand social and economic reform programs into reality.

> *Thus, we find that the Arab military leadership and the traditional ones as well, which have installed themselves in certain Arab countries since 1920, had their only justification in terms of meeting external danger. They have now given a public demonstration of their impotence in war. What reason do we have to suppose that they will be more successful in economic planning, development, education, foreign affairs or finance! They [the leadership] have divided the Arab world into camps on matters which are neither relevant nor along the lines that make sense.* *

> *... the new leadership has been able to prop itself upon the total, almost mystical support of the half-awakened masses without having to resort to the intermediary agency of political parties and groups: legality no longer needs the vote —it derives it directly from a mystic delegation of power by the people. This is perhaps the reason the attitude of the new leadership in the Arab world toward any form of political organization is expressed either by perfunctory assent to restricted party activity as in Iraq or by contemptuous sublimation of the energies through a single national organization shorn of any real power as in the United Arab Republic [Egypt].* **

---

* Cecil Hourani, *Encounter*, Beirut, November 1967.

** Hisham Sharabi, *The Arab Middle East and Muslim Africa* (New York: Frederick A. Praeger, 1960), pp. 60-61.

5) Identity Crisis: The identity crisis of young Arabs has originated from three main factors: 1) a sense of social and psychological uprootedness; 2) the breaking of ties with religious authorities; 3) a lack of coordinated purpose.

First, although Arab nationalism has spread rapidly since the turn of the century, the young Arab intellectuals who were army officers as well as those in the upper classes lacked the confidence to assert themselves in any attempt to effect change. The young intellectual was frustrated by his inability to grasp the challenge that Arab nationalism presented. For generations, Christian intellectuals and scholars had provided the young Arabs with the philosophical framework that made the need for developing their own unnecessary.

Second, the effect of the Moslem religion on the Arab masses has for centuries been powerful and uncompromising. The young Arab intellectuals, however, prided themselves on their freedom from this religious bondage. But what was to take its place, to fill the spiritual vacuum left once Islam was denied? Hopefully, a program of pure nationalistic fervor! But they could not make the transition because they lacked a well-articulated and appealing set of goals which the masses would willingly adopt. This hiatus continued to exist, even after several Arab countries gained political independence.

Finally, the various intellectual groups were further divided philosophically; each adopted a different set of political and social values. Behind the facade of intellectual unity, personal rivalry and sectarian animosities remained the general configuration. Thus we find that the young Arab intellectual, with all his enthusiasm and drive, could not rise above cultural and traditional barriers in order to contend with social injustice, economic exploitation, and corrupt political systems.

In sum, political instability within the Arab states did not arise out of the lack of political independence or the onset of independence itself. Most of the cuases of political instability are historical and relate to prior social, economic, and cultural conditions in the Arab countries.

ARAB NATIONALISM

The early Arab nationalist movements (1850-1920) remained confined to a small group of upper class intellectuals, who were unable to convince or attract the masses. Arab nationalism undoubtedly accelerated the process by which several Arab countries achieved political independence. At the same time, nationalism became a source of insecurity and fear to those countries which viewed it as a cause that might compromise their own independent political status.

Arab nationalism does not differ basically from the generally accepted meaning of "nationalism."* Yet several distinctions should be made. 1) Arab nationalism included a form of "Socialism" that advocates the central government's control of the major industries, such as oil, steel, transportation, and textiles. 2) Arab nationalism incorporated ideology, territory, language, religion, and history. 3) Arab unity, or Pan-Arabism, became the ultimate goal of Arab nationalism. 4) The destruction of Israel was viewed as essential to the realization of Arab nationalism.

These aspects of Arab nationalism have contributed to the Arab nations' political instability. It is quite natural that discrepancies in viewpoint and interpretation should arise since ideologies are born in turmoil. Thus today there is no one single way in which Arab nationalism is perceived by both revolutionary and conservative Arab governments.

The philosophical aspect of modern Arab nationalism was well-stated by the founder of the Syrian Ba'ath party (founded April 6, 1946), Michael Aflag:

> *If love is the soil in which your nationalism is nourished, then there is no scope for different views on how it ought to be defined and de-limited. Nationalism is racial in the sense that we hold sacred this Arab race which has, since the earliest historical epochs, carried within itself a vitality and a nobility which had enabled it to go on renewing and perfecting itself, taking advantage of triumphs and defeats alike.***

---

* Nationalism is a policy or an ideology that views the interests of a nation as separate from the interests of other nations or the common interests of all nations. Nationalism may also be viewed as a desire for national independence, subordinating all social and economic rivalries for the common cause.

** Michael Aflag, *Fl Sabil Al Ba'ath*, Beirut, 1949. Essay dated 1940. (Berkeley: University of California Press, 1962), pp. 242-243.

Aflag maintained that Arab failures are due to the decadence of the Arab spirit. By recreating Arab consciousness, the Arab nations could be reborn. Ultimately he thought there would be one Arab nation stretching from the Atlantic to the Persian Gulf.

The Ba'ath party of Syria today is probably one of the strongest instruments promoting Arab nationalism in its broadest scope. It is violently nationalistic; it views all Arabs as belonging to one "nation"; it is socialist in political orientation; it advocates the abolition of all class distinctions; its primary goal is Arab unity; it does not recognize the Arab states' political boundaries; and finally, it advocates unrelenting war against Israel.

> *Arab nationalism has become a living force, not to be justified theoretically by marshalling historical or sociological facts, but to be embodied in an all-embracing creed. This creed does not consist of any analytic findings about Arab nationality; it is represented as a philosophy of life as well as an ideal of government, a credo as well as a manifesto. It sets out, in fact, to be a complete ideology to match the rival world ideologies of communism and democratic capitalism.* *

President Nasser elaborated on the concept of Arab nationalism, although in principle his own ideas were based on Aflag's philosophy. Nasser, who was not so idealistic as to misunderstand the practical importance of mass support, tended to reduce the concept of nationalism to more serviceable terms he could easily relate to the public, such as his arms deal with Czechoslovakia in 1955, (which was supposed to demonstrate a break with old policies), the Aswan Dam project, and the nationalization of the Suez Canal. In his long, and at times furious, discussions with Aflag and Salah Al Buitar, both creators of the Syrian Ba'ath party, prior to the establishment of the Syrian-Egyptian union, (February, 1958) Nasser insisted on the following: 1) that all political parties be dismantled, leaving the Arab Socialist Union in Egypt as the sole political organization; 2) that a specific program of Arab socialism, unity, and freedom be prepared for the general public; and 3) that the Egyptian revolution

---

* Nessim Rejwan, *The Middle East in Transition* (New York: Frederick A. Praeger, 1958), pp. 145-146.

take the lead and supply the guidelines for all Arab nations in order to give "special meaning and cohesiveness" to Arab nationalism. "Our revolution," Nasser stated, "was the first to call for social democracy. This fact led us to socialism and to the inevitability of socialism as a prerequisite for true democracy." *

Nasser did not think Arab nationalism could be viable and complete, however, unless Egypt were the creator and promoter of the entire philosophy underlying Arab nationalism. It was for this reason that Nasser opposed attempts by Syria and Iraq to unite their forces, ideologically or otherwise, unless he himself played the main role in it.

Arab nationalism, despite differing views on how it was to be implemented, promoted a sense of national duty and purpose that were instrumental in achieving political independence for various Arab states. Yet the gains made by Arab nationalism also caused political disunity in certain instances. For Arab nationalism was not accepted by all the Arab states, both revolutionary and conservative, as the final political goal. Most of the revolutionary regimes subscribed to the general idea, but each reserved to itself a wide latitude for interpretation in order to further develop and enrich the concept as a whole.

The Arab nations today may be somewhat arbitrarily divided into three camps: the *traditionalist conservatives* and/or royalist (Jordan, Saudi Arabia, Lebanon, Morocco, Kuwait, Northern Yemen, and Abu Dhabi and a few other sheikdoms;) the *revolutionary moderates* (Egypt, Sudan, Algeria, Tunisia, Somalia); and finally, the *revolutionary extremists* (Syria, Southern Yemen, Libya, and Iraq). Although these countries share the same culture and similar historical and religious traditions to a great extent, the concept of Arab nationalism has not been understood to mean the same either to one of the above groups of states or even to two states in the same group. Thus, as Cecil Hourani, the renowned Arab spokesman, has commented:

> *The attempt to identify Arab nationalism with the "progressive" as opposed to the "reactionary" regimes has led to senseless and dangerous conflicts between some of the*

---

* Malcolm Kerr, *The Arab Cold War* (New York: Oxford University Press, 1967), p. 81.

Arab governments, just as it has inflamed and divided public opinion all over the Arab world. We must reject and resist the claims that any one Arab regime or party or leader has a monopoly on Arab nationalism and refuse to accept that differences of opinion or of interest provide an adequate basis for classifying regimes or individuals as genuine nationalists or traitors. *

The basis for the discrepancies in understanding, especially among the leaders of Egypt, Syria, and Iraq, is directly related to the ideological misconception of Arab nationalism.

The separate nationalisms of Arab countries were attacked in theory as being the heritage of colonialism, introduced and cultivated by the imperial powers as instruments to divide and control the awakening Arab world. Thus a Syrian diplomat told an American audience that he was ashamed to appear before them as a representative of Syria. "I should stand here," he said, "as a representative of the great Arab Nation." Some of the Arab states have expressed the same feeling in their constitutions, where it is stated that the country is a part of the Arab Nation, thus suggesting an ultimate loyalty higher than local patriotism.

The separate nationalisms of individual countries are an overwhelming factor in all the area's problems, yet in accepting this inevitable situation, Arab nationalists live with an accusing conscience and a wistful longing for the unrealized, which leaves them baffled and difficult to deal with. **

As indicated earlier, Arab nationalism sought a political and social system that would be applicable to the Arab masses. At the same time, it encompassed a wide range of social and economic reforms that were bound to raise fierce objections and diverse opposition on the part of some vested groups. The social and the economic

---

* Cecil Hourani, "The Moment of Truth", *Encounter*, Beirut, November 1967.

**Badeau, *op. cit.*, p. 48.

structures of the Arab states differed greatly from one another and could not be reconciled by ideology alone. What further deepened the controversy between the Arab states was not so much nationalism as a philosophy, but the lack of political tolerance in the process of implementing that philosophy.

IDEOLOGY OF ARAB NATIONALISM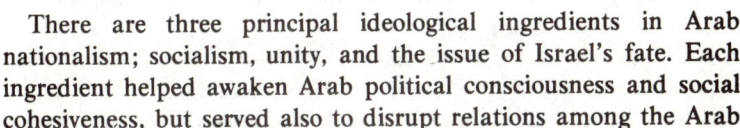

There are three principal ideological ingredients in Arab nationalism; socialism, unity, and the issue of Israel's fate. Each ingredient helped awaken Arab political consciousness and social cohesiveness, but served also to disrupt relations among the Arab states in their implementation.

Arab Socialism

Socialism as a basic component of Arab nationalism was an important source of disagreement among the various Arab states. Although in principle the Arab states, especially the revolutionary regimes, accepted the principle of Arab socialism, they differed in their interpretation of the term and thereby in their implementation of it. Some associated "socialism" with "communism" or semi-totalitarian state control of all important facets of the economy. By and large, however, Arab socialism is a combination of the western style of socialism, such as in Britain and Scandinavia, and Marxist-Leninist theories of socialism.

> *Thus it is not surprising that Arab socialism has varied from country to country. While having basic elements in common, the systems followed in Algeria, the U.A.R., Syria, and Iraq have been different. No single brand of Arab socialism has proved itself the regional pattern for development; and the accomplishments in the Arab countries which have adopted socialist systems have not yet demonstrated either its efficiency or its power to endure. The enthusiast for Arab socialism seen from afar [as in Libya or Jordan] has often revised his opinion when socialism has not proved that it is the wave of the future ...*
>
> *In Egypt the dilemma of Arab socialism is illustrated by two attitudes toward the state-operated economic system — "Arab socialism." One senior policy-planner in Cairo said,*

> *"The peasant has been so long deprived of even minimal decency that he cannot be made to wait much longer. In spite of everything, we must push on even more rapidly." In contrast, an Arab diplomat said that he had lost his faith in Arab socialism not because he disagreed with its theory, but because "when you take an already over-burdened and inefficient civil service, then add to it the huge responsibility of running an industrial system, the result can only be a complete breakdown."**

According to President Nasser, however, socialism meant less Draconian reconstruction and more self-reliance and social justice achieved through the elimination of monopolism, capitalism, and feudalism. These measures would include the reclamation and redistribution of land, provisions for health, education, and other social welfare services, and finally in the administration and the profit sharing of industrial firms. Privately owned big business concerns would retain only limited freedom. This new ideology, i.e., Nasser's Arab socialism, was geared to secure "economic liberty." According to Nasser, "no one should be allowed to exercise power over the economy of his country or its inhabitants." True liberty, Nasser asserted, is economic liberty and social equality.

Arab *socialism* is basically derived from Marxist-Leninist theory. However, Arab *nationalism* contained basic social, economic and religious tenets that contradicted the concept of socialism. Thus we find that

> *To some groups socialism might mean social justice, while to others it meant Marxist socialism involving all the forces of production and trade. Under such a brand of socialism, the state must take over all the wealth of the country. Another group of nationalists was prepared to settle for much less than this . . . What [the masses] believe in is their religion which certainly has nothing in common with pure Marxist ideologies.***

---

* Badeau, *op. cit.*, pp. 109-110, 39.

** Kerr, *op. cit.*, p. 164.

ARAB UNITY

Another ingredient of Arab nationalism is Arab unity, or as it is sometimes termed, Pan-Arabism. The continuous conflict of interests among Arab leaders until recently has hampered all efforts to achieve the economic and political common ground conducive to political unity. As they struggle for a renewed identity, the Arab states are in search of a formula that will fulfill their dream of regional unity. In their failure to find an acceptable answer to chronic internal political and economic problems, the Arab states find themselves haunted by the need for unity on the one hand and their inability to achieve it on the other.

What conditions have impelled the Arab states toward unity? First, and most obviously, a common history, language and religion, geographic proximity, and a common cultural heritage. Second, the felt need on the part of young Arab intellectuals to separate religious and civil authorities constitutionally so that religious traditionalism will not hamper social and economic reform. Third, the return of the Jews en masse to Palestine and the extablishment of the state of Israel gave a common cause for joint concern and action. Fourth, the leaders of politically unstable states, such as Syria and Iraq, have generally held that the durability and the territorial integrity of their respective countries would ultimately depend on Pan-Arab unity.

Most Arabs do not consider unity a luxury, but a necessity for survival, the essential prerequisite for social and economic reforms and as a defense against exploitation and conquest. Nasser and Syrian leader Michael Aflag assumed there was neither time nor need for a process of gradual integration, socially, economically, and otherwise. They indeed believed that unity could be achieved through the action of a single leader who had the stature and commanded the respect of the Arab people. During his long and elaborate discussion with the representatives of Syria regarding the creation of a union between the two countries, Nasser maintained that unity was a matter of mechanical arrangement. Once agreed to in principle, the rest of the pieces would fall into place. Yet the disasters of the "heroic" imagination of Nasser and Aflag and their passionate quest for "instant unity" turned out to be very costly. Unity was supposed to provide a remedy for their political frustrations, cultural revival, national regeneration, lost pride and humiliation. Disunity was considered the source of all ills and only unity could provide the cure.

In addition to the instability of individual Arab states, there were several factors that severely hindered efforts to achieve a lasting unity between two or more Arab states, let alone a Pan-Arabian union.

1) **Lack of economic and social preparation:** The Arab world is divided between the economic "haves" and the "have-nots." Borders that were arbitrarily drawn between the various Arab states by Britain and France did not take into consideration the economic viability of each independent country. Only in the last few years have the oil-rich states begun assisting the poorer states, and even now it is not done unconditionally but always with the expectation of some kind of political consideration. To date, Arab leaders have not learned that political unifications cannot survive unless they are based on strong and mutually beneficial economic considerations. This does not mean that the nations which contemplate unification should secure enough wealth in advance; rather, it means that whatever economic resources are available must be made equally accessible to the intended partners of the unified Arab world.

Social integration, despite a shared heritage, has been as difficult to achieve as economic integration. For example, in their short-lived union, the Syrians and Egyptians were soon to find that the mere *desire* for political unity is not sufficient. The average Syrian felt animosity, distrust, and suspicion toward the Egyptians who entered Syria, not as partners but as conquerors. The Egyptian-Syrian union lasted only three and one-half years (February 1958-September 1961) and was correctly considered by political observers to be an exercise in political futility, bound to collapse after a short period of time.

Another attempt at unification that failed was the planned merger of Egypt and Libya in September, 1973. In this instance, President Sadat of Egypt rejected the proposed union. Despite the enormous economic advantages accruing to both countries, Sadat felt that Libya was promoting — in fact imposing—unenlightened social and economic doctrines based completely on the rules of the Koran.

2) **Domination of the Egyptian military:** The preoccupation of the Arab states with military preparation and an ever-increasing influence of the military establishment in all walks of life gave rise to

dissent and antagonism among many younger intellectuals. In particular, this was the case in Syria. For these individuals the thought of being ruled and to a degree subordinated by "big brother" (Egypt) was simply unacceptable. The Syrian people rejected the excessive military presence of the Egyptian army in Syria following the short-lived Syrian-Egyptian union, while the Egyptian army looked upon the Syrians as if they were just a northern province.

The concept of Pan-Arabism was promoted particularly during the fifties and the sixties by the Arab revolutionary regimes of Egypt, Syria and Iraq, where the armies took over the political and administrative responsibilities. A non-military union could not be envisioned. Each Arab state that contemplated unity wanted its own army to remain the supreme power. Winston Burdett illustrated this rivalry during the process of unification:

> *General Kassem's revolution in Iraq in 1958 seemed, at first, to swell the oncoming Pan-Arab tide, but that strange dictator had other ideas and soon dominated and suppressed the Nasserites in his midst. Five years later, when the Kassem dictatorship was overturned and a regime led by the Ba'ath, the party of Pan-Arab nationalism, seized power in Baghdad, Nasser's credit soared again amid excited talk of an Egyptian-Syrian reunion and elaborate negotiations for a tripartite union including Egypt, Syria, and Iraq. But the interests of sovereign states and the jealousies of political factors defeated these ambitious schemes. The moments of euphoria were short-lived.* *

In principle, the army was supposed to keep itself out of politics, but this simply did not work. Egyptian officers with political ambitions carried on their intrigues and asserted themselves beyond their official capacities, citing the success of Egypt's experience in "proper" civil-military coordination. The Syrian military officers as well as civilian political leaders felt that for the sake of the union, they had turned into second-class citizens. The final word on all vital matters that concerned Syria proper came either from Egypt or from the Egyptian high command in Syria.

---

* Winston Burdett, *Encounter with the Middle East* (New York: Atheneum, 1969), p. 55.

3) **Lack of political tolerance:** One of the major points of controversy was naturally the political structure of any union. In the Syrian-Egyptian case, Syria insisted on a parliamentary regime with representation proportional to the populations of both regions. The Syrians wanted to allow political parties as separate entities while Egypt demanded the dismantling of all political organizations except the one ruling party — the Arab Socialist Union. The Egyptian demand was based on the premise that unless all parties were abolished, there would be a conflict over party loyalties and mutual confidence would never be solidly established.

The Egyptians, led by Nasser, and the Syrians, motivated by Aflag, were extremely anxious to "actualize" any kind of unity so that the Arab world could be quickly placed on a new historical course of fulfillment. Nasser, though he often demonstrated statesmanship and a remarkable political shrewdness, failed to understand that Arab unity could not be achieved through one magical stroke. Moreover, the political or military forces that opposed him in several Arab countries were suspicious of his own ambitions to see a great Arab empire in his own lifetime — perhaps with himself as supreme ruler. Arab leaders did not resent Nasser as a man so much as they resented the Egyptian bureaucracy and arrogance that he represented. Thus we find that Nasser, in his effort to accelerate the movement toward unity, was forced to resort to force and political espionage to rid himself of his political opponents. As the result of his policy, especially after the dismantling of his union with Syria, internal Arab turmoil reached its peak.

> *At the end of 1963, more Arab states were at each other's throats at once than ever before. Syria was feuding with Egypt, and since November, with Iraq. Egypt and Saudi Arabia were locked in a struggle for the future of Yemen, where 40,000 Egyptian troops had failed to win a final victory for the revolution there. Algeria had come to blows with Morocco over a border dispute and had another dispute with Tunisia. Tunisia and Morocco had been cool to each other ever since Tunisia had recognized the independence of Mauritania. Egypt was hostile to Jordan, as well as Saudi Arabia, as a matter of ideological principle, and took the side of the revolutionary Morocco, and was trading complaints with Lebanon over border incidents. Of*

> the thirteen member states of the Arab League, only three
> were on satisfactory terms with everyone: Kuwait [towards
> whom Qasim's successors in Baghdad had relented], the
> Sudan, and Libya. The majority of these quarrels, whatever
> their specific origins, pitted revolutionary against con-
> servative or moderate regimes: Egypt, Algeria, Iraq, the
> Republic of Yemen, and Syria, variously against the others.
> But of all disputes, the most bitter and least soluble was
> between the rival revolutionary movements of Damascus
> and Cairo.*

4) **The destruction of Israel:** One of the most crucial factors that crippled Arab unity was the goal of eliminating Israel as a political entity. This element was an integral part of the concept of Arab unity, at least since the advent of Nasser in 1952 and, most likely, since Israel's founding in 1948. Yet the repeated humiliation of the Arabs at the hands of the Israelis in the wars of 1948, 1956, and 1967 crippled their hopes for achieving unity at the expense of Israel.

The manifesto of the United Arab Republic (Egypt) that was published in April 1963, attached Arab unity directly to the destruction of Israel.

> Unity is especially a part of the revolution because it is
> profoundly connected with the Palestinian cause and with
> the national duty to liberate that country . . . It was the
> disaster of Palestine that revealed the conspiracy of the
> reactionary classes and exposed the treacheries of the hired
> regional parties and their denial of the people's objective
> and aspiration . . . It was the disaster of Palestine that
> showed the weakness and backwardness of the economic
> and social systems that prevailed in the country, released
> the revolutionary energies of our people and awakened the
> spirit of revolt against imperialism, injustice, poverty, and
> underdevelopment. It was the disaster of Palestine that
> clearly indicated the path of salvation, the path of unity,
> freedom, and socialism.**

---

* Malcolm Kerr, *The Arab Cold War* (New York: Oxford University Press, 1967), pp. 151-152.

** Excerpt from the manifesto of the U.A.R. that was published in April 1963. It was prepared in connection with an abortive attempt to establish federal union. The manifesto was signed by Gamal Abdel Nasser and the presidents of Syria and Iraq.

The repeated failure of Arab leaders to fulfill on what they promised their people — in terms of economic improvement, social reforms, and fairer land distribution has strengthened the need for a scapegoat on which they could put all the blame for the misfortunes encountered. Israel, which filled that role perfectly, became the indispensable means to divert the attention of the Arab masses from their more immediate economic problems.

The third and final component of Arab nationalism lies in the stimulating effect of Israel's existence on Arab nationalism and unity. The mere fact of the return of the Jews to Palestine in great numbers was a main impetus and stimulus to Arab nationalism. In fact, the beginning of the Jewish "revolution" that was eventually fulfilled with the establishment of the state of Israel, coincided with the awakening of an Arab political awareness (early 1900's).

President Nasser in his book *The Philosophy of the Revolution,* recalled his first sense of nationalism while in secondary school. "I used to go out in general strike with my comrades every year on the Second of November to protest the Balfour Declaration which Britain had made on behalf of the Jews, giving them a national home in Palestine, thus tyrannously wresting it from its rightful owners."

In another sense, the inclusion of Israel's destruction as an essential part of Arab nationalistic dogma was partly necessitated by expediency. It was adopted by shaky Arab regimes, such as Syria, as a means of focusing frustration outward, and as a pretext to cover internal failure, such as in Egypt. The existence of Israel in itself became a traumatic experience to every Arab.

> *Israel is an offense not to any particular Arab nation but to Arabism itself. It is the universal focus of frustration, felt by groups and sects and classes far outside the circle of the intelligentsia. Within that circle, the conviction has taken hold that Arabism is disabled by the mere presence of Israel, that it cannot be whole again as long as Israel exists, and that there can be no cultural rebirth or genuine reconstruction of society until this offense is redeemed.* *

Arab nationalism in relation to Israel has evolved in four distinct stages: from the early 1900's through 1948; from 1948 to 1956; from

---

* Burdett, *op. cit.,* p. 60.

1956 to 1967; and from 1967 to the present. The Arab-Israeli confrontation during the first stage was not significant in terms of Arab unity and its relation to th existence of Israel. During this period—1900 to 1949—Arab unity as a practical concept was still in its infancy. No Arab leader at the time could enviision the realization of Arab unity, when social, economic and political diversity prevailed.

While the objection to Israel's existence during the second stage served as a unifying factor on the one hand, it became a singularly potent and disruptive factor on the other. The Arab leaders quarreled among themselves in their search for ways to cover up their failure to deliver what they promised, and in their quest for prestige, managed to cause, or at least not prevent, military confrontations with Israel. The fact that the Arab nations fell victim to their bold assurances of strength and invincibility deepened the credibility gap between the people and the leadership.

Only President Nasser succeeded in capturing the imagination of the Arab people. He instilled a hope for a better future, a renewed sense of pride and of national fulfillment. His prestige was such that he was the only Arab leader who could even suggest detente with Israel without being subjected to removal or assassination. Nasser enjoyed popular support, particularly after recouping his losses suffered in the 1956 Sinai campaign. Although Egypt was defeated militarily by Britain, France and Israel, combined United States — Soviet pressure at the United Nations finally forced those three nations to evacuate Egyptian territory occupied during the fighting. Nasser's military setback was thus transformed into a political victory and his prestige and influence once again pervaded the Arab world.

Consequently, Nasser's views and aspirations for a Pan-Arabia deserve attention, particularly in relation to how he related his national goals to the state of Israel.

The political instability that engulfed the Arab nations between the years 1948 and 1967 mark the quickening of Arab political awareness. During Nasser's rule, there was hardly any Arab state that did not experience some sort of Egyptian-inspired political problem: revolution and a counter-revolution in Syria and Iraq, civil war in Yemen, conspiracies to overthrow King Hussein of Jordan and King Saud of Saudi Arabia, and last, a revolution in Sudan. During this period, Arab comity suffered at least three major setbacks. First, the Syrian-Egyptian union was dissolved; second,

Nasser's military aid to Yemen in its civil war was unsuccessful; and third, Nasser's own domestic, social and economic programs had to be abandoned to a large extent because of his preoccupation with both internal and external power struggles.

By 1967, Arab unity was on the verge of total disintegration. Israel was again the natural answer. For Nasser, Israel was a pawn in the power struggle among the Arabs. Israel was also necessary to distract the attention of the Arab people from the failure of Nasser's inexperienced and top-heavy military regime which lacked the expertise and resources to implement many of his domestic programs.

Nasser's search for "independence from imperialism," a prime goal of his revolutionary regime, developed into a more complex set of problems than he had anticipated. The Soviet Union's loans and grants for military and economic programs left the Egyptians with as little room for maneuvering as had been obtained under Western-style colonialism. Although he succeeded in extracting maximal concessions from the United States (particularly during the Eisenhower administration), Nasser steadily shifted his attention toward the Russians. In the give-and-take of international politics, Nasser's declared goals of "neutrality" and independence from the major powers meant little or nothing. By 1967, most of the national production of cotton for export was mortgaged to the Russians for at least ten years to pay for Soviet military aid.

In addition, Nasser committed a political blunder by over-relying on the Soviet Union to substantially influence Israeli policy. The Russians never showed any serious interest in eliminating Israel as a political entity solely to satisfy the Arabs. The elimination of Israel would have resulted in nothing less than the beginning of the end of Soviet influence in the Middle East, for a continuing Israeli existence compelled the Arab states to look to Russia for support in the wake of Israeli "aggression." Indeed, the creation of Israel in 1948 was whole-heartedly supported by the Russians as a means of promoting turmoil and instability in a region that was about to be evacuated by Britain. It was a historic opportunity for the Russians to penetrate the Middle East region, first by supporting the creation of Israel, and second, by promoting the philosophy of "unite and rule" among the Arabs. Unlike the Americans, the Russians fully understood that in order to gain Arab favor, they must first support the movement toward Arab unity.

Nasser's seeming misunderstanding of the Soviet role and his obsession with the state of Israel made him lose perspective. He underestimated the fact that the state of "no war, no peace" with Israel that prevailed between 1956 and 1967 served Soviet interests well, for such a condition kept political tensions high and hence Nasser's need for continual reliance on the Russians. He also failed to grasp that the only power that could exert any substantial influence over Israel was the United States, whose policy had consistently supported the security and integrity of Israel. Finally, Nasser failed to fulfill his announced national goals; empty rhetoric eventually caught up with him. "Western imperialism" was replaced by Eastern (Russian) imperialism, with far more rigidity and less freedom of choice on Egypt's part. In fact, he allowed the creation of a "state within a state." Many camps and military installations that were manned by Russians were off-limits even to Egyptian generals. The discontent of university students and young army officers over this situation arose once more. This time, however, Nasser's colorful speeches and promises would not suffice to calm the discontent.

This atmosphere of dissension and despair coupled with veiled Syrian charges of cowardice on Nasser's part for "hiding behind the UN forces," plus ever-increasing economic difficulties, "forced" Nasser to challenge Israel militarily in mid-1967. Nasser hoped by a show of force to revive unity, to give substance to national pride, and to fulfill his pledges to put an end to the Jewish state, which was supposedly the source of all the ills that the Arab nations had suffered since their independence.

> *The Arabs paid for their quarrels by stumbling into war with Israel. The Egyptian ejection of the United Nations Emergency Force from Sinai, which triggered the explosion of June 5, [1967] clearly reflected the UAR's quest for prestige in other Arab capitals . . . Once war began, other Arab governments lost control of their policies and were sucked in behind the UAR as hapless allies in a war to which their own rivalries had led them.* *

The Six-Day War of June 1967 and the events that followed comprise the fourth stage in the evolution of Arab nationalism. The

---

* Kerr, *op. cit.*, p. 168.

concept of "unity of ranks" that was promoted for the purpose of solidifying Arab nations irrespective of their internal systems finally collapsed after ten years.

"Unity of ranks" had been based primarily on one objective: the destruction of Israel. The unattainability of this objective for more than a decade (1956-1967) slowly diminished its value; the June, 1967 War signalled its demise as a viable unifying force.

The notion of "unity of objective" was invented to replace it, even though this concept unrealistically was intended to encompass all the Arab radical movements, socialist and revolutionary. Still no common language or agreeable formula had been found, not only with relation to Israel, but also with relation to the Arab "reactionary" countries that refused to subscribe to Nasser's philosophy of unity of objectives. This philosophy, the traditional regimes felt, was concerned more with Egyptian dreams and less with the actual interests and welfare of other Arab states.

The idea of a "unity of objective," which gained momentum after the Six-Day War, introduced several fundamental changes to the goal of "unity of rank." Most importantly, unity ceased to be spoken of in terms of changing the political system of any Arab regime by force; and secondarily, the new trend was for coexistence with Israel. The Arab countries—even Syria—came to the realization after 1967 that Israel would continue to exist, that Russia was incapable of changing this reality even if it chose to, without risking a total war, and finally, that the United States was committed to Israel's preservation.

President Anwar Sadat, who at first religiously followed his predecessor's foreign and domestic policies, gradually came to realize that total reliance on the Russians had produced neither Israeli withdrawal from the occupied territories nor a total commitment on the part of the Russians to bring it about. Arab unity could not be fully or even partially served by pursuing a pro-Russian policy. Thereupon, Egypt intensified its efforts to renew ties with the United States that had started even before the death of Nasser in September 1970.

Sadat also initiated an all-out effort toward reconciliation with the other Arab heads of state, regardless of their social, political, or philosophical tendencies. He realized that for more than twenty-four years Israel had been taking advantage of the disunity among the Arab states, and although now the objective was not to eliminate

Israel, co-existence with dignity would still require a united Arab front. Despite his strength and prestige, Sadat knew that he could not possibly reach rapprochment with Israel without the support, or at least the tacit consent, of the other Arab states.

In order to give more tangible meaning to Arab nationalism and unity, one of the principal objectives of the old concept of unity, the liquidation of Israel, had to be exchanged for something more realistic; the Arab countries could not suffer another military humiliation (as had been the case in 1967) and still cling to an outmoded dream. Once the idea of Israel's existence was accepted in principle, then a coordinated policy could be devised to meet the new conditions. Thus, emphasis was now put on the *liberation of the occupied territories* that Israel had captured in 1967, rather than on the elimination of the Jewish state altogether. Such a goal, in Sadat's mind, was at least partially feasible. Consequently, the media — radio, television, newspapers — in almost all Arab capitals began to express the new approach. Whether or not Sadat and the rest of the Arab countries were sincere in their new political moves, it was felt that Arab unity could not flourish any further on the concept of total "liberation of Palestine" through the elimination of Israel. Ashraf Gorbal, Egyptian ambassador to the United States, viewed the new Egyptian policy by stating:

> *We are dealing with a state, a sovereign state within the 5th of June 1967 lines . . . Egypt does not harbor any bad intentions against Israel's sovereignty as much as we want Israel to respect our sovereignty. I said to Jarring in February 1971, we are ready to sign a peace agreement with the state of Israel.* *

The views of Gorbal, reaffirmed by Sadat** were not, however, shared in all the Arab capitals. For example, a communiqué issued by the Arab heads of state at the Algiers summit meeting in December, 1973 indicated that the real intention of the Arab states was not, and has never been, just the evacuation of the territories

---

* "Face the Nation". November 1973.

** Sadat's interview with CBS news correspondent Walter Cronkite in June 1974.

captured in 1967. The communiqué stated that there are two "paramount and unchallengable" conditions for peace:

> *The cease-fire is not yet peace [although followed later by disengagement of forces*] and the latter presupposes in order to be achieved, a certain number of conditions. Among these are two that are paramount and unchallengable: first, evacuation by Israel of the occupied territories, and the rights of the Palestinian people . . . So long as these two conditions have not been met, it will be illusory to expect in the Middle East anything but a continuation of unstable and explosive situations and a new confrontation.*

In the minds of many Arab leaders, two goals must be achieved before Arab unity can become a fact as stated by Hassanein Haykal: One is the elimination of "the Israeli aggression in 1967"; the return of all territories occupied by Israel after the Six-Day War. The other is "the aggression of 1948"; the elimination of Israel altogether as a political entity. One Arab observer added that "we have committed the error of starting with the second before starting with the first."

But the pros and cons of the argument regarding the real objectives of the Arab states with respect to Israel have been shifting and will continue to do so as long as instability persists in any of the major Arab countries. And despite the increased aid of the oil-rich Arab nations, social and economic disparity continues to exist in the Arab world even though some of them appear to be seeing eye-to-eye politically.

The years of confrontation between the Arabs and Israel have left noticeable marks on both sides. While Arab nations today cannot claim total political unity, they were able to demonstrate a united political and economic front during and after the 1973 war. One indication of this is the widespread acceptance of Yasir Arafat as head of the Palestine Liberation Organization. Arab nationalism, a rather ambiguous concept from the early thirties to the late sixties, has not penetrated deeply in most Arab countries. Both the revolutionary and the traditional Arab regimes seem to have reached

---

*The disengagement forces between Egypt and Israel took place on January 18, 1974, and the disengagement of the Israeli-Syrian forces on the Golan Heights in June 1974.

a new era of reconciliation; the conspiracies, uncertainties and fears that marked Arab relations throughout the fifties and sixties (the Nasser era) have given way to more open dialogue, better understanding and increased cooperation among the Arabs.

President Sadat has assuredly played a major role in these developments. While he has not ceased to envision an Arab empire led by Egypt, he leans more toward Egyptian nationalism than Nasser-type Pan-Arabism. Sadat, unlike Nasser, has more attainable dreams. While Nasser tried to lead the Arabs by promoting an ambiguous concept of unity, Sadat is trying to lead the Arab nations by pursuing social and economic programs that must be an important precursor to any political unification. Above all, Sadat has not subordinated the economic and the social needs of Egypt to the cause of Arab nationalism, as did his predecessor. Sadat, in short, has been more realistic in his assessment of his own and his country's strengths and weaknesses.

Only men with vision can bring about change. The quality of such change and the speed with which it is achieved depend on the nature of the leadership. Thus the failures and the successes of Nasser and Sadat, Ben-Gurion and Golda Meir, King Hussein, and many other Arab and Israeli leaders were only a part of a political process that had to work itself out before today's multifold opportunities for peace could arise.

Historical events have awakened the Arabs and Israelis to a new set of values. Now political stability in the Arab countries, and a solid working majority in the Israeli government are required before peace is achieved. The Arab nations then would be able to carry out their needed social and economic programs. And a stable parliamentary majority in the Israeli Knesset would enhance the likelihood of a general settlement uninhibited by Israeli domestic political concerns such as a revisionist right wing party.

The Arab-Israeli confrontation was a historical circumstance that came about due to certain conditions that prevailed at the time. The Arab and the Israeli leadership may have slowed or accelerated, subdued or intensified the process of confrontation, but they did not create it in the first place. Although each leader, Arab and Israeli alike, may have hidden his own visions and dreams about his nation's destiny, they were all subject to internal and external, social, econimic and political imperatives that had to evolve and reach a certain level of "maturity." The leadership, by and large, reflects the needs, tendencies and awareness of the people. In the Middle East only two leaders had the vision and the ability to influence greatly the fate of their nations — Prime Minister David Ben-Gurion and President Nasser. Unfortunately, however, they too had to submit to the mood and the tone that their generations was experiencing.

The concepts of Arab nationalism, socialism, and unity were, unfortunately, often utilized in the service of the leaders' personal glamor and prestige rather than to further a Pan-Arab cause. The Arabs and Israelis are, of course, still at odds in their national aspirations. The disparity on that score is still great, but it appears they have both accepted several things in principle: that coexistence is not a luxury, that peace is the surest guarantee for social and economic prosperity, and that reconciliation, given purposeful leaders in the countries concerned, is only a matter of time.

Chapter IV

THE PALESTINIAN REFUGEES

One of the most crucial elements in any future general settlement to the ongoing Middle East confrontation is the Palestinian refugees' situation. At one time or another the Arab states, the various Palestinian organizations, and the U.S.S.R., together and independently, have assumed the position of "defender" of the Palestinian cause. Egypt, Syria, Jordan, Lebanon, and Iraq have each assumed the role of spokesmen for the refugees. Terrorist organizations — Al Fatah, Popular Front for the Liberation of Palestine (PFLP) — have even claimed the authority to act in the name of the refugees. Finally, the United Nations has acted on behalf of the refugees, but more in relation to social and economic matters than on a political level.

For almost twenty years (1948-1967) the "host" Arab countries, those Arab nations which permitted the settlement of Palestinian refugees within their borders after 1948, subjected them to conditions of social, political, and economic inequality. Internationally, too, the Arab states often subordinated the refugees' cause to their own. Israel in a similar vein, left the refugee problem to the Arab states; for two decades Israeli leaders myopically insisted that the ultimate solution rested with the Arab states alone.

The Palestinian refugee drama is rich in plot and protagonists: the creation of the refugees, the attitudes of those Arab states primarily involved, the position of the Israeli government over the years, the relationship of the Fedayeen (Palestinian resistance movement) to the refugees, and the role of the United Nations.

THE CREATION OF THE REFUGEE PROBLEM

There is no doubt, as was made clear by United Nations, British, and other European observers, that the Arab states declared war on Israel immediately after its birth. On May 14, 1948 the armed forces of Egypt, Syria, Jordan, Lebanon, and Iraq, supported by contingents from Yemen and Saudi Arabia, crossed their respective borders into Israel. On that day, there was no refugee problem, and there was no crisis of national proportions between the Arab Palestinians and the newly-declared state of Israel. The majority of Arab Palestinians in Palestine were caught in a war that they did not particularly want or believe in.

> *Nobody in 1948 had foreseen an Arab refugee problem; nobody expected it to be more than temporary; nobody expected the armistice agreements to provide boundaries which were going to have to last until another round of fighting, and then another. As is the custom, missions and commissions began to write reports and make recommendations. By the standards of the present age, this refugee problem was small and inconsequential.* *

There were conflicting reports about the causes and the extent of the mass exodus of Arab Palestinians in the early stages of the war.** Some reports supported the Israeli version, that the Arab states insisted that Palestinians leave their homes and return after a total Arab victory over Israel.

> *As early as the first months of 1948, the Arab League issued orders exhorting the people to seek a temporary refuge in*

---

*David Pryce-Jones, *The Face of Defeat* (New York: Holt, Rinehart & Winston, 1974), p. 19.

**There are contradictory views, since no actual census was taken as to numbers of the Arab Palestinians dispersed during the 1948 war:

1) Beirut: Palestine Research Center, 1968, pp. 65-66 indicates: In 1967, the Palestinian population numbered around 2.4 million of whom 47 per cent were refugees and 43 per cent Palestinians who on the eve of the 1948 war had lived, and continued to live, on the West Bank (20%), Gaza (6%), Israel (12%), and other places (5%). In 1967, the Palestinian population was dispersed in the following places: Jordan (52%), Gaza (17%), Israel (12%), Lebanon (7%), Syria (6%), and other places — North Africa, Persian Gulf, Canada, Australia, USA — (6%).

2) Today, there are approximately 2.7 million Palestinians, according to PLO sources. They include 750,000 in Jordan, about half the total population of Jordan; 620,000 on the West Bank, the area west of Jordan occupied by Israel; 380,000 in the Gaza Strip; 450,000 in Israel, most with Israeli citizenship; 180,000 in Syria; 160,000 in Lebanon; over 100,000 in Kuwait; and the remainder scattered in the Gulf states, in Egypt and elsewhere. The total includes perhaps 1.3 million refugees who fled from their homes, either in 1948 or in the June, 1967 war. The figure is controversial. The United Nations Relief and Works Administration, which helps support refugees, listed 1,471,220 on its rolls in 1971. This may be somewhat inflated. Nevertheless, the 726,220 refugees of 1948, plus those of 1967, plus the natural increase, probably adds up to a figure close to 1.3 million.

> *the neighboring countries, later to return to their abodes in the wake of the victorious Arab armies and obtain their share of abandoned Jewish property.* *

Certain Arab leaders confirmed this version. For example, on August 16, 1948, George Hakim, the Greek Catholic Archbishop of Galilee, recalled: "The refugees had been confident that their absence from Palestine would not last long . . . Their leaders had promised them that the Arab armies would crush the 'Zionist gangs.' There would be no need for panic or fear of a long exile."**

Emily Choury, a secretary of the Higher Arab Committee at the time of the Arab invasion, also supported the Israeli version when, on September 15, 1948, he declared on Radio Cairo: "The fact that there are these refugees is the direct consequence of the action of the Arab states in opposing partition and the Jewish state . . . The Arab states agreed unanimously on this policy (of encouraging the exodus for political gains), and they must share the solution of the problem."

> *Refugees in the camps today will say that they left because they were told to, on the understanding that they would be returning in the wake of the victorious Arab armies. Memory itself becomes an integral part of public opinion and realigns to keep up with it. For any rationalizations after the event, the refugees have so far stayed at the mercy of researchers whose concern in documentary material is to construct partisan briefs from it.* ***

Finally, a statement by Abba Eban, then the Israeli ambassador to the UN, provides another impression of the cause of the mass exodus.

> *Caught up in the havoc and tension of war, demoralized by the flight of their leaders, urged on by irresponsible*

**Research Group for European Migration Problems Bulletin*, Vol. V-No. 1, 1957, p. 10.

**Excerpts from a speech delivered by Abba Eban to the U.N. Special Political Committee, in 1957, quoting the Greek Archbishop.

***Pryce-Jones, *op. cit.*, p. 16.

> *promises that they would return to inherit the spoils of Israel's destruction — hundreds of thousands of Arabs [Palestinians] sought the shelter of Arab lands.* *

Some other observers claimed that it was the Israelis who spread fear and chaos among the Arab Palestinians, forcing them to flee by the thousands. Radio Damascus, on April 24, 1948, broadcast an appeal to the Palestinians to stay in their homes, asserting that "certain elements and Jewish agents are spreading defeatist news to create chaos and panic among the peaceful population. Some cowards are deserting their houses, villages, or cities . . ." It should be noted, however, that by this time (April 1948), the exodus of Arab Palestinians had reached its peak. Hence, some Arab leaders may have realized that they had committed an error in urging mass evacuation.

Christopher Sykes, in his book, *Crossroads to Israel* wrote:

> *It can be said with a high degree of certainty that if the exodus was only by and large an accident of war in the first stage, in the later stages it was consciously and mercilessly helped on by Jewish threats and agression toward the Arab population.*

In one of his articles, Erskine Childers, who worked for the British Broadcasting Corporation and subsequently became a leading official in Irish television, attempted to denounce the Israeli account by casting doubt on Israel's version of a widely-circulated statement by the Greek Catholic Archbishop that the Palestinians were urged to flee by their own leaders. Childers claimed that he had written to the Archbishop and that the Archbishop had denied any such statement, adding that "his name was quite often abused" by the Israelis.

Ahmed Shukairy, a Palestinian Arab who was at the time serving as Saudi Arabian representative to the UN and known in certain Arab circles (Egyptian and Syrian, as well as Jordanian) as a demagogue, periodically attacked the Israelis for "their evil acts against the Palestinians" and accused them of devising special

---

*An excerpt from a speech delivered by Abba Eban, November 17, 1958. Subsequently, he became Foreign Minister of Israel.

methods of frightening the Arab Palestinians. But he never produced any documentary evidence to support his arguments or accusations.

Based on many conversations I have had with Arab refugees in the Gaza Strip and on the West Bank, the only definite thing one can conclude about the drama of exile is that the exile itself did take places. The Arab refugees sometimes blame the Arabs and at other times, the Israelis; the blame shifts depending on prevailing political conditions. For instance, based on an informal survey I conducted in the Gaza Strip during 1956, I found that about half the refugees would blame Israel for their personal grief, but at the same time did not completely absolve the Arab states of responsibility. After the 1967 war, however, the moods slowly shifted. During my visit to Israel in 1969 I found, surprisingly, that almost four out of every five Palestinians of middle age in Jerusalem and on the West Bank held the Arab states responsible, plainly stating that in 1948 the Arab radio and other media had made constant pleas for them to leave.

In the Gaza Strip, however, two out of five refugees within the same age and occupational group (40 to 55 years of age — merchants, clerks, and school teachers) blamed the Israelis for forcing them to flee. Interestingly, Palestinians who were well off socially and economically refused to take a poisition in favor of either side. The difference in the attitude of the Palestinians in the Gaza Strip and those on the West Bank may be attributed largely to the Egyptian indoctrination of the Palestinians in the Gaza Strip. During their occupation from 1948 to 1967, the Egyptian authorities encouraged Arab Palestinian militancy which they supported with a vitriolic propaganda campaign against Israel.

By the time I visited these areas in September, 1973, the Arab inhabitants of both the West Bank and the Gaza Strip, irrespective of economic position, political philosophy or refugee status, had ceased trying to trace who was responsible for the original exodus. If pressed, they will acknowledge that *everybody* is to blame, not so much for the exodus, but because the Palestinians are still pawns in the games of local and international politics. Typically they indicate that they have been used by the Arab states, the Fedayeen, the various Arab movements, the superpowers, and Israel.

ARAB STATES' ATTITUDE TOWARD THE PALESTINIANS

For almost twenty years, most of the Arab states insisted that

Israel was the prime cause of the Palestinians' misery; therefore, the Arab states claimed no responsibility for resolving the refugees' problems. Instead, they placed the burden on the UN — the creator of Israel — and on Israel itself. The Arab countries, which insisted on repatriation, obstructed efforts by some Western European nations and the United States which, under the auspices of the UN, were trying to solve the refugee problem by means other than repatriation. Essentially, the Arabs' policy was to keep the issue of the Palestinians alive in order to capitalize on its emotional aspect and to get as much sympathy as possible from the international community.

While, as we have seen, there is conflicting evidence regarding the prime cause of the Palestinian exodus, there is little doubt that the Arab states attempted to avoid any resolution of the refugee issue. First, the rivalry for power, prestige, and leadership among the Arab states was not conducive to rational accommodation. The political instability within Lebanon, Egypt, Jordan, and Syria particularly, compelled the Arab leaders to assume a noncommittal position toward the Arab Palestinian problem for fear of alienating some crucial segment of domestic political opinion. At the same time, by perpetuating the hardships of the refugees, Arab leaders hoped to engage the Arab masses at large with an emotion-charged issue to distract their attention from the economic shortcomings and social ills of their own governments. Second, by maintaining the status quo, those Arab states directly involved with the refugees were able to muster support and sympathy from the international community. Third, most Arab states believed, at least until the Six-Day War, that Israel's liquidation was inevitable; therefore, settling the refugee problem by any means short of repatriation would be premature. In sum, the Arab states explained their inability to solve the refugee problem on social, economic, and political grounds. Lebanon feared upsetting the sensitive social equilibrium between its Christians and the Moslems. Syria was, and to a large extent still is, engulfed in constant political turmoil. Jordan feared a total takeover by its Palestinian Arab majority and thus attempted to keep the fragile unity without losing the monarchy. Egypt suffered chronic economic problems; any additional number of people would increase the economic pressure. In short, the perpetuation of the refugee problem by the Arab states has provided a useful political tool applicable to both internal or external political expediency.

> *A long-standing Western myth holds that the Palestinian cause unites the Arab states when they are divided on all else. It would be more accurate to say that when the Arabs are in a mood to cooperate, this tends to find expression in an agreement to avoid action on Palestine, but when they choose to quarrel, Palestine policy readily becomes a subject of dispute.* *

The representatives of the Arab states at the UN and in the various world capitals consistently advocated only one solution to the Palestinian problem: repatriation. Ahmed Shukairy, the UN representative of Saudi Arabia, repeatedly stated: "It is repatriation and nothing but repatriation. It is the only solution that does not dishonor but certainly does honor the UN charter."

In order to maintain world attention to the problem of the Palestinians, the Arab states kept the issue on the UN agenda year after year. Shukairy, in one of his numerous statements at the UN regarding the refugees, proclaimed: "The minute they (the Palestinians) lay their hands on their properties, they will be the first to thank you and plead the discontinuation of relief. It is only then that the UN responsibility ends, but not before."**

Studies of the refugee problem made by various international agencies and independent governments seem to have arrived at the same conclusion. The Carnegie Endowment for International Peace, for example, took a broader geographical and historical view when it wrote:

> *No large scale refugee problem has ever been solved by repatriation, and there are certainly no grounds for believing that this particular problem [the Palestinian refugees] can be so solved. Nothing can bring it about except wars which in our time would leave nothing to go back to ... The fact we must face forces us to the conclusion*

---

*Malcolm Kerr, *The Arab Cold War* (New York, Oxford University Press, 1967). pp. 151-152.

**Excerpt from a speech at the UN by Ahmed Shukairy in 1958 when serving as a member of the Saudi Arabian mission.

> *that for most of the world's refugees, the only solution is integration where they are.* *

Another survey** more pertinent to the Arab refugee situation reported that "the official attitude of the Arab host countries is well known. It is one of seeking to prevent any sort of adaptation and integration because the refugees are seen as a political means of pressure to get Israel wiped off the map or to get the greatest possible number of concessions."

In a survey on "Social Forces in the Middle East," published in 1956, Dr. Channing B. Richardson of Hamilton University wrote: "Toward UNRWA (United Nations Relief and Welfare Administration) the attitude of the Arab governments lay between suspicion and obstruction. It cannot be denied that the outside observer gains the impression that the Arab governments have no great desire to solve the refugee problem."

The Arab host countries placed many obstacles in the way of the Palestinian refugees themselves so that no solution short of repatriation could be found. Both the physical movement and economic opportunities of the refugees were restricted even though some Arab oil-producing countries, such as Saudi Arabia and Kuwait, lacked adequate manpower. They They were pressured by other Arab countries to refuse to accept Palestinian refugees.

> *To cross the border between Lebanon, Jordan, and Syria and sometimes even from one town to another in the same country, to visit a relative or conduct business, a Palestinian was required to wait for a Laissez-passer from the authorities. The issuance of this document was left to the discretion of local bureaucrats who obliged only when they saw fit — in a few weeks, a few months, or never. Socially, Palestinians were despised, persecuted, or at best ignored.* ***

---

*Excerpt from a document published by Carnegie Endowment for International Peace. Dr. Elfan Rees, adviser on refugees to the World Council of Churches, published September 1957.

**Published in 1957 by the Research Group for European migration.

***Fawaz Turki, *The Disinherited* (New York: Monthly Review Press, 1972), p. 40.

In his report to the eighth session of the General Assembly, the director of UNRWA described the Arab policies on free movement of the Palestinians in this fashion:

> *The full benefit of the spread of this large capital investment [in Arab countries] will be felt only if restrictions on the movement of the refugees are withdrawn. This is a measure which was proposed in the original three-year plan but little has been done so far to give effect to it. Such freedom of movement would enable refugees to take full advantage of the opportunities for work arising in countries such as Iraq, Saudi Arabia, and the Persian Gulf sheikdoms where economic development has already taken place.*

The Egyptians had held the Palestinians in Gaza under very tight control. Exit visas were very hard to come by. Curfews were imposed. Police surveillance was constant and police posts were constructed for around-the-clock watch. The refugee camps in Gaza looked like prisons.

Former Israeli Foreign Minister Abba Eban, in his speech to the UN on November 17, 1958, observed: "It is painfully evident that this refugee problem has been artificially maintained for political motives against all economic, social, and cultural forces which, had they been allowed free play, would have brought about a solution." The Arab states claimed only the role of "defender" of the Palestinian refugees.

Jordan, by virtue of the 1948 war, had captured the entire West Bank and with it a majority of the Arab Palestinians. Jordan was an exception among Arab states in that it maintained a policy of more or less equality between the native Jordanians and the Arab Palestinians. Several reasons lay behind this: (1) the Jordanians had annexed the West Bank and could not possibly create two classes of citizens and hope to keep the new territory indefinitely; (2) the close proximity of the West Bank to Jordan proper helped obliterate the social barriers between the two communities; (3) the Jordanian government's ambitious plans for the fertile land of the West Bank could not be accomplished without inheriting its people as well.

Yet the Palestinians still were not fully incorporated into the Jordanian structure.

> *The more they maintained their separate identity and their rights, the more they threatened the artificial unity of the*

> one country which had completely adopted them. If they set about liberating Palestine by force, they brought Israeli reprisals against Jordan. The Egyptians in 1955 and 1956 also fell into that trap. Sympathy for the Palestinian cause became a matter of speeches, unanimous in tone, perhaps, but cautious in committal. *

Some Arab and Palestinian observers held that the Arab states were not capable of absorbing all the refugees because of various internal socio-economic difficulties. Fawaz Turki, a Palestinian, in his book, *The Disinherited*, maintained that "it would have been impossible for Egypt to integrate the 200,000 Palestinians under its control into its overpopulated Nile Valley or into its economically depressed society. Thus the Gaza refugees, even in the event that they agreed to integration with Egypt, seemed destined to remain in the strip area."**

As to Syria, Turki continued, "While Syria might have been able to absorb all the Palestinians including those in Jordan and Lebanon, yet the country was continually shaken by *coups d'etat*, and slow in developing its resources for its own people, and in general, struggled with the budget showing a chronic deficit." Resettlement in Lebanon was ruled out, too: "Lebanon, with a delicate and, at times, precarious communal, religious, and social balance in its population, was hostile to the idea of welcoming as citizens any Palestinians whose loyalty was considered dubious, and whose members might overrun the structure of the legislative branches."

As to Jordan: "The Jordanian case was unique in this context, for although the Palestinians formed over half the population, the majority of them lived in the West Bank, originally part of Palestine. Thus a great number were refugees in their own country . . . Jordan had the highest concentration of Palestinians, but with its barren east bank and rocky, arid hillsides, has also traditionally been the most underdeveloped part of the Levant."***

It is interesting that the writer overlooked other Arab nations, such as the oil-producing countries of Iraq and Libya, which have a

---

*Pryce-Jones, *op. cit.*, p. 23.

**Turki, *op. cit.*, p. 36.

***Ibid., pp. 36-37.

manpower shortage. The Arab Palestinians are a cheap source of labor, yet systematically have been denied employment in these countries for fear that permanent resettlement of the refugees there would eliminate the refugee problem as an important bargaining chip in negotiations and as a mechanism for uniting domestic public opinion.

Regarding resettlement of Arab refugees in the oil-producing countries, David Pryce-Jones observed:

> *Resettlement was at first the UNRWA policy but it depended upon the willingness of Arab countries to accept Palestinians, and that was limited by politics, finance, and bias. Ambitious and expensive plans were drawn up for resettlement, plans which would have developed the overall economies of the region. Emptier Arab countries such as Iraq and Libya, badly in need of manpower and investment, allowed in over the years only a few token Palestinians. In the face of discouragement and rejection, UNRWA shelved its comprehensive projects and spent the money instead on routine relief.* *

The state of Kuwait, which had a far more liberal policy of refugee absorption, has allowed approximately 100,000 Palestinians to settle within its borders. Many refugees with whom I spoke, stated unequivocally that they would not hesitate to migrate to Iraq or Saudi Arabia, or even Libya, if they were allowed to do so. That is not to say, some added, that they would not want to go back to Palestine if they could. But if it were a choice between waiting and stagnating in the refugee camps or migrating to where they could work and produce, the answer was quite obvious.

The Palestinian problem has become an integral party of the inter-Arab rivalry. The refugees have been used by the various Arab states to promote their internal and external interests. The refugee cause was accorded subordinate or superordinate attention, depending on what seemed to serve the best interests of the host country at the time. This fluctuating policy of the Arab states served to perpetuate the refugee problem. Yet the Arab states alone should not be fully blamed for the persistence of the situation.

---

*Pryce-Jones, *op. cit.*, pp. 20-21.

ISRAELI ATTITUDES TOWARD THE PALESTINIANS

The Israeli attitude toward the Palestinian refugees was primarily based on Israel's perception of the cause of the original mass exodus of Palestinians after the war of 1948. This exodus, Israel maintained, was not only created by the Arab states, but was also nourished by them. The Israeli officials also claimed that the various emerging terrorist organizations obstructed rather than helped the Palestinian cause. Abba Eban, the former Israeli foreign minister, stated his government's position at the UN on November 17, 1958:

> *The Arab refugee problem was caused by a war of aggression, launched by the Arab states against Israel in 1947 and 1948. Let there be no mistake. If there had been no war against Israel with its consequent harvest of bloodshed, misery, panic, and flight, there would be no problem of Arab refugees today . . . Once you determine the responsibility for that war, you have determined the responsibility for that problem. Nothing in the history of our generation is clearer or less controversial than the initiative of the Arab governments for the conflict out of which the refugee tragedy emerged . . . Since these governments have, by acts of policy, created this tragic problem, does it not follow that the world community has the unimpeachable right to claim their full assistance in its solution. How can governments create a vast humanitarian problem by their action, then wash their hands of all responsibility?*

Through the years, the Arab states consistently defended the right of the Palestinians to return to their "homeland." Israel, however, rejected this concept of repatriation (apart from occasional family reunions) for three major and interrelated reasons:

1) Israel believed that the settlement of all the Palestinians in Israel would not be repatriation, but rather alienation from Arab society. In any case, differences of language, cultural heritage, national identity and loyalty would not permit easy assimilation of the Palestinian refugees with the Jews.

2) Over six hundred thousand Sephardic Jews from the Arab Middle East and North Africa emigrated to Israel, mostly between 1948 and 1955. Some came of their own will, especially before 1948, but the vast majority of them left their native countries to escape the domestic persecution that was expected to escalate after Israel's

independence. The property and other tangible assets of the emigrating Jews were confiscated by the governments of Iraq, Egypt and other Arab countries. The number of Palestinian refugees who left their homes since 1948 more or less equals the number of Jews who left the Arab countries in the same time span. Thus, argues Israel, if we with our limited resources, could absorb over one million immigrants from the Arab states and Europe (200% of our population) in a matter of a few years, then the Arab states with their vast lands and natural resources should be able to absorb at least the same number of people which equals only about one and one-half per cent of their total population.

3) Repatriation of the Palestinian refugees to Israel, it was argued, would create a social crisis that might lead to the disintegration of Israel's identity as a Jewish state. Even Arab spokesmen recognized that Israeli acceptance of the refugees would dilute the Jewish identity of the state. The population would eventually be dominated numerically by a majority of Arabs, if by no other means than the natural birth rate. Yehoshua Arieli, an Israeli writer speculated:

> *My argument, however, is with those circles who in the name of Jewish history, of the historic right of the Jewish people, of Israeli security as a Jewish state, want to annex this minority [i.e., Arab citizens in Israel] and thereby with their own hands destroy the character of our society as both a Jewish society and a democratic one. The state of Israel's uniqueness lies first and foremost in the simple fact that it was formed and exists in order to solve the problem of the Jewish people as a whole. However, there is a considerable difference between the situation of the Arab citizens in Israel and the large majority [i.e., Arab Palestinians in the occupied territories] we are adding to them, on whom we are imposing citizenship against its will, which has been educated in blind hatred for 20 years, has gone through the suffering of the refugee camps and therefore, justly or unjustly, looked upon this country as an expropriator. In practice, we can assume that this minority [i.e., after absorption] would never be ready to accept citizenship, and, if it accepted it with its 40 per cent minority, would form an irredentist movement, destroying the democratic structure of the country and compelling us, against our will, to move*

from a situation of equality and equal citizenship to increasing repression. *

If repatriation were accepted by Israel as a solution to the refugee problem, the emergent social and racial balance could easily threaten Israel's identity. Israel as a Jewish state, governed by and for the Jews, would no longer exist. Such would have been the case for instance if Israel were to have annexed the West Bank. Cecil Hourani, speaking of the Arab Palestinians on the West Bank and in the Gaza Strip, said:

> *If the Israeli government accepts the Arabs within the territories she controls as full Israeli citizens, with equal civil and political rights, the concept of Israel which has hitherto been incorporated into her laws will have to be changed. Israel will no longer be a Jewish State. It will become a Jewish-Arab state in which nationality will be a function of residence or citizenship. Israel, in other words, as she has been since 1948, will no longer exist, and Palestine with Arabs and Jews living together will have been restored.* **

The Six-Day War created a new wave of refugees. Having been blamed for the first exodus of Palestinians in 1948, Israel at the time of the 1967 war attempted to prevent a widespread panic that would cause the Arabs to flee. Israel determined that if a new wave of exiles were going to occur for reasons outside her control, it should be made abundantly clear to the Arab Palestinians, to the surrounding states and to the international community at large that the Israeli authorities had no hand in any new mass exodus.

> *By the end of June [1967] when the Arabs from the Gaza Strip and the West Bank were still leaving in hundreds every day, the Israeli authorities were making them sign a paper that they were leaving on their own free will. If the Israelis permitted the refugees to trek on foot, they were accused of callous indifference, and when they were*

---

*New Outlook (London), July 1969.

**Encounter (Beirut), November 1967.

> *provided transport, they were accused of systematic eviction.* *

The Israeli post-war occupation of a vast area, including the West Bank, the Golan Heights, the Gaza Strip, and the Sinai, presented the Israelis with a new set of responsibilities. One million Palestinians, most of them refuged in 1948, were thrust under Israeli control and in effect lost their refugee status. In a sense, they were repatriated.

The UN definition of a Palestinian refugee is anyone who lost his home or his means of living and was a resident in Palestine two years or more prior to the 1948 war. This definition makes no distinction between the Arab Palestinians who actually sought refuge outside the borders of Palestine as designated under the Mandate, and those who moved from one area to another within Palestine. A Palestinian Arab who did not seek refuge outside Palestine but either moved to or remained in the Gaza Strip or on the West Bank should not have been designated a refugee. The concept of repatriation that the Arab states advocate does not apply to a refugee or a prisoner of war who did not leave his country of birth in the first place. The Israeli occupation should have marked the end of the UN relief effort for these Palestinians. If it were not for the Arab states' need to perpetuate the refugees' dilemma on the one hand, and Israel's acquiescence in the matter on the other hand, the refugee problem, at least in the occupied territories, would have been solved by now.

The unforeseen and sudden occupation of the Gaza Strip and the West Bank also presented Arab states, Egypt and Jordan in particular, with a new set of conditions that they were not geared to meet, In addition to an economic loss, Jordan lost the political leverage it had held over the Arab Palestinians on the West Bank. For Egypt the loss of the Gaza Strip had significant strategic and political importance. Strategically, the Gaza Strip provided the Egyptian military easy access to the heartland of Israel. Politically, the Egyptians could no longer manipulate the Palestinians. Both Egypt and Jordan viewed Israeli dominion over these territories as a factor that would eventually separate the Palestinian refugees' cause from their own interests. The Jordanian and the Egyptian govern-

---

*Pryce-Jones, *op. cit.*, p. 11.

ments suspected that Israeli policy toward the Arab Palestinians would awaken the Palestinians to a new reality. The picture that the Arab propagandists had drawn of the Israelis, describing them as ruthless, monstrous, bloodthirsty, and vengeful, was soon to be tempered by a lenient and even-handed Israeli occupation policy.

Israel's attitude toward the Palestinians became clear soon after the first day of the occupation. The Israeli government, with an ear attuned to international opinion, committed itself to the principle that the inhabitants of the new territories would be treated in as equitable and humane a fashion as possible.

> *Israeli administrative methods in the occupied territory, firm and strict but humane and enlightened, with gradual relaxing of controls, influenced the great mass of Palestinians to remain neutral. They were certainly anti-Israeli occupation, but they began to see that the Israeli military government was much less oppressive than the Jordanian "civil" government.* *

When King Hussein of Jordan came under severe criticism from other Arab governments in 1970 for his suppression of the terrorist Palestinian Liberation Organization (PLO), he reportedly admitted: "We have reached the point when my people living in Jerusalem under foreign [Israeli] military occupation were ten times more secure in their homes than people living in Amman, our capital"**

A British observer of the scene reported the following behavior patterns among certain Palestinian irredentists.

> *An outside inquirer becomes familiar with quite a rigid cultural pattern. West Bank activists will begin by denouncing the Jews and all their work; they will elaborate this into recrimination of the Arabs for being so abject, blaming themselves exaggeratedly for their own faults and showing up everybody's behavior in the worst light. After which you become a friend, you may drop in whenever you please and treat their house as yours. So it ceases to be a surprise that someone who is on public record as wanting*

---

*John Laffin, *Fedayeen* (New York: The Free Press, 1974), p. 27.

***Ibid.*, p. 63.

> the death of every Jew, in fact spends weekends at a kibbutz, or that someone else who is proud of Fatah connections, takes loans from the Israelis, or that the rich and radical-chic Nabulsis set off in the Mercedes for good times and shopping sprees in Tel Aviv.*

The daily contact between many Israelis and the Palestinians in the occupied territories, it may be argued, slowly broadened the basis for understanding. Both sides came to the realization that if their national aspirations and objectives were not reconcilable in the past, at least they created the social, economic, and political basis for better understanding.

The Israeli introduction of industry, modern agricultural machinery, more adequate housing, improved public facilities, better educational curricula, more schools, and greater numbers of better-paying jobs helped to restructure a relationship that was once considered to be irreparably shattered.

> At least thirty thousand men — or about half the real work force of Gaza, are finding daily employment in Israel. They see nothing incongruous about it. For the first inconceivable time in their whole lives they are able to bring meat, tins of food, biscuits, shoes, fresh milk, into homes where hitherto everything has been a matter of scrounging and 1,500 UNRWA calories. Terrorism has failed to offer them any alternative.**

THE FEDAYEEN AND THE PALESTINIANS

The Palestine Liberation Organization (PLO), under which the various fedayeen resistance movements operate loosely, claimed the right to represent the cause of the Palestinian refugees. In order to better appreciate the new status that was conferred upon the PLO by the United Nations and the Arab summit meeting in October, 1974, the following brief historical background becomes relevant.

---

*Pryce-Jones, *op. cit.*, pp. 112-113.

**Pryce-Jones, *op. cit.*, p. 135.

For over a decade the PLO failed to receive recognition not only from the Israelis, the Arab states, and the international community, but also from the refugees themselves. Several reasons lie behind this failure to achieve legitimacy: (1) the alienation of the host countries that resulted in bloody clashes in Jordan and Lebanon during 1969 and 1970; (2) the indiscriminate acts of terror that alienated the international community: (3) the ideological and tactical differences among the various Fedayeen groups; and (4) Israel's successful economic and social policies in the Gaza Strip and the West Bank.

> *The Fedayeen story is an extraordinary contrast of success and failure. They aroused the world's sympathy and then alienated most of it. They raised the flag of Arab unity and then trampled it in the sands. They succeeded in drawing to the Middle East the press of the world, but failed to inspire their own people. They startled the Arab community but could not frighten the Israelis . . . They had deteriorated from dedication to desperation, and pathos had replaced pride.* *

Tension between the Fedayeen movements and the Palestinian refugees increased after the Six-Day War (June, 1967). One of the main reasons for this was Israeli policy toward the Palestinians in the newly-occupied territories. The Israeli administration gave every inducement to the Arab Palestinians to go about their business as before. More job opportunities, higher earnings, permits to buy and sell, or to visit relatives, all served to dissuade the Palestinians from collaboration with the Fedayeen. Finally, in retaliation and in a desperate effort to gain the necessary momentum that was imperative for their survival, the Fedayeen movements in 1970 intensified their acts of terror against those whom they were supposed to protect and represent.

> *Throughout 1970, the murder rate of Arabs killing one another in the Gaza Strip ran between thirty and forty a month. Whole families were wiped out, and while such murders were claimed to be punishment for collaborating*

---

*Laffin, *op. cit.*, p. 2.

> with the Israelis, more often they were a matter of pursuing vendettas and clan quarrels. *

The Fedayeen movements themselves indirectly caused a new exodus after 1969 of no less than 100,000 Arab Palestinians from the West Bank, when an intensified Israeli retaliation campaign on the Fedayeen compounds prompted many peasant farmers to flee across the river to Jordan. Fedayeen action unwittingly pushed the refugees further eastward to the desert, rather than westward to their former homes.

In the wake of the UN and Arab states' recognition of the PLO as the sole representative of the Palestinian Arabs in 1974, it became apparent that there were mixed emotions and different views regarding this issue. Some of the Arab Palestinians applied a sense of urgency to the Arab-Israeli dispute and tended to accept any formula of representation, provided, however, a settlement was soon to be reached. Others felt that their cause was betrayed by the PLO and therefore a new and legitimate representative should be sought. And there are those who, for ideological reasons, actively supported the PLO as being their sole representative. It would appear however, that in due course, Israel may well find herself negotiating with representative of the Arab Palestinians that might include some of the PLO leaders.

THE ROLE OF THE UNITED NATIONS

The UN position toward the Palestinian refugees has been somewhat ambiguous. As with most cases involving the interests of the major powers, the UN has lacked both the initiative and the power to bring the Palestinian refugee problem to a settlement acceptable to all. The Arabs, with the leadership and the veto power of the USSR in the UN Security Council, have successfully killed any attempt by the United States, Israel, or West European countries to promote their solutions to the problem of the refugees. For example, resolutions in the United Nations calling for resettlement (as distinguished from repatriation) of or full compensation to the Arab Palestinians have been consistently opposed by the Arab states. In fact, any resolution falling short of repatriation was immediately rejected.

---

*Pryce-Jones, *op. cit.*, p. 126.

While the UN has not succeeded in resettling the Palestinians in other Arab countries, it has made headway in rehabilitation programs, such as construction of shelters and distribution of rations. These particular programs were not rejected because they called only for improved conditions of the Palestinians.

Only with the compliance of the host countries could the UN do anything of substance on behalf of the Palestinian refugees. Although the vast majority of the Palestinian refugees ceased in effect to be refugees under the Israeli occupation, the UN relief program continued as if no change had taken place. UNRWA has therefore become static, unaffected by the political change; the refugees themselves have grown accustomed to permanently living hand-to-mouth, and in fact many of them prefer to cling to and maintain this status for want of other viable choices.

While UNRWA was unable to solve the political problem of the refugees, UNRWA did become a way of life. Enrollment in the relief program steadily increased, for UNRWA eligibility meant more than just a meal; it meant health care, education, and many other benefits. For this reason UNRWA received harsh criticism from Israeli and other Western observers who charged the agency with actually causing the swelling of the ranks of the refugees. The many attempts at reducing the number of refugees enrolled in UNRWA were unsuccessful.

The effectiveness of the UN in implementing any long-range program depends largely on the agreement of the superpowers who use the UN forum as an umbrella organization under which resolutions can be effected.

The Yom Kippur War was a surprise not only to the Israelis, but to many Palestinians as well. Few foresaw the Arab attack, particularly after the overwhelming and demoralizing defeat the Arab states had suffered in 1967. The initial success of Egypt and Syria in the 1973 War renewed the hope of some Palestinians that the return to the "old Palestine" might still be possible after all. But the Israeli forces moved swiftly from defense to offense and gained the upper hand on both the Syrian and Egyptian fronts.

What disheartened the Palestinian refugees the most, however, was the realization that the Arab states in their new offensive had openly stated and restated that their main objective in the 1973 War was the recapture of the territories taken by Israel in the Six-Day War six years earlier. There was *no mention* of repatriation of the

Palestinians to their "homeland"; there was no mention of settling their problem in any fashion. The Palestinians had to face once again a bitter reality — that indeed they had been abandoned by the same people who were partially responsible for creating their problem in the first place. The Palestinians, whose interests have been subordinated to those of the host countries, may reluctantly admit by virtue of their bitter experiences under the Jordanian and Egyptian regimes, that their future welfare is tied more closely to Israel than to the Arab states. They admit now that their cause was abandoned by the Arab governments long before the Yom Kippur War erupted. Many Arab Palestinians believe that even the late Egyptian President Gamal Abdel Nasser confided to other Arab leaders (and even later overtly announced) that he was seeking a peaceful settlement with Israel based on the 1967 borders regardless of the Arab Palestinians position.*

Many Arabs in Egypt, Jordan, Syria, Iraq, and other states may of course dispute the contention that they are no longer concerned with the Palestinian issue — to a point where they may go to war in an attempt to resolve the issue. However, the official news organs of Egypt and Syria, especially after the Yom Kippur War, repeatedly stated that the Palestinian problem must be *separated* from that of the Egyptian or the Syrian disputes with Israel, disputes which should, in their view, be limited to the return of the territories captured by Israel in 1967. President Anwar Sadat of Egypt clearly reaffirmed this position in July, 1974, in effect leaving the "Palestinian problem" to the Palestinians themselves.

Israel, on the other hand, long recognized that the crux of the Arab-Israeli conflict was the Palestinian issue. From 1948 to 1967 Israeli policy sought to incorporate the Palestinian problem with the problem of relations with the Arab states, treating the former as an integral part of the general Arab-Israeli dispute. Then after the Six-

---

*President Bourghiba of Tunisia was, in fact, the first Arab leader not directly involved with Israel, who suggested a peaceful solution to the Arab-Israeli crisis. On April 21, 1965, he proposed that the Arabs recognize the *de facto* existence of the state of Israel and seek peace. Israel in return would withdraw to the 1947 borders that were allotted by the UN. This proposal was rejected by the Israelis. Other Arab leaders were aghast at the spectacle of an Arab leader publicly advocating rapprochement with Israel. On April 23, 1965, Cairo's semi-official newspaper *Al Ahram* responded: "He (President Bourghiba) was moving according to a plan by the forces of Western imperialism." The daily newspaper, *Al Akhbar*, also published in Cairo, said: "Bourghiba has stabbed the Arab people in the back."

Day War, Israel sought to separate the Palestinian issue from that of Israel's relations with surrounding Arab states. It was the Arab states which, until 1967, adamantly refused to separate their own dispute with Israel from that of the Palestinians. However, since October 1974 (Arab state summit meeting, Rabat, Morocco) the Arabs have by and large ceased officially claiming to be the spokesmen for or the representatives of the Palestinians, having conferred this status on the PLO.

The settlement of the Palestinian problem remains for the Palestinians and Israelis to resolve. Perhaps with a third party acting as a mediator, they will eventually sit down and negotiate a settlement. Whatever the rights of Arab Palestinians, the Jews now possess part of Palestine and whatever were the Jews' historical rights in Palestine, Arabs possessed Palestine for the last twelve centuries. Any attempt to solve the Arab Palestinians' problem that falls short of direct mutual negotiations will most likely be doomed. For all practical purposes, the Jordanian occupation of the West Bank and Egyptian occupation of the Gaza Strip, both after the 1948 war, were in principle no different from the Israeli occupation of these territories since 1967. Neither Egypt nor Jordan has any greater right to these lands than the Israelis. Yet after twenty years of Arab occupation of the West Bank and the Gaza Strip, the Palestinian inhabitants themselves came to realize that the Arab states had been unwilling or unable to find an equitable solution to their problem. Now, under Israeli occupation and control, the Palestinians will most likely have to try to solve their problem with the Israeli authorities. Israel has the capacity to deal with them, not the Arab states.

A Palestinian who had experienced a refugee's life saw the development of events in this fashion:

> But what can we do now? What lies ahead for us in this crucial phase of our revolution? The Egyptians have defected from our cause, or at least they have reconsidered their priorities and concerns. The Jordanians want to crush us if they can. The Syrians and other Levantines want to reduce us to mere puppets and place us as they have done before under their erratic and irresponsible leadership. The Israelis have yet to acknowledge that we exist.*

*Turki, op. cit., p. 143.

The refugees do exist, whether Israel publicly affirms or denies it. By 1975, the majority of the Arab Palestinians were living either within the 1967 borders of Israel or in the territories occupied by Israel after 1967. It now becomes the Israelis' and the Palestinians' task to find a bloodless solution to their dispute, without a loss of national pride or prestige, without misery and agony, and even without the Arab states and the terrorist organizations in their present form.

Chapter V

THE FEDAYEEN

Among the elements that have largely contributed to the prolonged Arab-Israeli confrontation are the various Fedayeen* movements. Terrorist activities, particularly between 1967-1971, dominated the scene in the Middle East. The various Fedayeen organizations could not solidly sustain their impact on Middle East politics, nor could the major antagonists, Israel and the Arab states, ignore them completely. Their rise was overshadowed by periodic decline, and yet what might have been the logical and final decline turned out to be a renewed emergence hardly expected by either friend or foe. In relation to this development, however, one striking factor must be singled out. The PLO as a terrorist organization has failed in its effort to bring about the liquidation of Israel either by the use or the threat of force, and as such, it has collapsed. By the same token, the PLO as a political body seeking a peaceful solution to the Middle East crisis and recognizing Israel's right to exist, is probably in the process of emerging as a new factor in Middle East politics.

While many observers feel that the UN and the 1974 Rabat resolutions recognizing the PLO as the sole representative of the Palestinian Arabs may have signaled a new era of intensive terrorist acts, the author believes that the main thrust of these resolutions is political in nature. The future viability or impotence on the part of the PLO will not depend on "successful" acts of terror against Israel or the international community. Rather, it will largely depend upon its success in its transformation from a terrorist to a political organization without disintegrating in the process.

---

*The term "Fedayi" is the Arabic word for self sacrificer. "Fedayeen" is the plural of the word "Fedayi." Generally, these terms are used to describe the readiness of a certain individual to sacrifice himself for a national cause or a high and esteemed goal. Although other terms, such as "terrorist," "guerrilla" or "saboteur" are often used to characterize the Palestinian Arab resistance movement, the original Arabic term "Fedayeen" is here generally applied to the various movements. Other terms are used only when either quoting (someone else) or when that term is more precise in describing a certain act or event.

In order to better appreciate how and why these developments came about, the following historical background of the Fedayeen must be considered.

HISTORICAL BACKGROUND

The Fedayeen movement became official on August 31, 1955, when Cairo Radio announced:

> *Egypt has decided to dispatch her heroes, the disciples of Pharaoh and the sons of Islam, and they will cleanse the land of Palestine. Therefore ready yourselves, shed tears, cry out and weep, O Israel, because your day of liquidation is near.*

However, between 1955 and 1964 very few acts of terror directed against Israel took place. The Israeli authorities knew that the so-called "disciples of Pharaoh" were a criminal lot, mostly murderers from the Gaza Strip, who had been released by Egyptian authorities on the understanding that they commit acts of terror in Israel.

The rivalry among the Arab states to gain control over the Fedayeen organization encouraged the fragmentation of the movement into various groups; each group sought independence from the others and each Arab country supported at least one of the groups.

Between 1955 and 1967, numerous Fedayeen organizations were formed. By mid-1970 there were eleven guerrilla groups in operation, the most important and powerful of which were Al Fatah, PFLP, Al Saika and Black September.* The smaller ones were

---

*The other seven Fedayeen groups were:
1. Popular Liberation Front: 2,000 members, led by Zaid Haydar.
2. Democratic Popular Front for the Liberation of Palestine: 1,000 members, led by Nayef Hawatmeh; a Marxist splinter group of the PFLP.
3. Front for the Liberation of Palestine : 500 members, led by Ahmed Jibreel. This group was also a splinter group of the PFLP.
4. Action Organization for the Liberation of Palestine: 700 members, led by Dr. Issam Sartawi. This group was pro-Egyptian, an offshoot of Al Fatah.
5. Popular Struggle Front: 400 members, led by Bahjat abu Ghorbiya. This group was occasionally involved with acts of terror outside the Middle East region.
6. Palestine Arab Organization: 350 members, another splinter group of the PFLP.
7. Arab Liberation Front: affiliated with the Baath party of Iraq, its members were mostly trained and supported by the Iraqi army.

either ultimately absorbed by the largest group, the Palestine National Liberation movement (Al Fatah), or disappeared altogether.

Al Fatah (the reverse acronym of the first letters of Harakat Al tahrir Al Falastini) [Palestinian Liberation Movement] with approximately 10,000 members operated mostly from Jordan before moving its headquarters to Lebanon after September, 1970. Undoubtedly the most skillful of all the organizations, it met the Arab need to take action against the Israeli occupation on the West Bank and in the Gaza Strip. Al Fatah is led by Yasir Arafat (the head of the PLO as well), a colorful leader known for his decisiveness and vehemence. Arafat's first terrorist activities were irregular operations against British troops in the Suez Canal in 1954. In 1957 he fled Egypt when the Moslem brotherhood, in which he had some connection, was outlawed. Because of Arafat's strong leadership Al Fatah was able to mobilize substantial amounts of money and weapons from the oil-rich monarchs of Kuwait and Saudi Arabia, and from the military regimes of Libya and Egypt. In early 1975 Syria became the main supporter of the Al Fatah which is the cornerstone of the PLO.

The Popular Front for the Liberation of Palestine (PFLP), with approximately 3,000 members, came into being in 1967. The PFLP is led by George Habash who was born in Lydda (Lod) in what was then Palestine and studied medicine at the American University in Beirut. Habash organized and led an underground Palestinian movement years before Arafat became an acclaimed leader. Immediately after the Six-Day War of 1967, Habash founded a resistance group called the Youth of Revenge. By December 1967, three small groups, the Heroes of the Return, the Youth of Revenge, and the Palestinian Liberation Front were amalgamated into the PFLP in order to counteract Fatah's growing power.

Al Saika (Thunderbolt) with 7,000 members, was formed from the union of three Syrian-Palestinian groups in April 1968. Most of their recruits were members of the ruling Syrian Baath Party. The Saika was led by Colonel Taher Dablan, who was a sworn enemy of Al Fatah. The Syrian government supplied Saika with arms, training camps and propaganda facilities.

Black September (Ailul-Alaswad) numbers 500 members and was founded immediately after the civil war in Jordan in September 1970. This group eventually became the most violent of all Fedayeen operations. It committed spectacular acts of terror to attract world attention, such as the killing of the Israeli athletes at the Olympic games in Munich in September 1972. It is believed that this group is directly connected with Al Fatah and receives its instructions from Al Fatah leadership. The official leader of Black September in 1972 was Fakri-Al Amari, who led the team that assassinated the Prime Minister of Jordan, Wasfi Al Tel, in Cairo in 1970.

IDEOLOGY AND TACTICS

The various Fedayeen movements suffered from a profound inconsistency in ideology and tactics that subsequently led to internal crises and organizational breakdowns. Although the PLO attempted to coordinate most of the acts of terror against Israel, it often found itself at odds with its constituent members. Apart from the Fatah, no other organization saw eye-to-eye with the PLO. The main split was between nationalism and ideology. The nationalist elements such as the Fatah and the PLO concentrated on restoring a Palestinian geographical entity. Since the Fatah leadership gave that aim top priority, they subordinated all other considerations that did not directly complement it. The more purely ideological elements within the PLO, however, such as the PFLP and the PDF, sought a pan-Arab revolution, socialist in content, in which the "recovery" of Palestine had an important but secondary role.

> *Habash saw the terrorist movement not only as the forerunner of a struggle against Israel, but the nucleus of a profound social revolution in the entire Arab world. And for this revolution to be effective, Anglo-American interests in the Arab world had to be fought.* *

By 1968, there was clearly a third school of thought, led by Al-Saika, which viewed the question of Palestine as so unimportant as to warrant only minimal attention. The Palestinian issue was seen as only a small part of the larger pan-Arab goal.

The following excerpts from statements made by the various Fedayeen leaders clearly indicate the disparity in their thinking and in their approaches to revolution and war with Israel.

---

*John Laffin, *Fedayeen* (New York: The Free Press, 1973), p. 42.

The Fatah attitude:

For the aim of this war is not to impose our will on the enemy, but to destroy him in order to take his place [if-na'uhu lilhululi mahallahu] ... In a conventional war there is no need to continue the war if the enemy submits to our will ... while in a people's war there is no deterrent, for its aim is not to subjugate the enemy, but to destroy [ifna'] him. A conventional war has limited aims which cannot be transcended, for it is necessary to allow the enemy to exist in order to impose our will over him, while in a people's war, destruction of the enemy is the first and last duty. *

The PFLP position:

Our code of morals is our revolution. What saves our revolution, what helps our revolution, what protects our revolution, is very right and very honorable and very noble and very beautiful ... We were fully determined that in case they [the Jordanian army] smashed us in the camps, we would blow this building and the Philadelphia [i.e., the Philadelphia Hotel in Amman] all over ... You are not better than our people. **

The Saika thinking:
The organization's general director, Zahair Mohsen, who also headed the military department of the PLO, was quoted by the Middle East News Agency from Damascus on April 12, 1974, as saying: "Only by liberating the Arab states from the reactionary forces (i.e., the monarchies of Jordan and Saudi Arabia) can we hope to liberate ourselves from our bondage."

The PLO attempts to bridge the ideological and operational gaps among these various Fedayeen movements were in vain at the time and remain difficult for the present.

In April 1969, PLO-Fatah established the Palestinian Armed Struggle Command [ASC] and drew eight

---

*Voice of Fatah. Cairo, February 18, 1970. Quoted from BBC monitoring.

**Excerpt from a speech made by Dr. Habash on June 12, 1970. It was printed in a pamphlet produced by the PFLP information department [*Our Code of Morals is our Revolution,* 1970].

> *organizations into it. The major non-joiner was the Popular Front. The ASC's task was to sift and verify the military announcements of the member groups and so obviate the absurdity and ridicule of two or more groups claiming the same "victory." Also, ASC gradually became a military coordinator and planner, but it failed because it had no power to impose planning and many times the various groups went their own way — sometimes attacking each other by accidental confrontation on the same mission.* *

Since the main Fedayeen groups, Fatah, PFLP, and Al Saika, could not agree on a certain philosophy for a common cause, they also differed in their tactics, both those aimed at Israel as well as those aimed at the Arab states that gave them shelter. In a pamphlet published in early 1965, entitled "How an Armed Revolution Breaks Out," the Fatah strategists established the following guidelines for planning and tactics:

1) To establish a consolidated leadership.

2) To win the people's confidence in the Fatah leadership, to appeal to the multitude and incite them to revenge, and to clarify the movement's objectives.

3) To plant trustworthy, indoctrinated members in all possible organizations and institutions so that there would be a hierarchy of command which would maintain discipline.

4) To begin the military struggle against Israel.

Yet as early as August, 1965, the Fatah organization had forgotten completely about coordinated leadership, ignored the importance of gaining the people's confidence and neglected the planting of the right people in the right positions. In fact, they skipped guidelines two and three and went directly to number four. The lack of coordination coupled with Israel's military preparedness, however, caused disastrous results in many instances.

The tactical theory of the PFLP's leader, George Habash, differed substantially from that of Al Fatah. Habash was quoted by an Italian journalist as saying in effect that to kill a Jew far from the battlefield had more effect than killing a hundred Jews in battle.

---

*Laffin, *op. cit.*, p. 35.

"When we set fire to a store in London (referring to the incendiary bombs in Marks and Spencer, August 17, 1969) those few flames are worth the burning down of two kibbutzim, because we force people to ask what is going on."*

The spectacular acts of terror that Habash encouraged were not solely against Jews or Jewish property, but were directed, in addition, to what he termed the "reactionary regimes" of Jordan and Saudi Arabia and toward Western and Eastern imperialism. Chapter 6 of the PFLP platform stated:

> We must not neglect the struggle in East Jordan, for this land is connected with Palestine more than with the other Arab countries. The problem of the revolution in Palestine is dialectically connected with the revolution in Jordan. A chain of plots between the Jordanian monarchy, imperalism, and Zionism have proved this connection. The harmony of the struggle in the two regions must be realized through coordinating organs whose talks will be to guarantee reserves inside Palestine and to mobilize the peasants and soldiers in the border territories . . . This is the only way Amman can become Hanoi: a base for the revolutionaries fighting inside Palestine.

Subsequent events proved that Habash's tactics did not work as he had hoped. Amman did not turn out to be another Hanoi, for the civil war of September, 1970 between the Jordanian army and the Fedayeen groups brought the Fedayeen movement to its knees.

One tactic adopted by all Fedayeen organizations was the spread of false propaganda. To demonstrate their effectiveness, the groups exaggerated the numbers of acts of terror against Israel and claimed massive numbers of Israeli soldiers killed or injured. In a way, the organizations were forced to claim victories; the Arab states that supported them expected tangible results from the vast sums of money that they were contributing to the Fedayeen cause. Another reason for inflating the numbers was to stimulate recruitment.

The lack of tactical coordination among the Fedayeen resulted in a credibility gap. Two or three organizations would normally claim

---

*In an interview with Oriana Fallaci, *Life* Magazine, June 22, 1970.

credit for every act of terror in Israel. The PLO attempted to avoid such public embarrassment but failed because

> *There was no cohesion in the guerrilla movement. No less than ten organizations competed for the loyalty of the commandos; there were bitter jealousies and tensions among the various groups, and even between personalities within the groups; each group had its own ideology and its own source of finance. This left the guerrillas without any common policy, and without a disciplined command structure. There was precious little military or political liaison. When they found it convenient, all the organizations recognized Arafat's leadership of the movement, but when any of them disagreed with him, they went their own way.* *

Since they had failed to inflict heavy damages on Israeli military installations, failed to incite an intensified Israeli retaliation, and failed to provoke intervention and counter-retaliation by the Arab host countries, the Fedayeen decided in late 1969 to change their tactics in dealing with Israel, and to begin direct attacks against civilian targets. Bombs were placed in coffee houses, cinemas, and garages with the hope that demoralized and infuriated Israelis would rush out to the streets and kill Arabs in retaliation. Coexistence between Arab and Israel, especially in the occupied territories, would then become impossible. The Israeli authorities, however, remained constantly on the watch, with the result that these acts of terror diminished in number and significance. Once again the Fedayeen movements proved their inability to confront the Israeli military and to provoke the Israeli masses into direct actions against the Palestinians.

THE ALIENATION OF THE ARAB STATES

By and large, the Arab states initially supported the various Fedayeen movements. Although Egypt, Jordan, Syria, Iraq, and Libya supported *different* groups of Fedayeen between 1955 and 1964, they saw in the guerrilla movement as a whole a potential force

---

*Peter Snow, *A Biography of Hussein* (New York: Robert B. Luce, 1972), p. 209.

to disrupt Israeli civilian tranquility. The newspaper *Al Masam* (Beirut) stated on January 19, 1965:

> *Groups of fighters have begun the holy war by acts of sabotage in Israel... There is no doubt that the existence of these groups represents the aspirations of the Arab peoples, who do not believe in any other means but this of dealing with the Palestine problem ... The justification for the existence of this organization is the exploit which we can describe in no other way but as an act of glory.*

The support of the Arab states was given only reluctantly at the beginning and diminished as the Fedayeen movement gained in strength and popularity.

The battle of Karameh in Jordan on March 21, 1968 between the Israelis and the Fedayeen (mainly the Al Fatah supported by Jordanian units) was a significant confrontation. Some 150 to 200 Arab Palestinians and Jordanians were killed and scores were wounded, but the battle was interpreted by the guerrillas as a major victory for themselves, since the Israelis lost several military vehicles and twenty-three killed. Al Fatah's ability to face the Israelis in a major battle for the first time gave the organization an important psychological boost in the Arab world. The Fatah gained confidence now that they had shown their "effectiveness" in conventional warfare in contrast with the Arab armies discredited in the Six-Day War the previous summer.

Nasser's prestige was low as a result, and Yasir Arafat of Fatah had now become the Messiah that would soon bring the total liberation of Palestine.

The increase in popularity of Al Fatah among the Palestinians in Jordan, particularly after the battle of Karameh, became a serious source of worry for the Amman government. King Hussein, who at first supported Al Fatah for the sake of internal cohesion and a demonstration of solidarity against Israel, came to the realization that the restraint of Al Fatah within his own borders had become crucial if he were to retain his power. Fatah and the PFLP, however, demanded the unequivocal support of the Arab governments, with no restrictions on guerrilla activities. After small clashes between the Jordanian army and Al Fatah members on November 4th and 5th,

Yasir Arafat announced in a broadcast from Cairo on November 6, 1968:

> *The Palestinian organizations are alone competent to punish those Palestinians who deviate from the revolutionary line, and we reject controls [i.e., imposed by Arab states]. Arab frontiers must remain open for our operations and we demand immediate liberation of Palestinian revolutionaries detained in Arab prisons. The insecurity of Palestinian fighters inside Arab frontiers cannot continue and we cannot guarantee to remain quiet in the future. We shall not pay the price of a peaceful settlement.*

The disenchantment between the Fedayeen organizations, mainly Al Fatah and PFLP, and the non-revolutionary Arab states, such as Saudi Arabia and Jordan, was growing deeper. Saudi Arabia, for example, supported the Fedayeen financially but did not want them to become too powerful. The Saudis reasoned that if the guerrilla organizations took over Jordan, Israel might invade and occupy Jordan, thereby causing Saudi Arabia to lose that area as a territorial buffer zone and enhancing the likelihood of disruption of the 754 mile Trans-Arabian oil pipeline which cuts across Jordan.

The PFLP whose policies were designed to embarrass the Arab states and bring about the collapse of the Hashemite monarchy in Jordan, undertook a series of operations that alienated even a revolutionary extremist regime such as Algeria. The hijacking of an El Al aircraft from Rome to Algeria in July, 1968 is one example of an act that outraged the Algerian government. The blowing up of the oil pipeline carrying Saudi Arabian oil to the Mediterranean was an act that brought the Saudi Arabian relationship with the PFLP to a point of no return. Finally, in an attempt to secure the release of 60 Fedayeen in Jordan, the Black September launched a raid on the Saudi Arabian embassy in Khartoum on March 1, 1973. Shortsightedly, the Black September planned the raid for the eve of the first anniversary of the peace settlement which had ended 17 years of Sudanese civil war. Subsequently, the Sudanese government banned Al Fatah and the PLO from the Sudan, thus further damaging the Palestinian cause. These kinds of operations indicated to most of the Arab governments that the Fedayeen organizations were a source of danger to their own sovereignty.

After his military defeat in the Six-Day War, King Hussein believed that the West Bank could be returned to Jordan only through peaceful means. The terrorists opposed this policy of overt accommodation, using the slogan, "To liberate Tel Aviv we must first liberate Amman."

Biographer Peter Snow reported the situation as follows:

> By the end of 1970, the restless relationship between Hussein and the Palestinian commandos had become dangerously strained. The "Palestinian Resistance" was looking more and more like another state within Jordan. Unable to penetrate Israel's defenses, and driven from their advance bases by Israeli air strikes, the guerrillas swarmed about Amman as if it were a city they had newly captured. They rejected the discipline of Hussein's laws, policed their own areas themselves, and even registered their own vehicles independently of the Jordanian authorities. They were desperate, bitter men; Israel was the object of their hatred, but for the moment it eluded them, and many of them turned instead on Hussein. He had refused to throw the weight of his army behind their struggle to cross the Jordan since '67. He had even obstructed them. And he was committed to a settlement with Israel that would deny them their goal — the liberation of the whole of Palestine.*

So that people would better understand the position, King Hussein stated his case in the autumn of 1970, as follows:

> We have reached the point where my people living in Jerusalem under foreign military occupation [the Israelis] were ten times more secure in their homes than people living in Amman, our capital. No Israeli on a kibbutz has one millionth of the trouble we have had here. When people see the amount of arms and ammunition the guerrillas had in Amman, and the preparations they made for fighting here, they may well ask, how did we allow things to reach this pass? I can only answer that after the June war — the June disaster — I was so concerned with rebuilding the

---

*Snow, *op. cit.*, p. 208.

army, with the recovery of our lost territory . . . They [the guerrillas] talked about resisting Israel, but it was not a question of Israel at all. It was a question of takeover here. I was always puzzled by what they meant by "Palestine revolution." I could understand very well "Palestinian resistance" but not "Palestine revolution." We could not separate those who were genuine Fedayeen from those who were extensions of political movements in the Arab world.

Here was a resistance, or what was supposed to be one, doing its utmost to destroy the respect and support of its own people. I brought in a government which they practically chose [the Rifai government dismissed by the King the night before the fighting began] and a chief of staff [General Mashur Hadithi] who had some connections with them, in a last attempt to bring some sense to the situation. But our problems increased. There was not a single unit in the army or air force that had not been provoked, in terms of the families and homes molested.*

In September 1970, when neither party was willing to work out any acceptable compromise, a civil war broke out between the Jordanian army and the Fedayeen, especially Al Fatah and the PLO, which practically smashed the latter in Jordan. By mid-1971, there was virtually no resistance to the Jordanian army. This conflict marked a low point in the Fedayeen's standing among the Arab states.

While financial support continued from Saudi Arabia, Libya, Kuwait, Iraq, and Algeria, only Syria allowed the groups to operate from its own territory. Lebanon, in particular, was reluctant to allow the terrorists to move freely and wage acts of terror from her soil against Israel, and was, like Jordan, also forced to use her military to curtail the terrorists' activities. After a serious clash between the Palestinian organization and the Lebanese government in 1969, an agreement was reached to allow the Fedayeen, mainly Al Fatah, to operate from a limited stretch of land in the south of Lebanon. However, the intensification of the Israeli retaliation against the Fedayeen camps provoked the Lebanese government into taking retaliatory measures restricting the Fedayeen from launching raids

---

*Murray Sayle, *Sunday Times* (London), September 27, 1970.

against Israel. Yet Israel's freedom to move unopposed, to strike terrorist training camps and to destroy the houses of refugees who harbored them, made the life of the Fedayeen in Lebanon very difficult. In addition, Israeli warnings to the Lebanese government during 1974 to curtail terrorist movements in south Lebanon were taken seriously. However, Lebanon became the main springboard for terrorist activities against Israel; despite the intensive Israeli retaliation, the Lebanese government was and still is unable to control the Fedayeen movement.

In order to solve the crisis of legitimacy among the various Fedayeen groups in the Arab states (mainly Jordan and Lebanon) where the Fedayeen were not under strict control, several proposals were made. The Prime Minister of Jordan, Wasfi el Tel, once advised King Hussein to turn Jordan into a Fedayeen state and proclaim himself its leader. Another suggestion came from President Anwar Sadat of Egypt who proposed as late as 1972 that Fedayeen organizations go underground. The first suggestion was flatly rejected by Hussein, and the second was strongly dismissed by Yasir Arafat, who feared that in going underground, he would be in danger of being forgotten by the people he claims to represent.

DISENCHANTMENT OF THE INTERNATIONAL COMMUNITY

By the end of September, 1970, crushed by the Jordanian military and having suffered from Israeli retaliation, the Fedayeen movements, especially the PFLP and Black September, sought new ways of accomplishing their goals and gaining international attention to their cause. The terrorists spread their activities on a larger scale outside the region, mainly in Europe.

The resulting indiscriminate and ruthless acts of terror, however, alienated and outraged the international community, rather than arousing world sympathy for the Palestinian cause. Even countries such as the Soviet Union, which had been openly supporting the movement before, deplored such acts. The following partial list of activities over a five-year period gives some indication of their widespread nature.

November 27, 1969. A PFLP terrorist threw grenades into the El Al office in Athens, killing a Greek child and injuring 15 persons.

February 12, 1970. PFLP terrorists attacked an El Al plane at Klotan Airport, Switzerland, killing the pilot.

May 30, 1972. Three Japanese terrorists* arriving at Lod Airport, Tel Aviv, on an Air France plane, fired sub-machine guns and lobbed hand grenades into the crowded arrival hall, killing 24 people and wounding 72.

September 1972. Eleven Israelis were killed at Olympic Games in Munich.

September-October 1972. The PFLP posted sixty-four letter bombs in Amsterdam to Israeli diplomatic offices in eight cities. The one fatality was the agricultural counselor at Israel's London embassy.

March 1, 1973. The Fedayeen launched an armed attack in Khartoum, Sudan in order to secure the release of about 60 Fedayeen being held in Jordan, Sirhan Sirhan, criminals in German prisons, and Fedayeen in Israel. Two American diplomats and one Belgian envoy were killed. The terrorists were released from a Sudanese jail in June 1974.

April 9, 1973. A Cypriot policeman outside the residence of the Israeli ambassador to Cyprus was killed and a dozen bombs were thrown at the building.

In May and June 1974, the guerrillas attacked the communities of Kiryat Shmona and Maalot, killing some 50 Israelis, more than 40 of whom were children.

Although the PFLP and Black September interpreted their assaults and raids as demonstrations of bravery and selfless dedication, most of the world recoiled in revulsion. These acts were an expression of Fedayeen desperation and exasperation.

John Laffin observed in his book, *Fedayeen:*

> Black September's Munich operation should not be seen as the zenith of Fedayeen activity but the nadir. It alienated world sympathy for the Palestinians' cause to a degree that no other action has done.**

---

*Several dozen young Japanese had been recruited by Black September and other extremist Fedayeen groups to undertake suicidal missions in Israel, such as the one at Lod airport. After the Lod massacre, the Japanese government took a series of measures to avoid the repetition of such acts. Compensation was provided by the Japanese government to the families of the slain. This was the only time that Japanese terrorists were involved.

**Laffin, *op. cit.*, p. 156.

Indeed world-wide sympathy for the Fedayeen declined to a point where no Fedayeen group could count at that time on the moral support, the interest, and the attention that many in Eastern and Western European countries had once willingly supplied.

Finally, a note about the Soviet Union's ambiguous policy toward the Fedayeen groups. Although the Russians rendered moral, technical, and financial support — especially to Black September — the Kremlin, for reasons of its own, never took a clear position toward the Fedayeen. It was not the atrocities and the ruthlessness of the Fedayeen toward Israel that disturbed the Russians, but rather the fact that these Fedayeen groups were a cause of turmoil within the Arab states in which Russia had a special interest. Thus, the Russians, too, felt compelled to curtail their support, morally, technically, and politically, while leaving the door open for a change of policy.

THE APATHY OF THE ARAB PALESTINIANS

The Arab Palestinians initially saw in the Fedayeen movement a new source of strength that might one day force the Israelis to dissolve the state of Israel and restore the rights of the Arab Palestinians. Yet, the ideological, tactical, and political differences among the various Fedayeen groups at least during their early years (1955-1965) were not conducive to creating a trustful and long-lasting relationship with the Arab Palestinians.

In fact, the exact opposite has taken place. By intimidating those whom they are supposed to represent, the Fedayeen have systematically undermined their attempt to establish themselves as an integral part of the Arab Palestinian population. By attempting to take advantage of the Arab Palestinians' economic and political weaknesses, the Fedayeen ended up subordinating the Palestinians' interests to their own. They have demanded from their own people instant conformity to revolutionary doctrine and operations, setting aside the immediate social and economic needs of the Palestinian refugee populace. As if the "revolution" had the answer to every requirement, they asked for short-term personal sacrifice in the interests of long-term goals... Although the recognition of the PLO by the international community has restored some of the confidence between the Arab Palestinians and the PLO leadership, still many influential Palestinian personalities do not view the PLO as their representative; mutual distrust and lack of confidence continue to characterize their relationship.

The Palestinians, often subjected to sub-human conditions in the refugee camps, were torn between loyalty to the Fedayeen and physical survival. Although they provided shelter and food to the Fedayeen, the Palestinians often could not meet the stiff demands of the various Fedayeen groups who demanded absolute loyalty to whichever faction they represented. Between the empty protestations of the Fedayeen that Israel be eliminated and the failure of the Arab states to solve Palestinian problems, the Arab Palestinians' enthusiasm for the revolutionary movements of the Fedayeen slowly declined.

The Six-Day War and its aftermath provided the impetus for a new wave of Palestinian nationalist enthusiasm and hope. The humiliation of the Jordanian, Syrian, and Egyptian armies left a vacuum that was soon filled by the Fedayeen leadership, especially Yasir Arafat. By March, 1968, the Fedayeen groups could claim that they had finally become an indisputable element in the Arab-Israeli confrontation. Thousands of new recruits from all walks of life joined the nationalist terrorist organizations and the word "Fedayeen" carried the respect that had been sought for so long. Several factors caused this change, from skeptical ambivalence to enthusiastic acceptance, in the attitude of the Palestinians toward the Fedayeen: 1) being a Fedayi was a relatively well-paying job; 2) the growing numerical and military strength of the Fedayeen, especially in Jordan after 1967, allowed them to exercise greater power; 3) the battle of Karameh in March, 1968 gave the Fedayeen a great boost in morale; and 4) acts of terror, supposedly commited in Israel, and inflated through an intensified propaganda campaign misled many Arab Palestinians into viewing the Fedayeen as their saviors.

The harmony between the Fedayeen and the Arab Palestinians did not last long, however. Israeli operations against refugee camps that harbored Fedayeen and the Jordanian army operations put the Arab Palestinians in a very precarious situation. If the Palestinians refused to support a Fedayi, they would be accused of collaboration with Israel and shot, or at best become a target of constant harassment. If they helped a Fedayi, they were sentenced to jail in

Jordan, or had their homes blown up by the Israelis. The terrorist movement had failed in everything except complicating the lives of the Arab-Palestinians and implicating them in a quarrel which they did not seek or promote.

During a visit to Israel in September, 1973, many Palestinians told me, in effect, "we realize that some of us made bad mistakes by allowing the terrorists to come to our own homes." One Palestinian claimed that many terrorists were busy looking for men with whom they wanted to settle a personal problem. After a long pause, he added, "You know, it is indeed ironic that *we* became the targets, not the Israelis. My brother was shot; they said he collaborated with the Israeli authorities." Then he reluctantly said, "For twenty years we were pushed around by everybody; now that we can earn some money by working in an Israeli enterprise, we are called collaborators ... Well, such is life." This man was not alone. He was a Fedayi himself for a while, but left because of the mistreatment and the misconduct of the Fedayeen toward their own "brothers." The accusations of collaboration with Israelis or the Jordanian authorities and the severe punishment that followed — generally execution — created an extremely tense relationship between the Fedayeen and the Arab Palestinians.

> *Terrorists have killed many more of their own people than Israelis. Most bombs thrown at Israeli cars miss the target and then explode among Arab civilians. On Feburary 1, 1971, Fedayeen set off a bomb in a Gaza post office and injured 61 Arabs.* *

Some of the murders committed by the Fedayeen in the Gaza Strip and on the West Bank have been cruelly savage; at times whole families have been wiped out. Under such circumstances the majority of the Arab Palestinians became extremely reluctant to assist any Fedayi. Now that the East and West Bank of the Jordan River, as well as the Gaza Strip, have been meticulously screened by the Israeli authorities against any Fedayeen movements, the percentage of murders and armed robberies since 1968 has been reduced by 95 per cent. With these developments, the Fedayeen temporarily lost the basic foundation of their movement: the Arab Palestinians themselves.

---

* *Ibid.*, p. 82

THE ISRAELI COUNTER-MEASURES

The Israeli military succeeded in curtailing the terrorist organizations' activities by several methods:

1) **Instant reprisal.** Terrorist bases in Jordan, Lebanon, and Syria were repeatedly bombed, largely destroying the rebel sanctuaries.

> *The instant-reprisal method from the air — with the help of efficient intelligence reports — destroyed many sabotage units. Israeli planes kept saboteurs constantly on the move as they sought new hiding places. Fear of quick retaliation forced many sabotage units to use delayed action devices; they could then bolt even before the bazooka or katyusha rocket fired its charge.* *

2) **Mobility.** The special defense formation of the Israeli military, unburdened by stockpiles of supplies and ammunition, allowed it to be less vulnerable to attack and afforded it greater maneuverability. Moreover, the military posts along the borders (*Nachal*) were perpetually on guard while performing agricultural tasks. All these precautions made the Fedayeen activities much less fruitful militarily.

3) **Successful intelligence gathering.** Israel prides itself on its intelligence service. Units assigned to gather information about the Fedayeen were equipped with the most sophisticated equipment able to monitor every Fedayeen move. Ironically, the Fedayeen themselves were a great help to the Israeli authorities. These false stories about Israeli torture methods worked to the advantage of the Israelis:

> *Torture appears to be inherent in any clash between security forces and guerrillas, and there is no reason why Israel should differ from all countries which have practiced it as a counter-insurgence weapon. Since the Israelis need information from the Fedayeen, stories of torture are entirely to their advantage, predisposing prisoners into a panicky belief that they will be broken by interrogators who stop at nothing [so much so that some stories sound as if*

**Ibid.*, p. 122.

> *they have been helped on their way by the Israeli secret service]**

4) **Psychological interrogation.** Israeli methods of interrogation were especially tailored for each prisoner. By studying in advance his weaknesses, background, family ties, etc. an interrogator had a psychological advantage over his Fedayeen prisoner. In turn, the prisoner often assumed that the interrogator already knew almost everything, so the Fedayi, as an individual, became vulnerable and easily persuaded to release information.

General Narkiss, Governor of the West Bank, disclosed to foreign reporters early in 1968 that "for every terrorist captured, some thirty to forty others were rounded up through denunciation." Nothing could be kept secret in a society which was torn into factions, family allegiances, and enmities. At times, revenge, earning a few pounds and the starting of new quarrels, were the main motives behind the tip-offs.

5) **Credibility.** Israeli warnings of impending retaliation were never taken lightly by either the Arab states or the Fedayeen, for once an Israeli warning was made public, it became only a matter of time before the enemy was "punished." Once a retaliatory strike was carried out, the military spokesmen would announce generally accurate figures regarding the losses of men and material.

> *In contrast, among their own people the Fedayeen organizations have lost more credibility as a result of false or exaggerated claims of victories than through defeats at the hands of the Israelis and the Jordanians. Fatah's operational career began with a false claim and the history of the entire Fedayeen movement is lettered with clumsy lies and extravagances.***

6) **Consistency.** Having experienced repeated Israeli reprisals, the Jordanians were finally forced to wage a war of their own against the Fedayeen (September, 1970). Lebanon, too, fearing unimpeded

---

*David Pryce-Jones, *The Face of Defeat* (New York: Holt, Rinehart and Winston, 1973). p. 73.

**Laffin, *op. cit.*, p. 101.

Israeli attacks, decided in early 1970 to curtail the Fedayeen activities. The Syrians, however have managed to keep the Fedayeen under control at all times; consequently, Israeli raids on Syria have been less frequent.

7) **Pragmatism.** While the Fedayeen inflated the figures of Israelis killed or wounded in their "successful missions," Israel minimized the effects of its retaliation against the Fedayeen sanctuaries. Two reasons underlay this Israeli approach: a) The government was not interested in telling the world how often and how decisive its countermeasures were for fear of alienating the international community. b) Authorities in Jerusalem wanted to keep the Fedayeen constantly on the run and off balance, not knowing what to expect next. Between the middle of 1967 and the end of 1971, some 5,270 operations were carried out against the terrorist organizations across the cease-fire lines. Only 577 of these operations were announced by the military spokesmen.* Contrary to the Israeli policy of understating retaliatory activities, Fedayeen spokesmen overstated the extent of their own para-military actions.

> *In the four years from June 1967, the Fedayeen organizations officially claimed to have killed 8,619 Israeli soldiers and civilians, destroyed 351 tanks, 88 aircraft, 5,331 vehicles, and 312 bridges. Such catastrophic losses, had they occurred, would have badly damaged Israel's morale and fighting potential. Caustically commenting on these figures, the Beirut newspaper, Al Jarida, noted that Israel did not possess 312 bridges.* ***

8) **The Israeli policy in the occupied territories.** Under the Israeli occupation beginning in June, 1967 in the Gaza Strip and on the West Bank, the Palestinians soon came to realize that the Israelis were not the monsters Arab propaganda had painted them to be. The Israeli military treated the Palestinians as humanely as possible under the circumstances. It was the Israeli government's policy to prove to the Palestinians as well as to the international community

---

*The figures given by General Bar-Lev, former Israeli Chief of Staff, quoted in the Jerusalem Post, January 1, 1972.

**Laffin, *op. cit.*, p. 101.

that the Palestinian dilemma had become chronic, not because of the Israeli stand, but because of the positions of the Arab host countries. The daily contact between the Palestinians and the Israelis produced alterations in their previous relationship of mutual distrust and fear. More importantly, the Israeli policy helped substantially to alienate the Arab Palestinians from the Fedayeen movements. Arab Palestinians often stood to lose more than ever before, in terms of economic growth and possible political gains, if they sided with the Fedayeen.

THE IDEOLOGICAL CRISIS

By mid-1969 it became evident to the Fedayeen themselves and to Israel that the Fedayeen movements as a terrorist force were indeed in decline. The leaders of Al Fatah, PFLP, Black September, and others were unable to reverse the trend.

The experiences of other revolutionary movements in Algeria, Cuba, and Vietnam showed clearly that the guerrilla relationship with the surrounding countries that provide sanctuaries and shelter must be mutually beneficial or at least non-hostile at all times. By contrast, the Fedayeen movement, principally Al Fatah and the PFLP, had antagonized the governments of Jordan, Lebanon, Syria, and even Egypt. As Mohammed Yazid, an Algerian terrorist who became Algeria's ambassador to Lebanon, described it, "In Algeria we found it very important to use the surrounding countries as bases, and from the first we cooperated with those countries on a clear basis, i.e., non-intervention of the host country in our internal affairs, and non-intervention in their internal affairs."* Ignoring this Algerian experience, PFLP leader George Habash, in a press conference in 1972, stated: "The terrorist movement is declining because total impotence has come over the Arab bourgeoise regimes and the reaction of this impotence is seen in a hostile attitude toward the resistance movement."

The Fedayeen leadership also failed to understand that the success of the Algerian revolution did not necessarily guarantee their own success, even though they might try to follow the same path. Many writers have pointed out the significant differences between

---

*Journal of Palestine Studies, Beirut, Winter 1972.

the Algerian and the Arab Palestinian resistance movements. Hassanein Haykal, who was the chief editor of the daily newspaper *Al Ahram* in Cairo and President Nasser's confidant, discussed some of these differences.

> *The human ratio between the resistance forces and the enemy in the occupied territory is not like the ratio in Algeria . . . ten million Arabs against an enemy of four hundred thousand French soldiers. In Palestine inside the occupied area, the Arabs are less than a quarter of a million under arms.*
>
> *The nature of the Palestinian terrain is different from Algerian terrain with its rugged mountains . . . In Palestine, the plains are exposed and the mountains are not spacious. Furthermore, the Palestinian land is limited and narrow, in particular taking into account the extensive use of helicopters.*
>
> *Around Vietnam there are sactuaries in which resistance can prepare itself out of the enemy's reach, such as China and North Vietnam. The situation was similar in Algeria, with Tunisia and Morocco next door, and Libya and Egypt close by. The Palestinian resistance does not have such sanctuaries in which it can prepare itself out of reach of the enemy. The enemy is prepared to strike at any place in the Arab world, which in the present situation is defeated and has not yet recovered its strength.* *

One other striking difference was the fact that in Algeria the terrorists were fighting against a foreign power and seeking to compel it to abdicate its rule. In Palestine, the Fedayeen movements were not focused in ideology or tactics against any one enemy. Furthermore the Fedayeen movements were aiming at the destruction of a sovereign state and its people rather than rid themselves of a colonial power which was the case in Algeria.

In an attempt to improve their world image, the Fedayeen began to change their public relations campaign. Such understood propaganda terminology as "liquidation," "annihilation," or

---

*Al Ahram, Cairo, August 18, 1968.

"throwing into the sea," were eliminated from their slogans. In January, 1969, the central committee of Al Fatah passed a seven-point resolution, two of which made the important differentiation between the elimination of Israel's political entity and the elimination of the Jews.

> *Al Fatah, the Palestine National Liberation Movement, is not struggling against the Jews as an ethnic and religious community. It is struggling against Israel as the expression of colonization based on a theocratic racist and expansionist system and of Zionism and colonialism.* *

Point five of the same resolution put special emphasis on the characteristics that the "restored" state would have:

> *Al Fatah . . . solemnly proclaims that the final objective of its struggle is the restoration of the independent democratic state of Palestine, all of whose citizens will enjoy equal rights irrespective of their religion.* **

The change of slogans was not sufficient to generate world sympathy. A lack of consistency continued to plague the Fedayeen leadership. Within a matter of a few days, Arafat gave two totally opposing versions of his movement's aims:

> *A democratic, non-Zionist, secular state where we could all live in peace and equality as we did for thousands of years. If the Zionists would accept this principle, we could share power on a democratic basis. We would not insist on having an Arab majority.* ***

And:

> *The liberation of Palestine and putting an end of Zionist penetration, political, economic, military and propaganda, into Moslem states . . . is one of the duties of the Moslem*

---

*The seven points passed by the Central Committee of Al Fatah, part I, January 1969.

***Ibid.*, point 5.

***Time. December 21, 1970.

> world. We must fight a Holy War against the Zionist enemy, who covets not only Palestine but the whole Arab region, including its holy places...*

Reasons for the Fedayeen decline in 1970, however, go deeper than the failure in their public relations campaign or the lack of acceptance by the Arab host countries. The basic cause was the fundamental lack of unity within the movement. The fragmentation resulted in at least ten to twelve separate organizations with varying ideologies and competing leaders. Some groups broke publicly with the PLO,** such as the PFLP and the Arab Liberation Front; others met regularly under the PLO umbrella, spending most of their time on ideological controversies, causing a breach within their ranks and a gap between the leaders and the followers.

The Fedayeen Decline as an Effective Terrorist Force

By the end of 1969, Al Fatah claimed about 20,000 members, plus several thousand armed youths from the Palestinian refugee camps. But the fortunes and the membership of Fatah declined over the next several years so that by mid-1972, Arafat could claim only about 4,000 active members.

The Syrian-Egyptian attack on Israel on October 6, 1973 provided a source of new hope for the Fedayeen. The early successes of the Arab armies renewed their resolve. Israeli sources indicated that terrorist activity reached its zenith during the opening stages of the eighteen-day war. The Fedayeen were straining to prove their military value to the regular Arab attacking armies through a series of spectacular operations, which took the form of persistent shelling and mortar fire directed at the Israeli settlements along the border. This method of long-distance fighting became very popular with the

---

**Al Hayat,* (Beirut) December 25, 1970.

**In May 1964 at the Arab summit meeting in Cairo, a serious scandal, caused mainly by intra-Fedayeen competition, was averted when Nasser suggested setting up an umbrella organization which came to be known as the Palestine Liberation Organization (PLO). Ahmed Shukairy, a lawyer from Jaffa, was appointed to head the PLO, and was given the responsibility of coordinating the planning and consultation among the various Fedayeen groups. After the departure of Shukairy in 1967, the PLO was led by Yahya Hammoudia, a veteran Palestinian nationalist, though less colorful than Shukairy.

Fedayeen because their repeated attempts to penetrate into Israeli territory had failed for the most part.

When the cease-fire was finally accepted by the Arabs and the Israelis on October 24, 1973, the Fedayeen were astonished to discover that the Egyptians and the Syrians were preeminently concerned with the desire to recover their own lost territory. The Fedayeen movement was effectively bypassed; nobody seemed to pay more than lip service to the Palestinian cause.

By mid-1974, all Fedayeen organizations had fallen into complete disarray — they had no plan for the future, no strength, and neither friend nor foe to consider them a viable force. Al Fatah and the PLO admit, at least privately, that they were looking for a political settlement.

Thus the events that followed the Yom Kippur War have diminished what was left of Fedayeen hopes of destroying Israel by force. This realization coupled with other developments (Western economic vulnerability, Arab states' confidence, Communist political exploitation) have largely contributed to the rise of the PLO as a political, rather than a terrorist organization.

THE RISE OF THE PLO AS A POLITICAL FORCE

Due to the highly volatile situation in the Middle East, the long-range political impact of the newly-acquired recognition of the PLO remains speculative. Yet, the conditions that contributed to the present development have undoubtedly been promoted and sustained by various forces to whom the rise of the PLO is potentially advantageous. However, in surveying the process by which the PLO came once again to the fore, we find that the PLO remains a pawn of inter-Arab politics. What actually took place in the UN and in Rabat, Morocco, in October, 1974 was to some degree a demonstration of the extremist Arab states' (Syria, Libya, Iraq) political arrogance at the expense of the Palestinian Arabs. For if these states succeed in directing the PLO's future policies, then one might venture to guess that the rise of the PLO as a political organization will be doomed as well.

The UN Resolution: On October 14, 1974 the UN General Assembly voted in favor of a resolution sponsored by 71 Arab, African, Asian and Communist bloc countries, including the Soviet Union, recognizing the PLO as the sole representative of the Arab

Palestinians. The resolution was adopted by a vote of 105 in favor, 4 against.

There are several significant aspects to this resolution: 1) The economic influence of the Arab oil-producing countries played a crucial role in persuading the Afro-Asian countries to sponsor and endorse the resolution. 2) The Communist bloc, for political and economic reasons, maintained its traditional support of the Arab states; by sponsoring the resolution, the Communist bloc demonstrated its own initiative on behalf of the PLO. 3) The Soviet Union, which does not feel an equal partner to the U.S. peace initiative, saw in the rise of the PLO to prominence an opportunity to disrupt Secretary Kissinger's effort to achieve step-by-step agreements between the Arab states and Israel. 4) Many of the West European countries that supported the resolution were compelled to do so mainly because of their almost total dependence on Arab oil. In sum, the UN resolution of October 14 may have signaled a new era in international politics. For the first time in the history of the UN, (the Vatican representative excluded), a non-member state representative was not only allowed to address the General Assembly, but also was granted permanent observer status. Thus the PLO established itself as a member of the international community. Whether the recognition of the PLO will be of service to the Palestinian cause or further increase the Palestinians' agony remains an open question. One thing, however, is certain. Israel can no longer dismiss the issue of the Arab Palestinians as if it had never existed.

The Rabat Resolution: The Arab states' summit meeting in Rabat, Morocco also adopted a resolution recognizing the PLO as the sole representative of the Arab Palestinians. A compromise was worked out between King Hussein of Jordan and Yasir Arafat, the head of the PLO, whereby Hussein would concede any Israeli territorial concessions in the West Bank to the PLO's jurisdiction. The resolution also made provisions for the PLO to participate in the next round of the Geneva peace conference either as part of the Jordanian delegation or as a separate PLO delegation. The Jordanian parliament endorsed the agreement in November, 1974.

There were some indications that Hussein was actually forced to accept the resolution. His "compliance," however, did not preclude the possibility, given more favorable conditions, that he might renege on his promise.

A possible change of heart on the part of Hussein, however, did not seem to seriously affect the newly acquired position of the PLO, at least for the immediate future. The significance of the Arab summit meeting's resolution, however, transcended the immediate effectiveness of the resolution itself. 1) Once again the Arabs were able to demonstrate a capability for uniting their forces behind one objective. 2) Negative political repercussions that may have resulted because of the nature of the resolution, especially with regard to the peace negotiations with Israel, were overshadowed by the Arabs' sense of superior economic power. 3) While the extremist Arab countries (Syria, Libya, Iraq) saw the resolution as a way of slowing or disrupting the peace negotiations with Israel, the moderate Arab states, such as Egypt, supported the resolution as a way of avoiding responsibility for the fate of the Arab Palestinians. 4) The Arab states came to the realization that the PLO in its role as a terrorist force, had failed to liquidate Israel; therefore, by giving the PLO ultimate responsibility for the Palestinian Arabs, the Arab states attempted to separate their territorial dispute with Israel from the Palestinian dilemma. The effect of that separation might well help to obtain better terms on both fronts.

The UN and the Rabat resolutions have undoubtedly further complicated the prospects for peace between the Arab states and Israel. Yet given the new situation and an ample period of time, we might find that the opposing positions concurrently adopted by the PLO and Israel might be reconcilable. Yasir Arafat is well aware that, short of recognizing Israel's right to exist, his chances of playing the role of representative of the Palestinians bestowed on him by the UN and the Arab states will slowly weaken and probably diminish.

Many political observers, however, have expressed serious reservations about the ability of the PLO to assume a new political role without endangering its own existence. These observers point out that a few extremist splinter groups that believe in terrorism as the ultimate means by which to cripple Israel have already threatened to leave the PLO ranks permanently if the policy of peaceful negotiations with Israel is officially adopted. In the final analysis, however, the PLO might be compelled to choose between sustaining its old position as a terrorist organization seeking the destruction of Israel or assuming a political role, seeking a negotiated settlement with Israel. The former approach has proven futile, and the latter will undoubtedly have far greater appeal to both the international community and moderate Arab states which do not believe that Israel's demise is inevitable. Although the PLO has not, so far, overtly stated its new position, it is now widely accepted that it has acceded in principle to gradually adopting a policy of negotiation. Nevertheless the PLO's leaders seem convinced that if they do not completely abandon the option of force, they will keep the flexibility they need to maintain internal unity, as well as to remain a source of constant alarm to Israel.

The PLO's transformation from a terrorist organization to a political one might turn out to be a long and agonizing process. Failure to sustain the political ground will undoubtedly signal the total collapse of the organization. For this reason the PLO is maintaining an extremely cautious policy with respect to several factors over which it has only marginal control, but which could largely affect its fate.

Among these important factors are the following:

1) the conditions under which the Israeli government might agree to negotiate with the PLO,

2) King Hussein's willingness to adhere to the Rabat resolution,

3) the continuation of the Arab states' economic and political support for the PLO,

4) the attitude of the Arab Palestinians,

5) the position that will be adopted by the extremist splinter groups within the PLO ranks,

6) the containment and possible elimination of international terrorism.

If the PLO succeeds in negotiating with Israel while keeping King Hussein as an ally, if the Arab Palestinians recognize the PLO as their representative and the Arab states continue their support, if the PLO remains united and international Arab terrorism is eliminated (or at least substantially reduced), the PLO will go into history as one of the most extraordinary phenomena in international affairs. Since it is unlikely that all these conditions could ever be met, the question remains whether or not the PLO will succeed in its transformation from a terrorist to a political organization without disintegrating in the process.

Regardless of the PLO's future, one thing does remain certain. The moderate forces among the Arabs still have the upper hand in determining policy toward Israel in the foreseeable future. If Yasir

Arafat does not join the ranks of the moderates, he may lose his last chance to play the role of a political leader.

Chapter VI

THE ROLE OF THE SUPERPOWERS IN THE MIDDLE EAST CONFLICT

No step toward a peaceful settlement between the Arab states and Israel can be envisioned realistically without taking into consideration the role and the influence of the two superpowers, the United States and the Soviet Union. The fate of the entire Middle East region presently depends upon the position that either or both take.

For a brief period — between 1945 and 1952 — the Arabs and the Israelis might have been able to settle their dispute alone. During that time a political vacuum was created through the termination of the British mandate, and the U.S. and Russia had not as yet fully taken over where the British and the French left off. The Russians were probing Israel, hoping to bring her under Communist influence, while the Americans felt safe enough politically and economically to forego diplomatic and military action in pursuit of their interests.

It was not until 1952, when President Nasser of Egypt came to power through a military coup and Arab nationalism intensified, that the Americans and the Russians took another hard look at the development of events. What prompted superpower involvement in the Middle East was not a rediscovery of the importance of the region, but rather the realization, especially by the Russians, that conditions were now conducive to exploitation and penetration. Since that time, the Arab-Israeli crisis has taken on a global dimension, whereby the immediate parties to the crisis have, in effect, lost control over their own affairs and become an integral part of the rivalry for power between the U.S. and the Soviet Union.

THE REGIONAL IMPORTANCE OF THE MIDDLE EAST

From economic, strategic, and political perspectives, the Middle East has historically been considered one of the most important regions in the world. The empires of Rome, Persia, Greece, Turkey, and Britain were based on a control of the Middle East; their declines were in some way related to their inability to sustain their domain over the region. It is therefore little wonder that, with the decline of the British Empire after World War II, the U.S. and Russia as the emerging powers in the region attempted to increase their influence over the Middle East.

There are three considerations that make the Middle East crucial for any major nation seeking to protect its interests, assume global responsibility, and to a certain degree, ensure its national survival.

1. **Strategic.** The Middle East has long been the hub of communications between East and West. Therefore, any Western power that has interests and bears any responsibility in Asia and Africa would naturally attempt to entrench itself in the area. One might argue that recent technological achievements on the economic and military levels (such as high-flying planes that do not need the landing and servicing facilities of the Arab world; supertankers bypassing the Suez Canal en route to Europe; long-range anti-ballistic missiles that can be launched from any part of the world to targets anywhere; nuclear submarines that can stay under water for long periods of time without the need of refueling) have reduced the importance of physically controlling the Middle East. Yet physical control or access to landing facilities there from a strictly strategic vantage point remains essential. Conquest by a foot soldier or tank will most likely remain crucial, in spite of the overwhelming impact of nuclear weapons on military planning. Whether or not U.S. and Soviet policies presently envision such an eventuality is irrelevant. As long as the rivalry between the superpowers continues, such an eventuality cannot be ruled out.

2. **Economic.** The economic importance of the Middle East is related to its strategic importance. The very commodity that makes the region vital economically will continue to be for the foreseeable future the basic component that moves Western and Japanese industry: oil.

Arab oil has recently become not only an economic factor, but a political tool with as yet unimagined implications. During the 1973 Arab-Israeli war, when the Arab oil-producing countries imposed an embargo on all shipments of oil to the Western Hemisphere and to Japan, the importance of oil as a political weapon was brought home forcefully. An indefinite embargo could have brought the Western world to the brink of economic disaster. Therefore, in considering the importance of Arab oil to Western industry, we cannot separate it from the strategic component: namely, anyone who is in a position to control Arab oil can impose his own terms on Western Europe and Japan.

The American sensitivity toward Arab oil stems from three main sources: 1) Apart from her own partial dependence on Arab oil, the U.S. feels obligated to protect her allies' interests. Any serious threat of a possible takeover of the oil fields by the USSR for example — would bring a strong American reaction. 2) The U.S. is committed to protecting American investments in the Arab oil countries, which recently have been estimated to be in excess of 12 billion dollars. 3) Oil proceeds in Arab hands have reached astronomical figures (an estimated 60 billion dollars a year), and this has compelled Washington to reassess its policies toward the entire region. In brief, the U.S. can be expected to take a firm stance against further Soviet influence in the Middle East and will strive to insure further American economic collaboration with the Arab states.

3. **Political.** The political importance of the Middle East is an extension of its strategic and economic importance. What makes the political factor in this region crucial is that, like other regions in Asia and Africa, the Middle East has become a focal point of U.S. and Russian rivalry. For various political and economic considerations, the U.S. and Russia selected their clients in the Middle East based on a determination of how to gain maximum political leverage over them. The Russians showed a greater capacity, at least between 1950-1970, to understand the nationalistic moods of the Arabs and were able to cash in on it. The U.S., on the other hand, formulated its policies during the same period by adopting countermeasures in reaction to Russian initiatives that were either too little or too late. While the U.S. did not acquiesce in the Russian penetration in the first place, it maintained a policy of passivism as long as its immediate interests were not threatened. As one expert put it:

> *American policy toward the Middle East has been criticized as being at best inconsistent, at worst non-existent. Both*

accusations arise from the apparent lack of a single policy toward the area as a whole. *

SOVIET PENETRATION

The Russian dream of a strong foothold in the Middle East is centuries-old. Moscow's desire to control the region may be traced back to the time of the Mongols and Teutonic Knights and down to the times of Napoleon and Hitler. The reason lies in the Russians' obsessive fear of an outside invader. The German invasion of their homeland in World War II made the Russians more determined than ever not to allow Eastern Europe to again become a jumping board for aggression. When Eastern Europe became secure, the Russians pursued the second stage of their long-range policy, to secure a defensive "second line" of countries in the Middle East. Some political observers from non-Communist countries believe that Soviet expansionism will not stop with the Middle East. For if the Russian "waves" of political influence continue, the argument goes they will undoubtedly try to encircle the entire Middle East. And if they have a third stage planned, it would probably include control over Iran, Afghanistan, and Pakistan.

Essentially, Russian ambitions in the Middle East may be summarized as follows: 1) ensuring that the Middle East does not develop into anti-Soviet satellites from which her forces on the southwest would be threatened; 2) gaining access to and control over the rich oil-producing Arab countries; 3) encircling the Persian Gulf and acquiring access to its strategic waterways; 4) gaining a naval force in the Arabian Sea and a stronghold in Syria, Libya, and Egypt in order to apply leverage on the North Atlantic Treaty Organization (NATO) to obtain concessions. Since World War II, Soviet political shrewdness has made its entry to the Middle East possible and forced the United States to shift its strategy toward the Middle East as well as globally.

Russia's attitude toward Israel: The Soviet attitude toward the creation of the state of Israel was based principally on the belief and

---

*John S. Badeau, *The American Approach to the Arab World* (New York: Harper & Row Publishers, 1968), p. 81.

hope that an Israeli presence would create problems and instability in the Arab world, a situation that the Russians could then attempt to manipulate in order to gain the Arab states' favor in the long run. The USSR felt that the U.S. was not in a favorable position to immediately fill the vacuum left by the British.

While the Soviet long-range policy was aimed at currying Arab favor, Moscow nonetheless for almost six years (1948-1953) also apparently attempted to bring Israel into its camp. It was only after Nasser established himself in Egypt and in the Arab world that the Russians felt that a political move to woo the Arabs was timely. As Henry Kissinger observed in his book *Nuclear Weapons and Foreign Policy:*

> ... *in the Middle East the Kremlin used its new-found enthusiasm for Arab nationalism as a means to advance ambitions which had eluded Imperial Russia. In short, what many in the non-Soviet world considered the beginning of a relaxation of tensions was used by the Kremlin as a means to attempt to overturn the world balance of power.* *

The new Soviet tack: From late 1952 through 1953 the Russians were uncommitted to either the Arabs or Israel. But by the end of 1953, they began to demonstrate their full support for the Arab cause. This support was first given expression in the United Nations debate on the Arab-Israeli confrontation. The Soviet Union blocked a resolution calling on the Arabs and Israel to resolve their differences through direct negotiations. The Russians supported the Syrians in their 1954 attempt to block Israel's plan to drain the Hula swamp. By 1956, the Soviet foreign minister had blocked the debate on Israel's right to move her maritime fleet through the Suez Canal. Prior to that, the Russians stated in effect that Israel was responsible for the war of 1948 and hence should be condemned.

The Arab states, which conveniently ignored Russia's initial positive role in the creation of the state of Israel, willingly reciprocated the Soviet demonstration of support by, for example, abstaining from voting on a Western-sponsored measure to condemn the Communist aggression in Korea. Thus we find the Russian-Arab

---

*Henry Kissinger, *Nuclear Weapons and Foreign Policy* (New York: Norton & Company, 1969), p. 63.

collaboration, especially with the Arab revolutionary regimes, intensifying to the point where the Soviet Union was becoming a major political factor in the Middle East. This shift gave rise to an open, and at times dangerous, challenge to the U.S.'s interests and security.

> *To be sure, this power [Russia] has operated in the Middle East since the end of the war, and was the chief cause for the assumption of American responsibilities in the region. But with the 1955 Egyptian arms deal, the Suez debacle, and the ensuing collapse of the British position, the Soviet presence took on a new and more permanent character. By political support for Egyptian resistance to the West, the Soviets entered the Arab world not through the threat of force [as in Iran at the end of the war] or the support of local subversive movements [as in Greece], but by its identification with the aspirations of Arab nationalism. The Soviets offered a substitute for a European connection and were accepted on this basis in Egypt and other Arab countries.* *

The clash of the Egyptian government with the British and the French over the nationalization of the Suez Canal in 1956 allowed the Soviets to emerge from the crisis with an enhanced reputation and a closer identification with Arab national aspirations. The Eisenhower administration, by committing what might be considered America's worst political error in the Middle East, eliminated French a   .itish influence in Arab eyes and enhanced the likelihood of So⸌ ⸌t entrenchment in the region. During the period from 1956 to 1967, the revolutionary regimes of Egypt, Syria, Iraq and Algeria came to view the Russians as their savior. The implications of this relationship were far-reaching and probably beyond the Russians' own expectations.

The remarkable success of the Russians in a relatively short period of time may be attributed to five major factors:

1) Lack of American long-range policy for the region as a whole.

2) For economic reasons (oil), the U.S. was obliged to support

---

*Badeau, *op. cit.*, p. 10.

those traditional regimes that were considered "reactionary" by the nationalist revolutionary movements.

> ... the Soviet objective to seek and foster the polarization of the Middle East into traditional and radical camps, with the West labeled as the protector of reaction and the USSR as the champion of change and supporter of progress.*

3) The Soviets, lacking any direct responsibilities in the Arab world retained a freedom of action to pursue any policy deemed necessary to reach their goals. In addition, the Russians acted in such an ambiguous fashion that American policy-makers had difficulty assessing the situation and finding an ironclad basis to warrant a swift reaction. Thus inaction became America's usual prescription to remedy the situation.

4) The Russians never took any military action against Israel that would provoke a harsh American response. In fact, the continuation of Israel's existence was a prerequisite to Russia's continued influence. As long as Israel constituted a source of Arab frustration, the Russians were determined to "safeguard" that source and thereby perpetuate the Arab need for constant Soviet political and military support.

5) American commitments to guarantee the security of the state of Israel further alienated the Arab states, a factor that diminished America's influence over the revolutionary regimes, particularly between 1967 and 1973.

To what degree have the Russians succeeded in the Middle East? Is there a real reason for the U.S. to worry about the Soviet intentions, especially after the Yom Kippur War? Many political analysts maintain that, in fact, the Russians have been losing ground since the Six-Day War of 1967. The Soviets, like the U.S., have seen their influence fluctuate and, at times, have been frustrated by the Arabs' inability to commit themselves wholeheartedly to any one ideology or policy. The Egyptian government, under the late President Nasser and now Anwar Sadat, was to a certain extent ambivalent in its relation to the Russians. Nasser always kept the Americans informed about his willingness to normalize relations if only America could demonstrate a more even-handed stance in her dealings with Egypt and Israel.

---

*Badeau, *op. cit.*, p. 137.

The Soviets, too, have been ambivalent and much less generous to the Arabs than the U.S. in terms of outright grants, although since 1953 the Soviets have demonstrated consistency in their support of the Arab cause at all levels: political, military, technological and to a lesser degree on the economic level as well. As a veteran U.S. diplomat recently wrote:

> ... still, the Soviet Union has had no better luck than the United States in molding the Third World to its heart's desire. Outside of Southeast Asia, where the costs have been enormous, and Cuba, which is an unreliable satellite, communism has not gained an inch in twenty-five years; nor have flirtations with fellow travelers like Sukarno, Nkrumah, Lumumba, or Ben Bella proved rewarding.*

The Arab revolutionary regimes maintained by and large a position of nonalignment with the major powers. While they looked to Russia for help and support, they did not allow it to repeat its domination of Eastern Europe. Further, the Arab states have not permitted any Communist party to exist. The Arab states oppose becoming a Soviet satellite for two reasons. First, most of the Arab revolutionary regimes came to power and retained it on the basis of "independence from imperialism." Second, the Arab states, revolutionary and conservative alike, realize that the thrust, the power, and the influence of the U.S. could not be altogether disregarded. When President Sadat ousted 20,000 Russian "advisors" from Egypt in 1972, he intended to show the Americans his political independence as well as to extend an open invitation to the U.S. to take a more active part in settling his dispute with Israel.

The first Soviet setback: The Six-Day War inflicted the first serious setback on the Russians in the Arab world. A few months before, the Russians were faced with a problem and an opportunity. On the one hand, they wanted to save the shaky regime of Syria which was under tremendous pressure from intensified Israeli retaliation against terrorists encamped there. On the other hand, the Russians hoped to divert Israel's attention from the northern (Syrian) front by encouraging Egyptian provocation in the south. When Nasser demanded the withdrawal of the UN forces from the

---

*Charles Yost, *The Conduct and the Misconduct of Foreign Affairs* (New York: Random House, 1972), p. 119.

Sinai and sealed off the Gulf of Aqaba from Israel's shipping, he was indeed provoking Israel. He further dispatched some 80,000 men and heavy equipment to the Sinai, pronouncing the imminent destruction of Israel. Israeli reaction was swift and far-reaching, unexpected and disastrous to the Arabs.

Once the guns were silenced, the Arab-Israeli crisis had assumed a new dimension. The Russians belligerently assumed the role of Arab defender at the UN but failed to force through either the Security Council or the General Assembly their own resolution calling for total withdrawal of the Israeli forces from the occupied territories. To the Arab states, this diplomatic reversal was the first signal of Russian weakness. It became evident that the USSR was not strong enough to maneuver the community of nations into adopting their position, nor were they the true and honest friends who should have warned the Arab states not to confront the Israelis at that point in time.

> *These difficulties were a part of the general limits on Soviet diplomacy in the Middle East. It had not been able directly to challenge the U.S. nor to rally the support of the world community at the UN. While publicly and loudly supporting the Arab cause, it was at the same time privately urging the Arabs to come to some accommodation with Israel. Clearly, instability in the Arab world had come to such a point that even the Soviets found it in their interest to temper reckless policies. Arab representatives were angered; Algeria and Syria in particular showed sharp resistance to Soviet efforts seeking a modus vivendi between the Arab states and Israel. At the time of the Cuba crisis, one Arab chief of state had observed: "This proves that the Soviets will not go out on a limb for the sake of a small third country. They did not defend Cuba, and they will not defend us." If this lesson had been forgotten, 1967 taught it afresh to the Arabs.* *

Yet, since their armies were wholly supplied and equipped by Russia,**Egypt and Syria were compelled to maintain their pro-Russian policy, especially in view of the lack of American readiness

---

*Badeau, *op. cit.*, pp. 161-162.

**The Jordanian army was and is still equipped mainly with American weaponry.

to back their efforts. Therefore, although they had lost some of their glamour among the Arab states, Moscow was able to maintain the position and continue to demonstrate its unequivocal support of the revolutionary regimes. The U.S. was now faced with a strong Soviet challenge in the Arab world.

The Second Soviet setback: The results of the Six-Day War forced the Russians to reassess their position toward the Arab states; once again the Soviets were faced with a problem and a new opportunity. On the one hand, they were politically humiliated by their inability to translate into reality their protestations of willingness to come to the Arabs' aid. On the other hand, neither Israel nor the U.S. made any substantial political move to cash in on the Israelis' stunning victory. Egypt and Syria, having been forced into a corner were once again compelled to turn to Russia for help, military and economic. The Russians lost no time in re-equipping the Egyptian and the Syrian armies, this time with more and better equipment, which gradually brought the number of Soviets acting as advisors and instructors to over 20,000 in Egypt alone.

The Russians were determined not only to recapture what they had lost in prestige and influence in Syria and Egypt, but in addition, to enhance their reputation. Yet they were for the first time facing a serious problem — how to maintain their foothold in the Middle East when their continued presence depended on several conditions that were not favorable to them: 1) There was the problem of the inherent resistance of Arab nationalism to any foreign control. 2) The political instability of Arab nations made Soviet long-range planning difficult, if not impossible. 3) The unequivocal support of Israel by the United States stopped the Russians short of military intervention. Nonetheless the Russians became determined to extend this penetration into the Middle East.

The new Soviet strategy called for an increase in their Mediterranean fleet to afford them a greater presence; developing alternate bases to those in Egypt while trying to maintain their influence there; to be more active in patching up the relations between various revolutionary Arab regimes while trying to win their confidence; putting more effort into the training of the Egyptian and the Syrian armies while making available to them more sophisticated weapons in order to avoid another military humiliation; attempting to maintain the status quo, that is, a situation of no war no peace between Israel and the Arab states, while supporting the Arab "war of attrition" on Israel so far as it was confined to the exchange of shelling; and finally, continuing her subversive activities in those Arab states and sheikdoms that were ripe targets without provoking a confrontation with the U.S.

The new Soviet strategy seemed to work relatively well. Between 1967 and 1972, they entrenched themselves deeper than ever in Egypt, Syria, Iraq, Algeria, and Yemen.

However, in the autumn of 1970, the war of attrition between Egypt and Israel ended.* That U.S. Secretary of State William Rogers was instrumental in achieving the truce demonstrated once again to the Arab states that the U.S., unlike the Soviet Union, was not seeking to influence the Arab states by perpetuating the Arab-Israeli crisis. The fact that a continuous dialogue had been going on unofficially at a high level between the U.S. and Egypt since 1968 showed that the Egyptians never contemplated solving the Arab-Israeli crisis without American participation, influence, pressure, and desire.

President Sadat's decision to oust the Russian technicians and advisors in November of 1972 was not only because, as one Egyptian journalist observed, the Soviets had created in Egypt a "state within a state,"** but also because Sadat was convinced that the Russians' ultimate goal did not necessarily serve the interests of the Arab nations. While the Russians had, proven themselves willing to supply armaments, the success of a peaceful or a military encounter with the Israelis in the future would now depend on the U.S. more than on Russia.*** Other factors contributing to President Sadat's decision to oust the Russians might include the following: 1) to

---

*Israel's refusal to withdraw from the occupied territories captured in 1967 prompted the late President Nasser to start a war of attrition against Israel. This kind of war was intended to frustrate the Israeli military presence on the east side of the Canal. Israel retaliated severely against Egyptian compounds and other strategic targets within Egypt. The Israeli air raids were daily and it was estimated by military observers that Egyptian losses during this war exceeded 8,000 dead, plus over two billion dollars in damages to military equipment and other civilian and military installations. The war of attrition lasted from late 1968 to the autumn of 1970.

**The Russians in Egypt have established numerous military bases that were off limit even to Egyptian Generals.

***There was another widespread theory that the Soviet pullout was not caused by a unilateral demand by President Sadat, but by mutual consent. Yet the subsequent tense relationship between Egypt and the Soviet Union does not support this view. In addition, the Soviets would have spared no effort to capitalize on such an agreement in an attempt to demonstrate their non-imperialistic policies or intentions in the Middle Eastern region.

remove any suspicion that Egypt had become a Soviet satellite; 2) to tell the Israelis that they would be dealing with the Arabs alone; 3) to secure political and military flexibility; and 4) to ease internal tensions among Egyptian students and military officers who overtly resented the Russians' increasing presence.

The Soviet reaction to President Sadat's demands for withdrawal of their military presence was pointedly restrained. The Soviet media made the whole episode appear as if it were a joyful occasion. The Soviets, in fact, were faced with two rather unpleasant alternatives; either to withdraw with grace or keep their military units there by force. The latter could have developed into a new international crisis, possibly the end of Soviet influence in the Arab world. Thus, the Soviets swallowed their second humiliation with dignity, waiting for a new opportunity.

The third Soviet setback: The year that lapsed between the ousting of the Soviet advisors and the Yom Kippur War should perhaps be termed a year of reconciliation between Egypt and the USSR. Although the Soviets never came back to Egypt with the same strength, this reconciliation was still possible primarily because of President Sadat's failure to reach some sort of political accommodation with Israel. The internal situation in Egypt, socially and economically, was getting worse. The armed forces, trebled in size between 1967 and 1973, became restless, and young officers who had been trained for years were ready for action. The Russian assessment of the Egyptian and the Syrian armies was encouraging. While they had not told the Arabs that they could overrun the Israelis, they did indicate that the combined armies of Egypt and Syria stood a reasonable chance of making a good showing against the Israelis.

The early gains of the Egyptian and the Syrian armies in the first few days of the 1973 war showed that indeed they did have better-equipped and better-trained soldiers, excellent coordination, a superb military strategy that caught the Israelis by surprise, and a better fighting spirit and demonstration of courage. The combined early Egyptian-Syrian military thrust against Israel was made possible and successful by Russian technical aid. Egypt and Syria recognized this debt and the Russians were, of course, ready to capitalize on it.

The Israeli counter-thrust days later that drove the Syrian army beyond the 1967 lines, and the bridgehead to the west of the Suez

Canal that resulted in the encirclement of the 20,000-man Egyptian Third Army quickly and drastically reversed the military balance between the armies. Once again the Russians were put to the test, and again they failed.

The Russians took extensive military and political measures to save their clients from a total disaster. The airlift of armaments to Syria and Egypt was carried on with unprecedented speed and scope. Leonid Brezhnev, the Soviet Communist party chief, sent a message to President Richard Nixon that, in Nixon's words, "left no room for misunderstanding." It contained clear and overt threats of Russian intervention by force if the Israelis were not stopped. The Russians wanted to avoid another Egyptian and Syrian calamity at all possible costs. Yet the likelihood of a confrontation with the U.S. increased greatly once President Nixon submitted his stern answer to Brezhnev — a world-wide alert of American armed forces. The Russians were thus faced with two choices — to carry out their threats and bring about a greater chance of a catastrophe, or to join with the U.S. (with the loss of further prestige) in efforts to arrange a cease-fire. It was at this time that the Russians made their dramatic request to Secretary of State Kissinger, asking him to fly to Moscow for consultations.

The Egyptians and the Syrians obviously were well aware that until the U.S. was satisfied with the arrangement, the Soviet Union's threats to use force were almost meaningless. This conviction on the part of the Egyptians and the Syrians gave more credibility to the U.S. position than to that of the Soviet Union. The cessation of hostilities that the U.S. and Russia arranged, and the Arabs and the Israelis accepted on October 24th gave no clear-cut victory to either side. The cease-fire was in complete accord with Kissinger's doctrine that total defeat or total victory by either side was self-defeating because the victors would want to negotiate from a position of strength, and the losers might refuse to negotiate altogether. In the Arab-Israeli case, this imbalance has prevailed for the last 27 years. Kissinger was determined to change the balance just enough so that both sides would be willing to negotiate as equals.

When the second cease-fire was accepted and adhered to by both the Arabs and the Israelis on October 24th, most political and military observers around the world summed up their appraisal of the latest Arab-Israeli encounter more or less in this fashion —

Egypt, Syria, and especially Russia had emerged victorious; the U.S. and Israel probably suffered the most humiliation since the creation of Israel in 1948. But by January 1974 the entire political situation appeared to have reversed itself to a point where U.S. influence emerged. Washington has become, to a large extent, the determining factor in the outcome of the conflict, due to the following series of circumstances:

1) Since the Russians had not taken overt steps for military intervention, they did not find it embarrassing to withdraw their threat of intervention. At the same time, the U.S. alert gave a clear signal to Russia that America would oppose any Soviet threat even at the risk of nuclear confrontation.

2) The U.S. ignored the Soviet demands that Israel be forced to withdraw to the first cease-fire line of October 22nd. The two extra days gave Israel the opportunity to entrench herself on the west side of the Suez Canal. The U.S., especially, agreed on the date of the cease-fire and on the specific locations where the Israeli and the Egyptian armies were to "stand down," so that *both Israel and Egypt could claim a certain victory.* This situation of "contrived parity" was crucial in allowing both sides later to disengage their forces on January 18, 1974.

3) The U.S. airlift of armaments, missiles, planes, and ammunition to Israel in unprecedented quantities was an obvious signal to Egypt that the U.S. was committed to the security of Israel. The world-wide alert of U.S. forces provided additional assurance of this commitment and of the necessity of dealing with the United States, not Russia, in a post-war solution.

Events during and after the October, 1973 war clearly indicated that the U.S. had, by a superb coordination of military and diplomatic measures, in effect derailed what the Russians had been working toward for almost two decades in Egypt. That is not to say, of course, that the Soviet influence in Egypt today is non-existent. But what can be stated with certainty is that if the U.S. maintains a position of strength in her dealings with the Soviet Union, particularly in the Middle East, the U.S. will not only gain back any ground lost in the last twenty years, but will re-emerge as the dominant figure in that region.

Many political observers believe, however, that the failure of Henry Kissinger to achieve a second partial settlement between Egypt and Israel in March 1975, coupled with the fall of Cambodia,

South Vietnam and Laos to the Communists has significantly weakened the U.S. diplomatic thrust in the Middle East. Although this belief has definite merit, nevertheless the U.S. remains the principal factor in any peace negotiations between the Arab states and Israel. The retention of this position by the U.S. was possible due to a combination of intentional and circumstantial political moves that were adopted by the U.S. immediately upon the suspension of the talks:

1) Kissinger's failure was not attributed officially to either Israel or Egypt; by doing so the U.S. retained its impartiality and thereby its role as a mediator acceptable to both sides.

2) Privately the U.S. blamed Israel as being intransigent. As this unofficial position was leaked out to the media, the U.S. was able to keep Sadat committed to U.S. mediation and thereby less affected by Moscow's pressure.

3) The Cambodian capture of the Mayaguez and the ships dramatic release by U.S. forces was meant to signal to many countries, Israel and the Arab states included, that the U.S. intends to stand fast when her interests or prestige are affected. The Mayaguez incident was thus in a way a "blessing in disguise" that has partially restored U.S. credibility.

4) Due to the Israeli partial but vital dependence on U.S. military and economic aid, the U.S. was in a position to take a harder line toward Israel yet without a big risk to U.S. — Israeli friendship. Thus the reassessment of U.S. policy in the Middle East ordered by President Ford was designed among the rest to keep both the Arabs and the Israelis on alert, but warn the Israelis of a possible modification of U.S. commitments toward her. This situation, coupled with the Gromyko-Kissinger Vienna agreement in May 1975 to delay the Geneva conference, gave rise to the hope that a renewed U.S. effort may be underway. And indeed the resumption of the U.S. step-by-step approach during the second half of August 1975 found Israel and Egypt better geared psychologically for greater concessions. In the new interim agreement that followed Egypt and Israel agreed that the conflict between them will not be solved by military force but by peaceful means. In addition, Egypt agreed the UN force will not be removed without the consent of both sides. It should be noted here that although the new interim agreement contains more than forty clauses such as the exact lines to which the Israel forces will withdraw and the kind of armaments

that both sides may deploy and promises by Egypt to limit the economic boycott and psychological warfare against Israel and allow ships destined for Israel to pass through the Suez Canal, the most important aspect of the new accord is that Israel has agreed to concede the Gidi and the Mitla passes to Egypt in addition to the Abu Rudeis oil field. In return, Egypt has pledged to adhere to the new agreement and to continue the diplomatic efforts toward final peace agreement under the auspices of the Geneva peace conference

U.S. POLITICAL VULNERABILITY IN THE MIDDLE EAST

The emergence of the U.S. after World War II as the dominant international power gave rise to added interest and concern on the part of world leaders about how American policy might involve them or compromise the integrity of their respective countries. In essence, there were three regions on which world attention was focused and whose fate depended to a large extent on U.S. action: Europe, Asia, and the Middle East.

The critics of U.S. foreign policy seem always to out-number the supporters. The U.S. has been accused of adopting numerous kinds of unsuccessful policies. For example, there are those who accuse the U.S. of being unable to adopt a *long-range* policy outlined in stages and implemented accordingly. There are those who maintain that U.S. policy is based on prevalent events and usually only reacts to a *fait accompli*. Others criticize U.S. policies on the basis of the gap between massive American political, economic, and military power and a narrow perspective on how to use her potentialities. Some maintain that U.S. foreign policy lacks coordination between national interest and overseas commitments. And finally, there are those who insist that U.S. failures in foreign policy are due to the inflexibility that American policy-makers attach to their policies, basing them on certain rigid contingencies and leaving no room for political maneuvering, with the result that other options are never fully exercised.

The criticisms mounted on U.S. policy-makers between 1950 and 1970 in this area are for the most part valid. The U.S. policy in the Middle East between 1950 and 1970 might, therefore, be described briefly and with some overstatement, as inconsistent, uncoordinated, haphazard, unimaginative, and inflexible.

The Arab disenchantment with U.S. policy: Among the first to express disenchantment with U.S. policy after World War II were the Arab states. Especially after the creation of the state of Israel in 1948, there were basic differences between the American approach to the Arab world and the Arab expectations from Americans in the Middle East, associated with Western imperialism. The American hope of coming to the Middle East as a non-European state while attempting to protect European interests proved futile. What further alienated the Arab states was the unequivocal support of the U.S. for the state of Israel, beginning with the administration of President Harry Truman. Through the Eisenhower, Kennedy, Johnson, Nixon and Ford years, the U.S. remained committed to protect the integrity of Israel, while the Arab states, especially the revolutionary ones, remained committed to opposing American interests in the area.

Opposing objectives: American objectives in the Middle East at times ran contrary to the Arabs' national interests. While the U.S.'s main political objective was the containment of the Soviet Union, this goal clashed with some of the Arab states who were securing economic and military aid from the Communist bloc. The American interest in the defense of the area with its accompanying pressure to support Western regional defense pacts (e.g., the Baghdad Pact), plus the use of military facilities grated on the nationalist spirit of the independent Arab states. During the 1950's and particularly under Secretary of State John Foster Dulles, American pressure on the Arabs to align with the West stirred their fears that they would once again be bound to Western imperialism and be denied their own independent place in world affairs.*

Conflict of interests within the Arab states: The fact that the Arab states were divided politically into several groupings made it extremely difficult for the U.S. to follow any one policy that would conceivably please every Arab regime. In an effort, for example, to develop good relations with a revolutionary state, the U.S. would be charged with acting against the interests of the conservative regimes. Thus no matter what course the U.S. took, it appeared as if she were acting to promote her own interests against any political change that might lead to "Arab progress."

The pursuit of oil: One major determinant of U.S. policy toward the oil-producing states was their oil. U.S. interest in these countries

---

*Badeau, *op. cit.*, p. 176.

was three-fold: 1) heavy U.S. investments; 2) the need for oil as a crucial energy source for Western Europe; and 3) defense against a Soviet takeover. These three factors further deepened the schism between the revolutionary regimes and the United States. The U.S., unlike Russia, viewed the new nationalist revolutionary movements as a potentially disruptive factor that would endanger her vital interests.

American counter-measures: The lack of understanding between the revolutionary regimes of Egypt, Syria, Iraq and the U.S. forced the latter to take measures at times contrary to her long-term interests. Economic appropriations for Egypt were reduced substantially. The U.S. Congress was not willing to appropriate funds for countries, such as Egypt, which they considered "Communist satellites" and a source of continuous and annoying problems. The continuation of economic and military aid to the Arab governments that were considered "reactionary" by the nationalist and revolutionary ones further aggravated U.S. relations with the "progressive" regimes. This culminated in Egypt, Syria, Iraq, Algeria, and Yemen breaking diplomatic relations with the U.S. immediately after the outbreak of the Six-Day War, June 1967.

U.S. interests in the Middle East: What are the real interests of the U.S. in the Middle East? Do her interests or her commitments determine her policy there? And are these two compatible?

In view of the economic, strategic, and political importance of the Middle East, the U.S. should have for all practical reasons seen to it that her interests coincided with those of the Arab countries, since they are the predominant factor in the region. The U.S., however, did not adopt this line of reasoning despite the fact that between 1947 and 1973 American influence among the Arab states was declining.

The decline was precipitated by the Truman Doctrine of 1947, which effectively subordinated the interests of the Middle Eastern nations to the foreign policy goals of the United States to contain Soviet expansion and to further world stability by adopting a global policy. The various nationalistic movements, young intellectuals and leftist extremists in the Arab states interpreted the Truman Doctrine as anti-Arab, and opposed it.

Israel was immediately recognized by the U.S. in 1948. While sentimental, moral, and political affiliations with the new-born democracy were important in determining the U.S. position at the time, one important factor was the American view of Israel as a potential *obstacle to Soviet expansionism in the Middle East.* Thus we find that the U.S. commitment to preserve the state of Israel has been maintained to date by all administrations in the United States.

Many observers have argued that the U.S. commitment to the state of Israel is not in line with, and is even contradictory to U.S. interests. This contention, however, is based on narrow regional considerations limited to oil, rather than on global considerations that transcend the purely economic motivations. In fact, the defenders of U.S. policy toward Israel go one step further. They argue that unless the U.S. continues to view the Middle East as an integral part of her global policy in her confrontation with the USSR, there will be no future economic benefit for the U.S. to consider, once the region has been lost to the Soviets.

The main antagonism of the Arab revolutionary regimes did not stem from continued U.S. support for Israel. The Russians, after all, pioneered in supporting the state of Israel from its inception through 1953, and that was not held against them by the same Arab revolutionary regimes. Their objection to U.S. policy was based mainly on the fact that the U.S. preferred the status quo in the Middle East and was reluctant to support and endorse the new revolutionary spirit that engulfed the Arabs after the rise of Nasser in 1952.

In early 1957, several interrelated events prompted the U.S. to review her policy toward the Middle East, and particularly toward Egypt, the most important nation in the region: 1) the Egyptian arms deal with Czechoslovakia that was sponsored by the USSR and gave Russia the key to the Egyptian door; 2) the Egyptian nationalization of the Suez Canal in 1956; 3) the subsequent invasion of Egypt by Britain, France, and Israel later in 1956; and 4) the Egyptian-Russian contract to build the Aswan Dam. All of these events, destined to plunge the Middle East into upheaval and instability for years, took place during the Eisenhower Administration. Despite the so-called "even-handed policy" that Secretary of State Dulles was applying toward the Arabs and Israelis, the general attitude of the revolutionary regimes toward the U.S. did not change, and by 1958 the U.S. was still cast as the enemy of the Arabs.

When the above events are considered in chronological order, the contradictions of the Eisenhower Administration's political maneuvering in the Middle East become rather obvious. In November, 1955, when John Foster Dulles learned about the Czech-Egyptian arms deal, with Soviet blessing, he expressed astonishment. The disclosure undoubtedly prompted the cancellation of negotiations to finance the Aswan Dam by the U.S. and the World Bank. In retaliation, Nasser announced the nationalization of the Suez Canal.

Although the U.S. sided with the Soviet Union in condemning the attack on Egypt by Britain, France and Israel and threatened Israel with economic sanctions unless it withdrew to the old lines, relations with Egypt did not materially improve. Less than two years later, the revolution in Iraq, in which Nasser conspired, put an end to the Baghdad Pact,* and by the end of 1958, U.S. relations with Egypt and Iraq further deteriorated. Although the Eisenhower Administration thus took diplomatic action against Israel in favor of the Arabs, the basic antagonism and distrust between the U.S. and Egypt never really changed, irrespective of what policy the U.S. adopted toward Israel.

U.S. psychological gains among the Arab States: The relationship between the Arab states and the U.S. remained clouded despite the numerous attempts by the Eisenhower Administration to appease Nasser, Yet, neither the U.S. nor the Arabs were psychologically geared to change their approach fundamentally. The Six-Day War, however, was a turning point for the U.S. in the Middle East. Some political observers maintain that the U.S., as a result of support for Israel in that conflict, further damaged her interests in the Middle East, and that U.S.-Arab political relations deteriorated further. On the other side of the argument, it was the 1967 war that gave the U.S. her first political, and especially psychological, advantage over the Arab states and Israel, an advantage that made her role in the October war of 1973 instrumental in ending the crisis the way it did. Furthermore, it forced the Soviet Union to assume a secondary role during the disengagement of forces negotiations, even when dealing

---

*The Baghdad Pact was established in February, 1955 between Iraq and Turkey. The pact, engineered by the Eisenhower Administration, was aimed at deterring the Russians and insuring Western influence over the Middle East region. The pact was economic and military in nature and was designed to include other states, such as Pakistan, Iran, Syria, Jordan and even Egypt. The pact was dissolved in 1958 immediately after the military coup led by General Kasem in Iraq put an end to the Iraqi monarchy.

with the most ardent opponents of Israel and the U.S., Egypt and Syria.

The repercussions of the 1967 war compelled the Arab leadership to review the role that the U.S. and the Soviet Union played during the war and afterwards. It became unequivocally clear to the Arab leadership that the U.S. honored its commitments; despite her involvement in Vietnam, the U.S. had stood fast against the Soviet threats. President Johnson at the time clearly informed Prime Minister Kosygin that the U.S. would not tolerate direct Soviet intervention in the Middle East. The determination of the U.S. and her credibility had enormous psychological effects on the Arabs. Twice, in the 1962 Cuban crisis and in 1967, the U.S. had challenged the Soviet Union, and it was the latter which backed away. This experience remained vivid in the minds of the Arabs during the last encounter with Israel in October 1973. The consistent position of the U.S. in 1967 was thus the beginning of the re-emergence of the U.S. in influence and importance in the Arab world.

The anti-Americanism that engulfed the Arabs after the 1967 war was an expression of anger and frustration, and though it resulted in the severing of diplomatic relations with the U.S., America did not really lose any ground. Publicly, the outraged Arab revolutionary regimes denounced the U.S. for her role in giving Israel military superiority. They accused the United States of being an accomplice in the Israeli lightning stroke. Yet secretly, the dialogue between some Egyptian and U.S. officials continued. One Egyptian official in the U.S. told me that "in fact, a few weeks after the June 1967 war, President Nasser himself instructed his foreign minister to see to it that some form of dialogue with the U.S. should be established irrespective of the level." Nasser was convinced, he added, "that without the full participation and involvement of the United States, the future of the occupied territories will be uncertain and probably gone forever."

What might have appeared to be an almost instant change of heart and policy between Egypt and the U.S. was not that "instant" at all. I believe, without taking away any of the credit due Kissinger, that the Egyptians were psychologically prepared to enter into a new era with the U.S. many months — and probably three to four years — before the Yom Kippur War. The failure to establish better relations prior to the Yom Kippur War was due to: 1) American preoccupation with Vietnam; 2) relative stability in the Middle East region with Israel and Egypt both observing the truce that was arranged by Secretary of State William Rogers in 1970; 3) American confidence in Israel's ability to defend herself; and 4) no pressure from either the Soviet Union or Israel for a settlement.

In sum, the U.S. has undoubtedly tilted the scales of influence and responsibility to its own side. The Arab states, revolutionary as well as traditional, have come to the realization that total reliance on the Soviet Union will not produce the results they seek: Israeli withdrawal from the occupied territories. Where the Russians stand and how effective they might be in future negotiations between Israel and the Arabs depend largely on the degree to which the U.S. and the Soviet Union are willing to cooperate.

SOVIET-AMERICAN INTERACTION IN THE MIDDLE EAST

American and Soviet rivalry did not start in the Middle East, and it will certainly not end there. Their rivalry is based on a global contest for power and influence. The nations of the Middle East — Israel and the Arab states alike — have become, willingly or not, subject to this rivalry. As long as the U.S. and the Soviet Union can't agree on a certain accord with regard to the Middle East, their clients will remain paired against each other.

The U.S. is in a better position than the Soviet Union to influence both the Arabs and the Israelis. This condition, however, will be sustained only if Moscow decides not to disrupt what Kissinger has accomplished to date, namely, the disengagement of forces accords between Egypt and Israel in January, and then between Israel and Syria in June of 1974 followed by a new interim agreement between Israel and Egypt in September 1975.

The significance of Kissinger's successes, however, outweigh the mutual pull-back of armed forces. The U.S.'s re-entry into the Arab revolutionary camp as a mediator or a peacemaker is significant, for it not only re-established the diplomatic relationship between Egypt and the U.S., but more importantly, it brought the U.S. into Egypt with economic programs that will involve billions of dollars in the next five years. The reopening of the Suez Canal and the building of a crude oil pipeline, plus new projects geared to rebuild the destroyed cities of Port Said, Ismailia, and others, all give Egypt a stake in maintaining a cooperative, non-belligerent stance.

But one may ask, why should the Soviet Union remain silent and help the U.S. try to find a peace formula for the Arabs and Israel? Have the Russians given up hope of restoring their position in

Egypt? What about the Soviet clients, Syria and Iraq? These questions boil down to the fundamental query of whether or not the Russians have abandoned their hopes and plans to control the Middle East following the October, 1973 war. According to Communist ideology, the means of accomplishing a goal may change, but not the ultimate objective.

Henry Kissinger's views on this subject are of special significance in this regard, since the entire concept of detente that he is promoting uniquely applies to the Middle East crisis.

> Communists believe that Marxism-Leninism supplies an invaluable tool in understanding historical trends and the relation of forces existing at any particular moment. According to it, "subjective" factors, such as the personal convictions of statesmen, matter less than the "objective" factors they reflect. These objective factors include the social and economic conditions of society, the nature of the economic process and, above all, the class struggle. Communists consider that Marxism-Leninism enables them to distinguish between appearance and reality, to avoid the "subjectivism" inherent in an excessive reliance on personality and the "adventurism" that risks a historical movement on one throw of the dice. *

> "Until the final issue [between capitalism and communism] is decided," said Lenin, "the state of awful war will continue... Sentimentality is no less a crime than cowardice in war." "We... have no use for stupid scruples about benevolence, righteousness, and morality in war," wrote Mao. "In order to win victory, we must try our best to seal the eyes and ears of the enemy, making him blind and deaf." **

Kissinger believes that in the final analysis, Soviet vulnerability and strength depended largely on the ability of the United States to break away from her preconceptions and on her readiness to meet the prospects and opportunities of limited war. In connection with

---

*Henry A. Kissinger, *The Troubled Partnership* (New York: McGraw-Hill, 1965), pp. 196-197.

**Kissinger, *op. cit.*, p. 54.

penetration by the Soviet Union into the Middle East, Kissinger said, "Thus the Soviet leadership has been able to blackmail the West both in its strength and its weakness. We recoil before Soviet power, but we also fear to exploit Soviet difficulties.*

Kissinger did not find any contradiction between working for a greater unity among America's allies and seeking greater American strength, yet at the same time working for the relaxation of tension (detente) between the Soviet Union and the U.S. Even after the Soviet invasion of Czechoslovakia in 1968 and the near confrontation in the Middle East in 1973, he remained committed to his idea of creating a new "world order" that presupposed improved Soviet-American relations. However, Kissinger is cautious in his definition and application of the concept of detente. In his book, *The Troubled Partnership*, he observed:

> ... that the current period of relaxation of tension has been initiated by the Soviets not because a few individuals have overcome the opposition of some unnamed Stalinists, but because conditions require it. To the West, the challenge presented by this detente can be defined as follows: When the Communist world faces internal difficulties, should we bask in the relative calm of the Communist tone, or should we use the opportunity to press for the settlement of issues that produced the tension in the first place?
>
> Domestic considerations impel many Western leaders to present themselves to their electorate as the architects of a lasting peace. The temptation is, therefore, strong to treat a more conciliatory Communist tone as a permanent conversion to a peaceful course and to gear everything to a personal diplomacy.
>
> Such attitudes will cause the West to squander its opportunities, as has happened so often in the past. The prospects for peace are not served by leaving the Soviet leadership with the impression that any action, no matter how belligerent, can always be reversed by a change of tone. Negotiations will prove empty if they are confined to vague protestations of good will. If detente is not to be part of

---

**Ibid.*, p. 100.

another cycle leading to renewed tensions, it is essential that negotiations be concrete and programs specific. *

DETENTE** AND THE MIDDLE EAST: PROS AND CONS

There is no doubt that Kissinger himself is the most ardent defender of "detente," although he does not take it for granted that detente, as far as Russia is concerned, is an end in itself. The Russian subscription to detente may be viewed as a result of economic and social imperatives that compelled the Soviets to search for a new political approach. By the same token, these imperatives are subject to changes in intensity, which gives rise to the question that the critics of detente often ask: Would the Russians change their tone again once they have extracted all they can from detente?

There is, of course, no single easy answer offered by informed observers of detente. As far as Kissinger is concerned, detente is prerequisite to improved relations with the Soviet Union. He is not, however, advocating U.S. abdication either of its commitments or its principles for the sake of detente. He is saying, basically, that if the Soviet Union desires to work with us on global problems or on regional matters that directly or indirectly affect both our futures, then let us talk. But he is also certain that such talk or negotiations must not be made in a vacuum. The scope of negotiations should be predetermined and predefined, so that failure in negotiations does not worsen the situation, but at least maintains the status quo.

---

*Kissinger, *op. cit.*, p. 203.

**By definition, detente is a relaxation of international tension. The Russians are interested in detente because it has produced significant gains for the Soviet Union, namely, stabilization of the Soviet western front, as Soviet fears about China's intentions in the east grow greater, and the expansion of trade agreements with the U.S. Detente has also given the Russians access to Western technology to improve their industrial system. From the American point of view, detente can lead eventually to limitation of arms, and maybe to partial disarmament. It also means new markets for American businessmen, and Russian cooperation and support in solving local or regional crises (such as in the Middle East). Some American observers in political and scholarly circles are skeptical about Soviet intentions. They cite the Arab-Israeli war of October, 1973, when the Russians overtly called on other Arab nations to join in a holy war against Israel. And the arms race continues unabated. The Soviet-American competition in the Middle East will most likely continue, as the Soviet Union seeks to regain some of the ground lost to the U.S. However, despite the U.S.-Russian differences over the need for detente or in the interpretation of the term, one aspect remains valid: the growing desire by people everywhere for a policy of cooperation between the superpowers.

Fundamental to detente is the give and take of negotiations. The U.S. will not and cannot negotiate only from a position of strength. The Russians so far have hardly ever compromised their position, especially on the ideological level. But they cannot survive on ideology alone; their realization of this makes them today, more than ever before, ready to negotiate. This particular point is of crucial importance. Supporters of detente find it very hard to defend in the face of both Soviet and Chinese statements, repeated time and again, that ideologically Communists everywhere will remain committed; that everything else will be subordinated, including temporary accommodation with the West, to the goal of eventual world domination. Melvin Laird, the former Secretary of Defense, viewed detente in this fashion:

> *I am one of those who does not believe that an apparent easing of relations with the Soviet Union — some will call it detente — necessarily means there has been a fundamental change in their objectives. There is talk of detente, but the security of the U.S. is not assured by such talk — it takes deeds and ironclad guarantees as well.*
>
> *The Soviet Union is in a position where they will use those five years of arms control that were agreed to the SALT I talks to their advantage. I think they feel they've lulled Western Europe and the United States into a feeling that the Russians really aren't doing much in the national security field.*
>
> *The fact is they are progressing all the time. The Soviet weapons momentum continues.* *

Kissinger's defense against this position is based on what is termed "social and economic imperatives" — the Russians' dire need for technological aid from the U.S., in addition to her growing need for agricultural products, both of which "compel" the Russians to adopt a softer approach to the capitalist world, whether or not they change their ultimate objectives. America can defuse Russian ambitions, not only by military buildup and more sophisticated weapons, but also through the "bread basket." Soviet-American relations should be built on continuous economic and

---

**U.S. News and World Report,* September 17, 1973, p. 39.

cultural exchanges. Strengthened relations should produce an increase in mutual needs and subsequently reduce any desire for change by the use of force. One factor that Kissinger emphatically stressed is that the Soviets should under no circumstances be given the impression that our desire to cooperate emanates from weakness. Only the opposite of that can assure the continuation of detente. In his words spoken during the last Arab-Israeli war, "Detente cannot survive irresponsible acts" in any area on the part of the Soviets. Detente did indeed serve a purpose and did survive when the U.S. challenged the Soviet Union on that occasion by alerting her forces world-wide.

Experienced American and European diplomats ask whether the survival of detente will always depend on America's strong military posture and preparedness. If so, why does the U.S. need detente? The reason is that if military preparedness and expenditures must remain high at all times — regardless of the extent of tension between the U.S. and the Soviet Union — detente can only have a good effect. Several important points support this position. 1) New markets will open up for many American companies, which in the long run, will help balance U.S. exports and imports. 2) It might bring about the limitation of arms and consequently, a reduction in military expenditures. 3) It might also produce a more relaxed Europe and the end of dangerous confrontations between the superpowers. 4) Detente will induce the Soviets to work closer with the U.S. in solving regional crises, such as in the Middle East. The supporters of detente argue in this particular instance that were it not for detente, the latest Arab-Israeli crisis of 1973 might have escalated out of hand.

On the other side of the argument, the staunchest critics see only Soviet exploitation of detente. They maintain that there are several reasons behind Soviet promotion of this policy. 1) The Russians will use detente so long as they have internal economic difficulties. Once these have been conquered, they will be in better shape to resume their drive to spread Communism everywhere. 2) The intensification of Chinese pressure on the Soviet border compels the Russians to ease tensions in Europe and stabilize their Chinese front. After this has been achieved, the Russians will be able to concentrate again on their European front. (Presently there are over fifty Russian divisions with nuclear capability facing China.) 3) Some Russian leaders actually believe that the Arabs are not reliable allies, in addition to their being an economic burden. Thus a trend toward economic cooperation with the U.S., even at the expense of making some concessions in the Middle East, will be in the long-term interest of the Soviet Union. 4) Other internal problems in Russia compel her to pursue detente, e.g. the problems of Jewish emigration and dissenting Soviet voices, such as Andrei Sakharov and Alexander Solzhenitzin.

The debate may well go on for years. Despite the criticism and the skepticism about the workability of detente, and despite the fact that the euphoria over detente is beginning to fade, one thing remains valid — the need for cooperation between the two superpowers has become every nation's business. For in the long run the relationship between the Soviet Union and the United States will surely affect the fate of all countries.

Several basic reasons for the soundness of this cliché warrant restatement:

1) Food and energy shortages create a need for international cooperation. The superpowers hold the technological key, not only to the survival of civilization, but also to the *kind* of survival the world will see.

2) Whether or not the Russians change their final objective, the Soviets are not interested in either a destroyed America or Western Europe. There is too much at stake materially for them to risk world-wide conflagration. Therefore, they will continue to pursue their objectives by the threat of force rather than the use of force. Detente will work for the betterment of mankind. The prerequisite condition, however, is that the U.S. must not confuse Soviet intentions with deeds. The Soviets will most likely proceed with their calculated policy of ambiguity, without overtly provoking the U.S. into hostile action. Therefore, it behooves the U.S. to continue its negotiating posture from a position of strength and to make its intentions clear. Detente is a two-way street and it will not long withstand conspiracies and provocations that hamper the interests of either side.

3) If detente is a means and not an end by itself, it should not be difficult to test its effectiveness periodically. Any conciliatory moves that are undertaken by the U.S., such as better trade relations, credit, loans or the granting of the status of "most-favored nation"

to Russia* (MFN), should immediately be followed by reciprocating action from the Russians.

For instance, the granting of MFN status to Russia was held up in Congress for over two years due to Senator Henry Jackson's amendment that called on the Soviet Union to ease its regulations with regard to the emigration of Soviet Jews. In late August, 1974 Senator Jackson announced he had received assurance that the Soviets would indeed apply a more flexible policy regarding Jewish emigration. However, when MFN status was finally approved by the Senate, the Soviet Union repudiated the 1972 trade agreement with the United States.

Although the Soviets linked their repudiation of the 1972 trade agreement to the stipulation on Jewish immigration that was attached to the agreement, many political and economic observers believe the main reason that motivated the Soviets to cancel the accord was the limitation in the overall credits that the bill provided. This point, however, has raised an issue of special significance: whether to link trade relations to internal Soviet problems. Senator Jackson's position was based on the principle of freedom that America has sacrificed so much for.

> *It was not just a Jewish issue, but an American issue in this nation of immigrants. I would not be in this chamber today if Norway, the country of my parents' birth, had practiced the sort of emigration policy that the Soviet Union has today.* **

Conversely, Kissinger, the pragmatist, does not see fit to mix ideology and trade relations. He wrote: "Interest is not necessarily amoral; moral consequences can stem from interested acts." He went on to say: "A new American administration confronts the challenge of relating our commitments to our influence and our obligations to our purposes."***

---

*At present, the U.S. extends most-favored nation treatment — which simply means that a country's goods can be imported at the lowest tariff rates in effect — to all of its non-communist trading partners, as well as to Poland and Yugoslavia. MFN status would make Moscow's imports much more competitive; the U.S. tariff on Russian vodka, for example, would drop from $5.00 a gallon to $1.25. *Time Magazine,* March 26, 1973.

***Ibid.*

***Badeau, *op. cit.,* p. 261.

It would seem that a basic relationship between detente and human rights does exist. Kissinger has avoided the issue, but the question remains valid.

> *Andrei Sakharov, the Soviet nuclear physicist and outspoken dissident . . . chose the SALT Conference in Geneva to link the question of detente with the violation of human rights in the Soviet Union, insisting in the most public way that "true detente is impossible given the repressive conditions in Russia."**

Undoubtedly, there is a fine line between "live and let live," the relaxation of tensions that put an end to the cold war, and detente that extends beyond rational borders and reaches the heart of every citizen in the world, i.e., detente that produces a new set of agreements and arrangements that might lead to what Kissinger terms "new world order." Such an order cannot be achieved by disregarding the internal affairs of any country, not to mention those of the superpowers. Internal affairs have become global affairs. The economy of the U.S., for example, directly affects the entire free world, and even the Communist world now that it is developing a closer economic relationship with the West.

The racial minorities problem in the U.S. is affecting and will continue to affect U.S. relations with sub-Saharan Africa and with many other nations that "profess" social equality and justice. On the military level, more and more of the free world depends largely on the American military "security blanket," whereas the Communist world relies mostly on Russia and, to a lesser degree, on China. This centripetal trend of social, military, and economic international integration since World War II has removed the myth that the internal affairs of a certain power should not be considered in the conduct of diplomacy on the international level. Kissinger has consistently maintained that the internal structure of a country has immediate and direct effects on its conduct of foreign policy. Why then, should the Russians be able to separate the two? Whether the question is moral or strategic, the effectiveness of detente should only be tested on the basis of give-and-take. The U.S. cannot afford to fully trust the Russians or the Chinese, but should try to convince

---

*Newsweek, September 24, 1973.

them that if they decide to abandon detente, their loss will be greater than their gains.

THE ARAB-ISRAELI CRISIS AND DETENTE

U.S.-Soviet rivalry in the Middle East is based on the principle of protecting one's economic, strategic, and political interests. There is, however, at least one striking difference between the U.S. and the Soviet approach: while the U.S. is attempting to achieve its goals primarily by fostering economic and political stability, the Russians have generally adopted a policy of subversion and conspiracy that results in frequent upheaval and instability. The question today is not whether the Russians have abandoned their long-range global objectives, but rather to what degree they have modified their approach for the sake of preserving detente. Have the Russians acceded to the notion that they cannot pursue a policy of subversion and promote revolutionary trends against American interests and stop just short of direct confrontation with the U.S.? Probably not, nor would the U.S. give up its clandestine operations as long as it perceives them to be in its best interests!

The Soviet position with regard to the Arab-Israeli war of October, 1973, for example, was in complete contradiction to the spirit of detente. Only when U.S. forces were put on alert did the Russians come to the realization that calling for both subversion and incitement against U.S. interests in the Middle East and a policy of detente in the same breath would no longer be acceptable to the U.S. Detente, the Russians were told, cannot survive irresponsible acts. They could not expect American favors while encouraging the Arab states to maintain their oil embargo against the U.S. and Western Europe. The United States' firm position in this respect left no room for ambiguity. The basic condition of detente, U.S. officials insisted, is the avoidance and prevention of the kind of crisis that took place in the Middle East, not its encouragement and support. The Russians cannot hope to exploit both ends, as they attempted to do after the 1967 war.

Soviet cooperation in the efforts by Secretary Kissinger to achieve the 1974 disengagement accords between Israel, and Egypt and Syria was based on practical calculations. Whether their decision to pressure the Egyptians and the Syrians into accepting the agreement was a result of their desire to keep detente alive is debatable. Several facts, however, do remain indisputable.

1) President Nixon's reaction to the Russian threat to intervene with force placed the Russians in a secondary position in influence in relation to their clients, Egypt and Syria.

2) By October 12th, the Russians had given up any hope of an Arab victory, as well as any hope that the U.S. would not commit whatever was required to ensure the security of Israel.

3) President Sadat of Egypt had made it very clear by October 24th that he could not fight the U.S. and that he would welcome U.S. intervention for a peaceful solution.

4) The Egyptian Third Army was trapped on the east side of the Canal. American pressure on Israel not to force the surrender of that army saved both Egypt and Russia from the most severe humiliation. Since the Russians were apparently not ready to commit troops to the scene, they were compelled to ask the U.S. for assistance.

Faced with these problems, the Soviet Union attempted not only to save face but also to extract as many political and strategic concessions as possible from all parties involved in the crisis. Therefore, the Soviet acquiescence in the disengagement was most likely based on the following assessment of probable benefits.

1) The Egyptian-Israeli disengagement agreement allowed Egypt to re-open the Suez Canal. This factor is highly significant from the Soviet point of view. For the previous eight years, the Russians had been pushing for the re-opening of the Suez Canal, so that both their commercial ships and war ships could have access to the increasingly strategic oil-rich Gulf area and to the Indian Ocean.

2) Soviet support of the disengagement accord also was to gain U.S. favor. The hard-pressed Russian economy is in dire need of credit, better trade agreements, and all the technological aid it can get from the U.S., including capital goods and industrial facilities to produce all kinds of household equipment and consumer items.

3) The Russians are extremely interested in cooperating with the U.S. in areas other than economics, for example, troop reduction in Europe, and the continuation of the SALT negotiations. Moreover, Brezhnev himself has staked much of his personal prestige on accommodation with the West. He was committed not to allow the Middle East crisis to shatter this foundation of good will.

4) The Soviet Union's loss of prestige among the Arab states since 1967 prompted the Russians into demonstrating support for the Arab cause in order to recoup some status.

These were the considerations that prompted the Russians to demonstrate responsibility as well as sensibility in their confrontation with the U.S. in October, 1973.

China and the Middle East

China's political role in the Middle East, would seem to be limited in scope, at least in comparison with the roles of the U.S. and the Soviet Union. The Chinese view the Arab-Israeli confrontation as an integral part of the "third world" struggle for political and economic independence. Although the Chinese do not draw a clear line among the states that comprise the three world categories, the Arab states fall into the same third world as China. According to Chinese Vice-Premier Teng Hsiao-Ping, the world today consists of three parts, both interconnected and in contradiction with each other. The U.S. and the Soviet Union make up the first world; the developed countries, the second world; and the developing countries constitute the third. Since China is a socialist country and a developing one as well, China, asserted Vice-Premier Teng Hsiao, belongs to the third world. China is not a superpower, nor will she ever seek to be one.*

Although Peking clearly leaves its options open as to which countries should comprise the second or third worlds, potentially, the third world includes the vast majority of the independent states and population, which could become, as expected by the Chinese, a third force politically.

The Chinese feel that the Arab states have been exploited by both the U.S. and the Soviet Union. They believe that, in principle, the Arab states as a part of the third world oppose the political philosophy that has been pursued by the superpowers. The Chinese insist that the present cooperation between some of the Arab states, for example, and the Soviet Union, or the Israeli-American collaboration are primarily based on prevalent circumstances that will not survive future tests.

In order to further Chinese favor among the Arabs, they have consistently identified themselves with the national aspirations of the various Arab states and especially the Palestinian Arabs. When

---

*Excerpt of a statement made by the Vice-Premier of China, Teng Hsiao-Ping, taken from the official English translation published as a supplement to the Peking Review, April 12, 1974.

the Arab states imposed the oil embargo of 1973, the Chinese immediately voiced support for the Arab position. In a statement made in the UN by the Chinese delegation on April 6, 1974, the Chinese fully endorsed the use of oil as a political weapon during the Arab-Israeli war. The Chinese hailed the Arab action as a "pioneering action" and suggested that "what was done in the oil battle should and could be done in the case of other raw materials."

Beyond verbal support for the Arab cause, the Chinese have supplied the Arab extremist groups, such as the Popular Front for the Liberation of Palestine and the Arab Liberation Front, with weapons, ammunition, and training. However, no major arms deal or direct Chinese intervention in the Middle East have so far been consummated. Many political observers do not envision a major Chinese shift in the Middle East in the foreseeable future. In support of this argument these observers cite:

1) The intense rivalry between the U.S. and the Soviet Union over the fate of the Middle East leaves very little space for Chinese political maneuvering in that region at the present time.

2) The growing Chinese concern over the Soviet threat has undoubtedly contributed to the process of "normalization" of U.S.-China relations, which climaxed with President Nixon's trip to China in 1972.

3) The U.S.-Chinese "detente" further limited the Chinese political initiative in areas vital to American interests. It would, therefore, be politically expedient for the Chinese to promote tension between the U.S. and Russia without direct involvement, and thus engage the Soviets even more deeply in the West, if possible. By following such a policy, the Chinese hope that the Soviet Union will not readily be able to transfer important forces from Western Europe to the East.

In sum, the Chinese present influence over the Middle East political affairs is limited. The U.S. and the Soviet Union do not consider the Chinese a party to the Middle East crisis, or to the present indirect negotiations between some of the Arab states and Israel. It would also seem that the Chinese will not take part in any future Arab-Israeli peace conference, and therefore, their involvement will undoubtedly remain limited to the support of extremist Fedayeen groups.

With this background, some tentative projections and conclusions can be drawn:

1) There is an overriding interest on the part of the U.S. and the Soviet Union to have a settlement between the Arab states and Israel reached. Any renewed hostilities will most likely draw the two superpowers to assume the positions they assumed in the last confrontation of October, 1973. Neither can expect to improve its position if hostilities erupt again. The Soviet Union may further damage its own deteriorating influence among the Arab states, while the U.S. may lose the prestige she gained in the eyes of the Arabs.

2) The Egyptian government continues to face severe economic conditions. The multi-billion dollar program to re-open the Suez Canal, to rebuild the ruined cities around the Nile Delta, and to construct the Suez-Mediterranean oil pipeline — all these and many more vitally important projects undoubtedly make renewed hostilities with Israel increasingly unattractive. In addition, it was through U.S. meditation and "pressure" that the first and second withdrawals of Israeli forces from the east side of the Canal resulted. It does not seem likely that President Sadat would want to venture another war which might not see the same kind of American leaverage over Israel.

3) Israel, too, has come to the bitter conclusion that the only ally she can depend on for economic and military aid is the United States. The Yom Kippur confrontation clearly drew the line between Israel's friends and adversaries. Israel has already been subjected to pressures from Washington, although both sides know what Israel's limitations might be in terms of territorial concessions. Still, Israel today is more apt to listen to any reasonable suggestions regarding territorial boundaries, provided her national security is not jeopardized. Although the general consensus inside and outside Israel is that a renewed war would probably result in another military defeat of the Arab armies, the economic cost to Israel of such a war would be so formidable as to constitute a pyrrhic victory.

4) Western Europe and Japan will remain dependent on the flow of oil from the Middle East for at least a decade or so. Anything that endangers the continuation of that flow would likely provoke intervention by the U.S., the chief protector of Western Europe and Japan. The U.S. has never ruled out a takeover by force of the Arab oil-producing countries in order to insure the survival of her

allies.* An oil-consuming nations' agreement on sharing seems a logical next step, however, rather than an invasion. The Arab states today, apparently, are convinced that the Soviets will not risk a war with the U.S. to protect Arab interests. All but a limited oil embargo seems very unlikely.

5) The Arab oil-producing countries will accumulate an enormous amount of money, probably 250-300 billion dollars by 1980. The only viable market where these vast sums can be invested and absorbed with some degree of security is in Western Europe and the U.S. The Arab oil-producing countries will have to act extremely foolishly to allow their emotions to take over sound economic reasoning. This, too, makes the prospect of renewed hostilities unlikely.

6) While Soviet *long-range* policy may not be in accord with present detente, the general trend in the Soviet Union's international relations is toward reconciliation with the West, particularly the U.S. This policy did not begin with Brezhnev, for there is a growing vocal need among Russian consumers for a higher standard of living. These are perhaps the most compelling factors that open the new era of detente. The desire for economic prosperity is the key. Whether their final objectives (Lenin's Doctrine of a Socialist world) have changed or not is immaterial at this juncture. Full U.S.-Soviet cooperation in the social-economic sphere may, in the long run, have far more power than a thousand atomic bombs. If detente continues for the next ten to fifteen years, it might become an irreversible trend. The U.S. will certainly not turn the Soviet Union into a capitalist country, nor will the reverse happen, but one thing is certain — the ideological gap between the two systems is narrowing. More and more social reforms are taking place in the U.S. and other parts of the free world, while the Russians are upgrading their standard of living and classes of different economic bases are developing. The economic and the social imperatives that today exist in Russia favor the United States. Therefore, these new conditions should be used to generate maximum help and

---

*Secretary of State Kissinger said in a *Business Week* magazine interview published the first week of January, 1975 that he did not rule out the use of military action if Middle East oil policies were strangling the industrial nations. However, he insisted that "the use of force would be considered only in the gravest emergency." Kissinger also said that it would be unwise for the U.S. to try trading Israeli concessions to the Arabs for a reduction of oil prices because that would create the basis for pressures in the opposite direction. Later in the same month, President Ford stated that Kissinger had reflected the administration's views on the subject.

cooperation wherever the Soviet Union can provide them. The Middle East is one such case.

7) The rivalry between the USSR and the People's Republic of China is another opportunity that should not be neglected by the United States. Washington's position vis-a-vis the two Communist giants can prove to be most useful in solving regional crises. The Chinese are not presently interested in provoking the Americans in any fashion. In fact, they welcome the U.S. presence in Southeast Asia, and they are against the reduction of American troops in Europe.

8) The influence of the Soviet Union on the Arab extremist revolutionary regimes — Syria, Iraq, Algeria, and Yemen — is large. Yet most of these states, individually or united, cannot have a detrimental effect on peace in the Middle East, due mainly to the geographical distances between them and Israel. Even Syria, considered the country most antagonistic toward Israel, might eventually accede to an overall agreement with Israel provided the Soviet Union uses its leverage there, and provided the U.S. and the Soviet Union "neutralize" Egypt's interest. Therefore, the closer the relationship between the U.S. and Egypt becomes, the harder it will be for Syria to initiate any major move on her own. Current U.S. cooperation with Egypt, if it continues, will most likely soften the Syrian position, especially if it is in the Russians' immediate interests to dictate that Syria do so, also.

9) The U.S. can and should initiate the next move toward the Arab states, toward Israel, and the Soviet Union for,

> *the advantage of initiative is that each move opens the possibility of several further steps. If carried far enough, it will force the opponent to protect itself against an ever-growing number of contingencies and, therefore, to concentrate on purely defensive measures.*
>
> *This does not mean preventive war. Considerations of principle would prohibit such a course, apart from the enormous destructiveness of modern weapons. However, we should be as ready to profit from opportunities in the Soviet orbit as the Soviet bloc feels free to exploit all the difficulties of the non-Soviet world. In foreign policy, courage and success stand in a causal relationship.* *

*Kissinger, *op. cit.*, p. 246.

And finally, those who advocate a settlement imposed by the superpowers either on Israel or on the Arab states or on both, ignore the natural social, economic, and psychological factors involved in the Arab-Israeli crisis. There will always be a limit as to how far the U.S. and the Soviet Union can pressure their clients for concessions. For no nation, for the sake of harmony and international comity, will bargain away conditions which it considers essential to its survival.

Chapter VII

ISRAEL'S NATIONAL SECURITY SECURE BORDERS AND ANNEXATION

Israel's sensitivity regarding national survival has always been at the heart of her long-standing confrontation with the Arab states. For Israel, peace does not necessarily guarantee her survival. Only a combination of 1) a formal peace with the surrounding Arab states of Egypt, Jordan, Syria and Lebanon; 2) a strong military posture to deter future Arab attacks; and 3) secure borders or, as they have been termed by Israel, "defensive borders," will afford her the highest degree of safety for the maintenance of her political integrity and hence her survival.

There are essentially three conflicting views regarding the validity of Israel's contention that secure borders are directly related to her national security. 1) The Arabs, by virtue of their resolve to get back the territories they lost in the 1967 war, argue that if real peace is to be achieved, the question of secure boundaries from the point of view of military strategy becomes irrelevant. 2) The Russians also discredit Israel's stand on the basis that in a nuclear age with long-range missiles, secure borders in the traditional sense hold no real meaning. They contend that Israel is only attempting a cover for her expansionist policy. And 3) such U.S. policy-makers as William Fulbright and Henry Kissinger have suggested that a permanent defense alliance between the U.S. and Israel might substitute for Israel's demand for secured borders.

A thorough examination of Israel's stand is warranted, particularly in view of the fact that the problem of secure borders may ultimately determine whether another round of hostilities between Israel and the Arab states will take place and if so, how soon.

The Arab states' contradictory statements: The Arab position on peace with Israel is at this point neither consistent nor completely clear. One cannot speak of the Arab nations as if they had one voice, even in their protestations against Israel; however, two trends of thought appear to be prevalent.

The more moderate states, such as Jordan and Lebanon, maintain that once peace is achieved, there will be no need for secure broders. The word "peace" (*salaam*) in this context by the Arab leadership means "co-existence," rather than the peace indicated by the word *"sulh"* which connotes a peace of reconciliation. When the moderate Arab spokesmen speak of peace, they refer to the UN Resolution 242.* This resolution, according to their interpretation, calls for *total and complete withdrawal of all Israeli forces from the occupied territories taken in the Six-Day War*, whereas Israel maintains that the resolution calls for *secure and recognized boundaries, without unilateral Israeli withdrawal to the 1967 borders.*

Extremist Arab countries such as Libya, Algeria, Syria, and some of the guerrilla resistance movements, have disavowed any intention of reaching any kind of peace with Israel; the solution to the Arab crisis, they believe, hinges primarily on Israel's total destruction. "We might change the means of our dealing with Israel—that might be taken or interpreted as being reconciliatory —" President Hafez Assad of Syria observed in November 1973. "However, the ultimate goal reamins unchanged, namely: Israel's elimination." This vociferation by the extremist Arab leadership certainly does not help assuage the deepest fears of the Israelis.

Since Israel has agreed to the disengagement accords with Egypt and Syria (early 1974) and committed herself to possible further

---

*The Security Council resolution on the Middle East, November 22, 1967. The Security Council...

1. affirms that the fulfillment of Charter principles requires the establishment of a just and lasting peace in the Middle East which should include the application of both the following principles:

(i) withdrawal of Israeli armed forces from territories of recent conflict.

(ii) termination of all claims or states of belligerency and respect for and acknowledgement of the sovereignty, territorial integrity and political independence of every state in the area and their right to live in peace within secure and recognized boundaries free from threats or acts of force.

2. affirms further the necessity

a) for guaranteeing freedom of navigation through international waterways in the area;

b) for achieving a just settlement of the refugee problem;

c) for guaranteeing the territorial inviolability and political independence of every state in the area, through measures including the establishment of demilitarized zones...

withdrawal in the future,* Israel cannot help viewing this ambivalent Arab attitude with strong reservations. While some of the Arab countries have stated their willingness to negotiate a peace settlement, there remains the question of the durability of such a negotiated settlement as long as other Arab countries have pledged themselves to no negotiations and no peace. Witness, for example, the statement made by President Sadat of Egypt on July 23, 1974 before the central committee of the Arab Socialist Union in Cairo on the 22nd anniversary of the Egyptian revolution. "The good cards in our hands are continuously increasing, not becoming fewer. I shall not speak with two tongues, only with one. I shall speak frankly. The world will not let us totally defeat Israel and we will not fight against the world. But we do not pretend to represent the generations to come. We shall only pass the flag on to coming generations for them to fulfill their task."**

On February 9, 1973 Colonel al-Qadhafi of Libya said in answer to a question by foreign reporters on how he envisaged the next battle with Israel: "This is a confrontation as a result of which Israel will be destroyed or the Arabs will be defeated but no regrets [if the Arabs are defeated] because it is possible that Israel will be annihilated at a certain stage."***

Arab domestic instability: Even if the Arabs were to relinquish their desire to bring an end to the state of Israel, and even if they remained committed to the present stage of negotiations, Israel argues there would still be no guarantee that the peace would survive. The political instability of most of the Arab regimes puts the prospect of lasting peace in a very precarious position.

Who is to guarantee that if the regimes of President Sadat of Egypt, King Hussein of Jordan, or for that matter, President Hafez Assad of Syria were to be overthrown, their successors would adhere to any peace formula agreed to by their predecessors? Most of the

---

*On June 2nd 1975 Premier Rabin announced a unilateral Israeli thinning of forces. And in August, 1975 a new interim agreement between Israel and Egypt was concluded that resulted in an additional Israeli withdrawal including the relinquishing of the Gidi and Mitla passes as well as the Abu Rudeis oil field.

***Brief Middle East High Light*, July 16-31, 1974 bi-weekly, Tel-Aviv, p. 2.

***Press conference given to foreign reporters on February 9, 1973.

Arab regimes who would deny Israel's existence are revolutionary and have not as yet gained enough political stability and popular support to be accepted by their own people without any new challenges. Had the Arab countries enjoyed a traditional legitimized political system supported by popular vote, and had they worked cohesively with the international community, Israel would not be so concerned with the durability of any negotiated peace.

The political instability of the Arab extremist states and the threatening pronouncements of their leaders have forced Israel to insist on what she terms "secured boundaries." Such boundaries, it is felt, will give Israel the independence, the security, and the time that she may need in a moment of sudden renewed hostilities.

Israel's experience in the Yom Kippur War reinforced her belief that ultimate security depends on a wide buffer zone. In that war, the zone of formerly conquered territories allowed Israel time to mobilize her forces and move from a defensive to an offensive position in a matter of three days. The initial loss of territory was for all practical purposes nothing more than a temporary strategic retreat.

The psychological effect of the wide buffer zone that prevailed prior to the Yom Kippur War seemed to have influenced Israel's military thinking. The decision not to undertake a pre-emptive strike at that time was partly based on the belief that a wide buffer zone had created a "psychological margin of safety." Without it, Israel's sense of insecurity might have prompted another pre-emptive strike by Israel, such as in the Six-Day War.

Missiles and Nuclear Weapons

To the argument that the missile age has made defensive borders obsolete, Israel responds that while a missile attack may inflict severe damage on an enemy, still, foot soldiers or tanks would have to move in to occupy the conquered land. Secure boundaries, thus, can still play a major role in preventing an enemy advance even though industrial and urban centers may have been demolished.

More importantly, small powers such as Israel, Egypt, and Syria that have access to relatively long-range surface-to-surface missiles tend to allocate to this kind of weapon the job of deterrent only.

The experience of the Yom Kippur war indicated that there probably was some kind of unofficial agreement between the leaders of Egypt and Israel not to deploy any long-range missiles. Only when

Sadat was on the verge of total defeat did he voice threats of using his long-range missiles against Tel Aviv. Golde Meir's answer at the time — that the distance from Cairo to Tel Aviv is the same as that from Tel Aviv to Cairo — forced Sadat to re-assess his threats and to appeal to Russia to interfere in order to stop Israel's advance. The mutual vulnerability that long-range surface-to-surface missiles have created makes them almost obsolete as offensive devices.

The possession of a nuclear arsenal by one side would no doubt change the balance of power in the region. Israel knows that three small nuclear bombs, equivalent to a few thousand tons of TNT (twice as big as the one dropped on Hiroshima), dropped on its three major centers — Tel Aviv, Haifa, and Jerusalem — could destroy its society. The Arabs also understand that any nuclear retaliation would be a devastating one that might include far greater numbers of cities with an incalculable toll in lives.

If both sides face these possibilities, the thought of nuclear confrontation becomes inconceivable. With this in mind, several possibilities may develop. First, the possession of nuclear weapons by the Arabs and Israel would, of course, constitute mutual invulnerability; both sides would presumably take all necessary measures to avoid any nuclear confrontation.

Second, the possession of nuclear arms by Israel alone would most likely not tempt her to strike any Arab state pre-emptively for any type of gain. She would fear not only a total isolation by the international community, but also the possibility of a massive counter-strike, nuclear or conventional, by a larger power with special ambitions in the Arab world. Israel would, therefore, risk nuclear retaliation *only* if her very survival were at stake. Third, the possession of nuclear arms by the Arabs alone might drastically shift the equilibrium of power in the Middle East. However, the only conceivable nuclear strike on Israel is one that might be initiated by an extreme Arab leader, a fanatic nationalist, who would miscalculate the catastrophic outcome to both parties.*

---

*The buildng of a nuclear reactor in Egypt by the U.S. or any other Western power, cannot or should not pose any danger to Israel's security. Such reactors, if well supervised, make the building of nuclear weapons a very remote possibility. Israel has been operating similar reactors for more than a decade. Furthermore, the proliferation of atomic reactors in the hands of smaller nations is an inevitable process due to the ever-growing need for more and better sources of energy. It would be preferable that the U.S. take the lead in the Middle East, rather than compel the Arabs to seek atomic assistance elsewhere.

In addition, it is most unlikely that the Arab states as one entity (or several unified Arab states) would strike Israel with nuclear weapons for the purpose of total destruction. The fallout of radiation generated from a massive nuclear strike would certainly inflict severe damage on the neghboring states as well, not to mention the fact that after such an attack, there would be no "Palestine" to go back to. As one famous expert on nuclear energy has written:

> *There has been, in recent years, the development of small nuclear weapons having yields equivalent to a few thousand tons of TNT or less. The day will come, if it has not already, when there will be nuclear weapons of smaller yield than the largest high explosive weapons. When that day comes, will there be no longer a distinction between nuclear and conventional weapons? Some have argued to that effect. But they are mistaken. There is and will remain an important distinction, a "firebreak", if you like, between nuclear and non-nuclear war, a recognizable qualitative distinction that both combatants can recognize and agree upon, if they want to agree upon one. And in the nuclear age, they will have a very powerful incentive to agree upon this distinction and limitation, because if they do not, there does not appear to be another easily recognizable limitation on weapons — no other obvious "firebreak" — all the way up the destructive spectrum to large-scale thermo-nuclear war.* *

Nevertheless, Israel feels that she must take all necessary precautions to meet such a contingency, including nuclear defensive installations as well as a nuclear strike capability. This does not mean that Israel today must commence the buildup of nuclear arms — assuming she has the know-how and the resources. Rather, Israel would follow very closely her adversaries' intentions. Once it became obvious to Israel that an Arab country possessed nuclear arms, Israel would most likely announce her own intentions, the extent of her possession of nuclear arms and her striking capability, so as to lessen the chance that a miscalculation by either side could take place. The possession of a nuclear arsenal by Israel or the Arabs or

---

*Henry A. Kissinger, *The Troubled Partnership* (New York: McGraw-Hill, 1965), pp. 102-103.

by both is only a contingency that might become a reality some time in the future. However, the existence of such a contingency makes it necessary for both sides to be constantly on the look-out for new developments.

Israel today, however, is more concerned with secure borders in relation to conventional weapons. She cannot jeopardize her security today on the assumption that secure borders would prove inadequate in the case of nuclear attack in the future.

U.S. Defense Treaty with Israel: How Viable?

The United States' growing understanding of Israel's sensitivity toward the issue of secure borders, especially after Kissinger's deep involvement in arranging the disengagement accords in January and June of 1974, and in September of 1975, prompted some U.S. officials to send out feelers regarding the possibility of a mutual defense treaty between the U.S. and Israel. Israel, however, does not consider a defense treaty with the U.S. an adequate substitute for defensive borders or a shield against a sudden attack by the Arabs — who might be supported directly by Russian forces.

Israel at this particular juncture does not doubt America's sincere intentions to preserve her sovereignty. She is more concerned about the possibility of a sudden devastating blow by the Arabs, inflicted when she did not have the flexibility to react as she saw fit. The U.S. will always respond to a regional crisis in a manner befitting a world power, but such intervention might not always serve Israel's immediate interests.*

The involvement of the U.S. in Vietnam is still fresh in the minds of the Israelis. America's experience there illustrates the inability of the U.S. military to solve those particular regional crises which do not allow for the total defeat of the enemy. In an effort to avoid direct confrontation with either the USSR or China, the Israelis observe, the U.S. made de-escalation of the war an objective in itself, and the so-called "Vietnamization" of the war became a face-saving cover under which U.S. troops were withdrawn.

---

*Turkey's invasion of Cyprus and her refusal to withdraw her forces is a case in point that prompted the U.S. Congress to take a "disciplinary action" against Turkey by imposing an embargo on all military shipments to Turkey. It should be noted that both the U.S. and Turkey are members of Nato (North Atlantic Treaty Organization).

U.S. withdrawal from Vietnam has, therefore, clearly demonstrated that, although America may be willing to sacrifice money and manpower, she cannot win a war if she is unwilling to bring about a total defeat of the enemy. Moreover, fighting in Vietnam continued for three years after Kissinger negotiated a "peace treaty" there. Consequently both Vietnam and Cambodia fell to the Communists followed by a communist political take over in Laos as well.

Finally, the U.S. experience in Vietnam raised overwhelming domestic opposition, a factor that the U.S. government cannot afford to overlook in future overseas commitments.

Israel, therefore, would prefer to maintain her military posture with the support of the U.S. but with secure boundaries, and in this way assume the task of protecting her own interests as well as those of the U.S. indirectly. A United States defense treaty with Israel would definitely increase the uneasiness among the Arab states, who might retaliate against American interests, particularly in the Arab oil-producing countries. Renewed Arab antagonism toward the U.S. would lessen U.S. influence even over the moderate Arab states, and over Egypt especially where the U.S. today carries substantial weight. All this would subsequently open new or renewed opportunities for the Soviets to increase their spheres of influence.

The continuation of the present relationship between the U.S. and Israel is far more effective than either of the two other frequently mentioned alternatives: a defense treaty between the U.S. and Israel, which would no doubt inhibit Israel's response to threatening conditions; or, the permanent stationing of Soviet and American troops* (a notion supported by Russia) between the Arabs and Israel, which would not only inhibit the U.S. from taking unilateral action in an emergency, but would also give the Russians legitimized permanence as "peace-keepers" for an indefinite period of time.

It should be the U.S. and Israeli goal, leaders in Israel argue, to retain maximum flexibility and utmost preparedness to meet any contingency even after a peace agreement between Israel and the Arabs has been reached. The Russian long-range policy in the Middle East is still ambiguous. This ambiguity allows them the flexibility *they* need in case of a change in their priorities or at-

---

*This is notwithstanding the presence of a limited number of U.S. civilians in the Sinai for the purpose of providing both Israel and Egypt with advance warning **against any attack.**

titudes. Undefended borders are nothing less than an open invitation to renewed hostilities particularly if the Russians can derive new advantages in the future. Again, Kissinger writes:

> *The challenge of our leadership is all the greater if we consider the inevitable spread of nuclear technology. Within a generation, and probably in less time than that, most countries will possess installations for the peaceful uses of nuclear weapons. And even if this should not prove to be the case, the Soviets may find it advantageous to increase international tensions by making nuclear weapons available to other powers, on the model of their arms sale to Egypt and Syria. But nuclear weapons in the hands of weak, irresponsible, or merely ignorant governments present grave dangers. Unless the United States had demonstrated a military capability that is meaningful for the newly-independent states, many parts of the world will play the role of the Balkans in European politics; the fuse which will set off a holocaust. The United States, therefore, requires a twentieth-century equivalent of "showing the flag," an ability and a readiness to make our power felt quickly and decisively, not only to deter Soviet aggression, but also to impress the uncommitted with our capacity for decisive action.* *

In sum, the question of secure borders, from the Israeli point of view, is the crux of the Arab-Israeli dispute. Israel does not seem likely to give up her demands notwithstanding the stated good will or the guarantees of either the superpowers or the Arab states. Israel's position has deep-rooted psychological and political origins. No Israeli government can last if found neglecting the sensitive aspects of defensible frontiers.

SECURE BORDERS AND ANNEXATION

There are four areas of territorial dispute directly related to Israel's understanding of "secure and recognized boundaries": old Jerusalem, the Golan Heights, the Gaza Strip, and Sharm el-Sheik.

---

*Henry A. Kissinger, *Nuclear Weapons and Foreign Policy* (New York: W.W. Norton & Co., Inc., 1969) p. 220-221.

Apart from old Jerusalem, which has special historical and religious meaning to the Israelis, the rest of the occupied territories were left subject to further negotiation with the Arab states. The territories mentioned above, bordering Israel's pre-1967 lines, are considered by the Israelis as vital in terms of either security or economy or both.

Jerusalem: The annexation of the old city immediately after its occupation in 1967 war was considered by the vast majority of Israelis as a matter of course. The annexation of Jerusalem, the Israeli government insisted, is not and will never be negotiable. Although some Israelis, mostly leftists, advocate a certain accommodation with Jordan, or possibly with a new Arab state of Palestine that might be formed later, such proposals speak only of allowing the Arabs and the Christians to have a direct control and supervision of their holy shrines, not of returning old Jerusalem to the partitioned situation that prevailed prior to the 1967 war.

Jerusalem is unique in terms of Israel's national, psychological, and political needs. "If I forget thee, O Jerusalem, may my right arm forget its cunning." This cry from the Psalmist has for 2,500 years inspired the Jews to go back to Jerusalem and to rebuild it. Only Jerusalem could be conceived as the capital of modern Israel. The unification of the old city with the new has fulfilled the dream of generations, a dream that was a constant source of renewed vitality and hope for every Jew. Furthermore, the entire existence of Israel was primarily based on historical "rights," on cultural heritage and on a relationship between the people and the land. Jerusalem has always been the focal point of that claimed historical right. Its renunciation would be nothing less than a denial by the Israelis of their cultural heritage and of one of the basic imperatives of the entire Jewish faith. Israel thus made it clear from the beginning that the annexation of Jerusalem was a historical fulfillment, and as such was not negotiable.

Moreover, the Israelis cite their plight during the eighteen years of Jordanian control of the old part of Jerusalem, when they were not permitted to visit the relics of their holy shrines. Now, Israel maintains, the holy places for the Jews, the Arabs, and the Christians are open to all and have been from the very first day of the Israeli occupation. The Israelis left the management and actual administrative functions of the Moslem shrines to the Moslems, the Christian shrines to the Christians. Israel insists that the present conditions will have to continue, no matter what the cost or suffering that Israel may have to bear in the future. Israel refuses categorically proposals for the "internationalization" of Jerusalem* as did the Jordanians before them.

One other important step taken in connection with the annexation of Jerusalem was that Israel granted citizenship to the Arabs who resided in Jerusalem as of June 1967. There are approximately 75,000 Arabs who had the option to become Israelis (many of them did), and thus Israel felt that she had fulfilled her moral obligation. There were, however, a few Arab subversive factions determined to foil Israel's attempt to create an integrated social and economic life that would allow the united city to function normally.

There is no doubt that many Arabs wish to see Jerusalem separated again and be given back to their jurisdiction. Yet it seems that the Jordanian authorities, including King Hussein, have come to the realization that the city will not be divided again, either through the free will of the Israelis or through peaceful negotiations. Since King Hussein himself and other Arab leaders, including President Sadat of Egypt, have apparently ruled out the possibility of ousting the Israelis from the old part of Jerusalem by force, the general consensus now is that a certain formula should be achieved, so that the Arabs will have autonomous rule over their shrines. Israel in principle does not object to such a possibility, provided that the

---

*United Nations General Assembly resolution on the internationalization of Jerusalem. Resolution 181 (II) of November 29, 1974, and 194 (III) of December 11, 1948 ...

(1) The City of Jerusalem shall be established as a *corpus separatum* under a special international regime and shall be administered by the United Nations; (2) The Trusteeship Council shall be designated to discharge the responsibilities of the Administering Authority...; and (3) The City of Jerusalem shall include the present municipality of Jerusalem plus the surrounding villages and towns, the most eastern of which shall be Abu Dis; the most southern, Bethlehem; the most western, Ein Karim (including also the built-up area of Motsa); and the most northern, Shu'fat ...

2. To request for this purpose that the Trusteeship Council at its next session, whether special or regular, complete the preparation of the Statute of Jerusalem, omitting the new inapplicable provisions, such as articles 32 and 39, and, without prejudice to the fundamental principles of the international regime for Jerusalem set forth in General Assembly resolution 181 (II) introducing therein amendments in the direction of its greater democratization, approve the Statute, and proceed immediately with its implementation. The Trusteeship Council shall not allow any actions taken by any interested Government or Governments to divert it from adopting and implementing the Statute of Jerusalem.

II. Calls upon the States concerned, to make formal undertakings, at an early date and in the light of their obligations as Members of the United Nations, that they will approach these matters with good will, and be guided by the terms of the present resolution.

unity of the city under her control will not be affected. Thus we may sum up our discussion in reference to Jerusalem as follows: No internationalization of the city but Arab-Israeli coordination in controlling the holy places will be accepted so that Moslems will be given complete freedom to handle their shrines the way they see fit with no Israeli intervention. The international community seems to be ready to agree to the Israeli position, although by and large it is not officially recognized.

The Golan Heights: Perhaps the most intense negotiations will surround the future sovereignty of the Golan Heights. The paramount difficulties in reaching the Syrian-Israeli disengagement accord in mid-1974 were only a prelude to what the future holds in store for both sides. The Syrians on the one hand are adamant that no peace negotiations with Israel can be meaningful unless and until Israel withdraws from *all* the Golan Heights. For the Syrians it is a matter of national pride and prestige, in addition to the fact that the loss of the Golan to the Israelis in 1967 forced some 20,000 Syrians to flee, which further complicated a settlement. The Israelis, on the other hand, insist that control over the Heights is necessary for Israel's security. Israel argues that for eighteen years, between 1948 and 1967, the Syrians had used the Heights' geographical proximity and topology to continuously bombard Israeli settlements. The Israelis maintain that unless a wide buffer zone separates the Syrian and Israeli forces, the conditions of pre-1967 will soon prevail again, and the endless harassment and killing of innocent people will begin again.

In addition, Israel believes that with the Golan Heights under her control, she will be able to reduce the terrorist infiltration from Syria proper. The establishment of some twenty Israeli settlements in the Golan Heights was not only a symbol of Israel's intentions to retain most of the area, but also concrete evidence of the role the area plays in the whole scope of national security. Israel does not consider Syria a reliable party, even after a peace agreement is achieved. Syria is known to the Israelis for its belligerency and determination to find a "permanent solution" to Israel, by dismantling it as a political entity. Israel is skeptical about the Syrians' intentions. Although President Hafez Assad may show a degree of flexibility in his dealings with Israel, most of the Syrian leadership is far more extremist than Assad himself. Yet if the Syrian-Israeli dialogue continues, there is a way by which both sides may find a satisfactory answer to their dilemma. If Israel were to retain a narrow stretch of the Heights, while leaving a buffer zone between the two nations, possibly occupied by UN forces with Israeli and Syrian contingency units as well, the whole problem of the Heights would become a question of technicality rather than a matter of principle or survival.

The Syrians might agree in principle to the inevitability of some limited Israeli presence on the Golan especially on the slopes overlooking the Israeli settlements. On the other hand, Israel understands that retaining the whole or most of the area would simply be unacceptable to the Syrians. The experience of Kissinger with both the Syrians and the Israelis over the Golan Heights indicates that both sides have agreed in principle to find a formula. Israel's relinquishing of the city of Kuneitra and the strategic Mount Hermon, in addition to her general withdrawal along a narrow stretch of two or three miles behind the 1967 lines, indicate its readiness to compromise even in the Golan Heights, which, according to most political, and especially Israeli military observers, is the most crucial sector endangering Israel's security. Until a final agreement is reached, the likelihood of renewed hostilities over the Golan Heights is a strong one. But apart from attracting world attention to the crisis, any renewed fighting would result in only slight change. Israel may advance once again toward Damascus in the event of another war, but in the last analysis, the final lines will be drawn as indicated earlier. President Assad has so far demonstrated a greater willingness to compromise than his predecessors. If he succeeds in holding his position, the threat of renewed hostilities might remain only a threat, and eventually the development of events will propel the parties toward settling the Syrian-Israeli territorial dispute by negotiations.

The Gaza Strip: The Gaza Strip was part of Palestine, allocated by the UN for a Palestinian state. In 1948, the Gaza Strip was occupied by Egyptian forces and remained under their control until 1967. The Egyptian government never annexed the territory nor incorporated it into their social and economic system. In spite of its strategic importance to the Egyptians, the Gaza Strip was an economic and political burden on Egypt, which makes its reacquisition by the Egyptians unattractive.

Israeli insistence on not returning the Strip to Egypt is based on several considerations: 1) During the Egyptian occupation, the

Gaza Strip was used as a jumping off point for raids against Israel. Short of Israeli control, the entire stretch will once again constitute a threat. 2) The Egyptians have openly stated time and again since the October, 1973 war that they do not speak for the Palestinians, and that their main dispute with Israel is over the occupation of their own territory, namely, the Sinai. Since the Palestinians constitute the overwhelming majority of the Gaza Strip's population, it stands to reason that they should decide the fate of that land. 3) Israel has integrated the Strip into her social and economic systems. This relationship has been beneficial to the Palestinians there as well as for the prospect of Israeli-Arab cooperation in the future. 4) The economy of the Gaza Strip, whether or not it is incorporated with the West Bank, will remain extremely weak without help from the Israelis. Since economic prosperity, Israel argues, is essential in curtailing Arab hostilities and antagonism against her, it would seem that continuous Israeli social and economic relations with the Arabs in the Gaza Strip will always remain a crucial consideration. 5) If reinstatement of Egyptian control is ruled out on the basis of security as well as economic considerations, the only two options left are either to incorporate the Strip with the West Bank and declare both sections a new Palestinian state, or for Israel to annex the Gaza Strip, giving the indigenous Arabs the option to remain and become full-fledged Israeli citizens or to leave for the West Bank, with full compensation and guaranteed rehabilitation.

It seems, however, that Israel is leaving her options open at this juncture. Whether or not Israel annexes the Gaza Strip, which might be preferable to both the Arabs and the Israelis, the territory should under no circumstances become once again the enclave of various factions hostile to Israel, nor should it be given to a Jordanian regime that does not enjoy either the support of the Palestinians or a political system guaranteeing legitimate succession without political upheaval. Thus we find that the only sound solution to the Gaza problem is either annexation by Israel, or its incorporation with the West Bank into a united Palestinian entity. In either case, Israel will be able to secure her boundaries by taking upon herself the protection of the newly-autonomous Palestinian entity, or by stationing a residual military force there for a period of time, say 10 to 15 years. Such a transitional period would stabilize the Arab Palestinians' and the Israelis' relationship, and put any peace treaty to a practical test.

No matter what course is taken by the Israelis, the Gaza Strip will undoubtedly constitute an agonizing problem in any future peace negotiations. If Israel annexes the area, it will have to absorb over 300,000 Arab Palestinians into the Israeli social structure. What most Israelis are concerned with is how would additional numbers of Arabs of that magnitude affect the Israeli social composition? The Gaza Strip then poses a moral and social problem that must be weighed against the demands of national security. Would Israel's security needs be served better by having some 700,000 Arab Palestinians as Israeli citizens, or by incorporating the Strip with the West Bank under Palestinian or Jordanian jurisdiction? One thing is certain, however; Israel will not allow the Egyptians to resume control of the Gaza Strip. Nor can the present status quo be maintained indefinitely. Nor will Israel hand it over to Jordan. A viable solution will have to be found by excluding these three presently unworkable possibilities. A solution must be acceptable to both the *Arab Palestinians* and *Israel*.

Sharm el Sheik: Unlike the Gaza Strip, Israel has no hesitation regarding the fate of Sharm el Sheik. Israel in this respect will not abdicate her control over the Straits of Tiran without receiving absolute guarantees that her right to the use of international waterways is observed. Israel does not view the joint U.S.-Soviet guarantee or the UN and the Egyptian guarantees as workable enough to safeguard her rights. In the Israeli mind, the only absolute guarantee is when the Straits are under Israeli control. However, that does not necessarily mean Israeli sovereignty over the Straits of Tiran. President Sadat of Egypt seems to have indicated that he might not reject Israel's demand on this issue, if and when Israel withdraws from all of the Sinai Peninsula. During 1974 there was some talk about an Israeli option to "rent" Sharm el Sheik for a period of 100 years, or possibly granting Israel a narrow stretch of land from Elath in the south to the Straits of Tiran along the Red Sea. It is possible that once Israel finds a Sinai formula acceptable in principle to Egypt, the presence of Israeli forces in Sharm el Sheik will be accepted by Egypt. However, Israel will have to allow Egypt to declare its sovereignty over the entire Sinai area, or Sadat may not be able to concede Israeli rights in Sharm el Sheik.

The bulk of the territory Israel has occupied since 1967 is divided into two regions — the West Bank and the Sinai Peninsula (see map). An Israeli military withdrawal from these areas will not be as controversial as will be the attempts to negotiate an Israeli withdrawal from the four other areas, all of which are crucial to an understanding of what Israel considers to be at the heart of the problem of security.

The Sinai Peninsula: The withdrawal of the Israelis from most of the Sinai might turn out to be relatively easier than their withdrawal from the other occupied territories. In fact, Israel has announced time and again her readiness to withdraw from most of the Sinai provided that the withdrawal is only a part of an overall peace treaty. Israel's main concern with the Sinai is that this vast desert remain *demilitarized* and that UN forces be stationed between the countries. Such a UN contingency force should not be withdrawn without the explicit consent of either the Security Council, or the mutual consent of Israel, the U.S. and the USSR, or to say the least, the consent of the Arab states in question and Israel.

This provision is extremely important, for leaving the presence of the UN forces to the discretion of only the host countries will actually be meaningless. Israel cites that the incident precipitating the Six-Day War might have been avoided had the UN forces remained in the Sinai and not been withdrawn merely on Egypt's insistence. Egypt and Israel may find that their territorial differences are not so controversial, once Israel can secure her right to free navigation in international waterways, and insure that the Sinai desert will not become once again a shelter for Egyptian troops poised against her security.

The West Bank: Israel so far seems to favor the return of the West Bank to Jordanian authority. Apart from minor changes in the borders and the annexation of the old City of Jerusalem, it would seem unlikely that Israel would consider the annexation of the entire West Bank. The implications of such a step are immense. First, Israel cannot hope to annex the area without resistance from the Palestinians and the Arab states. Second, the absorption of more than a million Arab Palestinians (in the Gaza Strip and the West Bank) will endanger Israel's Jewish identity, and would ultimately create two kinds of citizens, an unacceptable situation to both Israelis and Aabs. Third, the West Bank does not have the strategic importance of, say, the Golan Heights, and it is not isolated from the rest of the Arab states. In other words, topographically, the West Bank is almost an integral part of the east bank of the Jordan River. Arab Palestinians live on both sides of the river. The separation of the two would not only be very difficult to institute, but also impossible to implement. A Palestinian entity on the West Bank, however, with the consent of the people, could retain an open economic and social exchange between the sides with the mutual cooperation of Israel and Jordan.

In summation, the present status quo on the West Bank will have to be altered and cannot be maintained indefinitely. The most viable solution to the Arab-Israeli crisis must include a permanent and just solution to the problem of the Arab Palestinians. The viability and life of any agreement between the Arabs and Israel will largely depend on whether or not the Arabs and the Israelis have understood that the continuation of military confrontation is self-defeating and fruitless.

Chapter VIII

CONDITIONS FOR PEACE IN THE MIDDLE EAST

Throughout this book, we have attempted to explain the Arab-Israeli crisis by surveying all the relevant factors that have either contributed to the Arab-Israeli impasse or have paved the way toward a peaceful dialogue in the near future. It should be apparent, therefore, that during the seven decades of Jewish-Arab confrontation, both sides were compelled by general cultural and political circumstances to act as they did. Even today, both are victims of outside forces beyond their control, although present conditions are far more conducive to peace than ever before. A stage of social, economic, cultural, and political "adjustment" was a precondition for peace.

Although the Arab and Israeli leadership throught this period determined to a large extent the direction, pace, and scope of the Arab-Israeli confrontation, the leaders were compelled to submit to the pressures of groups in both camps who were not ready in any fashion to reconcile their differences through negotiation. Thus, the Arab-Israeli confrontation developed to the present mutually recognizable state in which both sides feel equally vulnerable. Their basic differences have reached a conciliatory point whereby *the "imperatives" have evolved into a "choice"; and co-existence is an integral part of that choice.*

Peace between the Arab and the Israeli must be the choice, despite the present danger of renewed large-scale hostilities. If peace is the ultimate and only reasonable option, what types of realistic concessions are required and which can be accepted by both sides? Establishing an independent Palestinian entity is essential to a lasting peace.

Why Peace Must be the Choice

The prolonged Arab-Israeli confrontation has compelled both sides to come to grips with a new reality, but one that is likely to be resisted for some time by the hawkish factions on both sides. Nevertheless, it is a reality that the vast majority of Arabs and Jews cannot ignore any longer: *military means by themselves are not sufficient to produce their desired ends.* Although the military on both sides have played the major role in setting the stage for a peaceful dialogue, the military machines should take a back seat at this juncture and allow diplomacy to consolidate and go beyond the military gains.

Israel and the Arab states have come to recognize that the wars of 1948, 1956, 1967, and 1973 were nothing more than battles in a larger conflict. In all four wars, Israel has not been defeated nor has one Arab state abandoned its implacable opposition toward Israel; the cessation of hostilities was achieved each time by mutual acceptance of a ceasefire imposed by the UN and sponsored by the big powers. The Arabs and the Israelis have never had the opportunity to fight to the end, nor is it likely they ever will. The stake of the superpowers in the Middle East region is so great that continued Arab-Israeli hostilities to the bitter end has become unthinkable and unallowable. Both sides have lost the power to determine their own fates. If either the Arabs or the Israelis had forgotten this, the Yom Kippur War came with a resounding reminder that the days of political independence, especially in foreign affairs, are, in fact, over, if indeed they ever existed.

What would have happened to the Israeli economy had Israel been able, assuming she had the desire, to conquer Damascus and Cairo? How long could the Israelis have held such vast territories without formidable resources of money, manpower, and equipment? Some of these requirements Israel may have been able to mobilize for a certain period of time (probably a month or two); but under no circumstances could it have continued such an effort indefinitely without direct involvement by the U.S. The October war brought Israel to the brink of economic disaster in less than three weeks of fighting. The Israeli economy would have been seriously damaged without the speedy disengagement of her forces from Egypt so that substantial numbers of reserves could be spared to go back to their work!

The Arab states, and Egypt in particular, are very much aware of this Israeli handicap. But they also know that their desire to "wipe Israel off the map" is also unattainable. On this score, the Israeli military plays the primary role. After decades of constant confrontation, and particularly after the war of 1967, the Arab states accepted in principle the reality of Israel. Co-existence became a "necessary evil" to which they were compelled to adjust. The United States' consistent policy of supporting Israel combined with Israel's military and technological superiority were major factors that made possible the tolerance of Israeli existence by the Arabs.

The numerous gaps between the Arab states and Israel have gradually narrowed, and the antagonists have now reached near equilibrium. The need to negotiate as "equals" was a crucial psychological prerequisite to meaningful negotiations. One can negotiate territorial differences, but not issues of national existence or national pride. That is not to say, of course, that the Arab states may not feel compelled in the near future to resort to force to recapture their lost territory. Yet, while the recapture of those territories may be the ultimate goal, the use of force will not by itself accomplish this goal. Renewed warfare would recreate the status of insecurity, danger, and instability that would compel outside powers once again to intervene.

Hence, as long as the U.S. and the USSR can agree in principle that peace in the Middle East serves *their* purposes, neither Israel nor the Arabs will find it practical or advantageous to go totally against the wishes of the superpowers. It would seem that the superpowers are in agreement in this respect, and that they will hold to their position as long as they can retain their influence in the Middle East and extract maximum concessions from each other in other spheres, such as arms limitation troop reduction in Europe, trade, and possibly, disarmament. President Sadat is indeed aware that Egypt is as dependent as Israel on the good will of the superpowers and on their ability to effect a change.

The Arab states failed to stop the Jews and the international community from creating the state of Israel. For the last twenty-seven years, they have also failed to eliminate what has become a recognized political entity, instrumental, at least from the American viewpoint, in stopping or slowing the Soviet expansion in the Middle East. The Arab states had to concede this reality. Now that they appear to be edging toward accepting the existence of Israel, they have set various conditions to announcing it publicly. Although these demands may seem substantial and at times, impossible to meet, both the Arab states and Israel are far more prepared today to reach an agreement than they were a few weeks prior to the Yom

Kippur War. Both sides have been conditioned by circumstances to make greater concessions than might have been thinkable before the conflict. The choice, therefore, is not peace or war, but what concessions must be made to insure a durable peace.

Peace and Concessions: No peace formula can possibly be drawn without major concessions on the part of both sides. In the search for peace, however, Israel is not dealing with a single Arab entity; each Arab state has its own individual requirements. By virtue of their physical proximity, military force, and potentialities, Israel is faced with paramount difficulties, and no set of concessions that she makes to one Arab state is likely to fit or be suitable to another. For this reason, any future peace formula may well be constructed in various stages, to include one Arab state at a time.

Egypt: The key to a lasting peace in the Middle East is an agreement between Israel and Egypt. One of the conditions for the continuation of the present peaceful dialogue between Egyptians and Israelis must be the adherence by both sides to *all* the provisions of the disengagement accords of January 18, 1974 and September, 1975. The explicit fulfillment of the disengagement accord is a crucial test of the intentions of both sides, for unless future negotiations are based on faith and credibility, both sides once again will negotiate out of skepticism, fear, and reluctance, conceding nothing without guarantees of "absolute security." But absolute security for one side, as Kissinger observed, would mean insecurity for the other. Consequently, both sides will go backwards in their negotiations, arguing discrepancies in the compliance with past agreements.

Israel might be willing to withdraw from almost all of the Sinai Peninsula, present statements to the contrary notwithstanding. Some territorial adjustments may have to be made. A compromise at this point might entail Israel's declaration of Egyptian sovereignty over the Sinai, including Sharm el Sheik, in exchange for Israel's maintaining her own residual forces over the Straits of Tiran until normalization of her relationship with Egypt is well-established. The issue of removal of UN forces that would be stationed at Sharm el Sheik along with Egyptian and Israeli forces should be in the hands of the UN Security Council with the consent of the parties involved. The Israeli presence in Sharm el Sheik in this fashion would satisfy Israel's strategic demands, while Egyptian sovereignty over the Straits of Tiran, camouflaging the Israeli military presence and making it less offensive to the Egyptian pride, would satisfy Egypt's known wishes. Such an arrangement will require free passage of all Israeli personnel along a narrow corridor beside the Red Sea.

All these territorial arrangements could be worked out, providing two conditions exist and remain valid. The Sinai Peninsula must be a demilitarized zone whereby the presence of the UN force is irrevocable and does not rest with the host country. And Israel should have the right of passage through the Suez Canal, which would daily symbolize the reality of Egyptian-Israeli peaceful coexistence. In both matters, the Security Council should issue a resolution sponsored by Russia and the U.S. granting Israel free navigation in international waterways. Israel and Egypt only stand to gain by these measures. Israel will be able to disengage from a permanent war footing, while Egypt would recover almost all of its lost territory. Once the territorial issue is settled, diplomatic and commercial relations would follow. Further, it is probable that Egypt will not insist on administering the Gaza Strip. The Egyptian government could be induced to leave the problem of the Strip to negotiations with either the Arab Palestinians or the Jordanians. However, a full-fledged agreement could be reached with Egypt and Israel based on a mutually satisfactory solution with regard to Sharm el Sheik and the Sinai.

An Israeli peace agreement with Egypt might supply the psychological thrust to enable Syria to negotiate with Israel. It is important to understand that the *de facto* separation of Egyptian interests from the other Arab states will discourage extremist Arab countries from initiating any hostilities on their own against Israel. Therefore, the immediate resolution of the negotiations between Egypt and Israel is crucial and should be given top priority. Israeli agreements with the Jordanian, Syrian, or Lebanese governments will come only after an Egyptian-Israeli accord has been achieved. President Sadat will be acting very shortsightedly if he pushes Israel for major concessions on behalf of other Arab states prior to his achieving a settlement with Israel because the peace with Egypt is crucial in Israel's negotiations with the rest of the Arab states. Therefore, Israel will not be apt to concede her control over the various geographical fronts unless a margin of safety is secured first on her southern, most critical frontier. For this precise reason, neither the U.S. nor Egypt should demand from Israel what she cannot deliver. In other words, no Israeli government will be able to make any major concessions on other fronts and remain in power unless some kind of a solid substitute has taken place already.

By the same token, Israel should demonstrate maximum flexibility in her dealings with Egypt. The unilateral thining out of Israeli forces in the Sinai, announced by Premier Rabin, for example is a move in the right direction. The Israeli action was intended to coincide with the Ford-Sadat summit meeting in Salzburg on June 2, 1975, in order to achieve the following: to revamp U.S.-Israeli relations, especially when President Ford himself has embarked upon a new peace offensive; to put to rest the circulated view that it was Israeli intransigence that caused Kissinger to fail in achieving a second partial agreement between Egypt and Israel in March 1975; and finally, to create a new atmosphere that might enhance Israel's position in future negotiations through the mediation of the U.S. The new Israeli-Egyptian interim agreement of September, 1975 was at least in part facilitated by the modified Israeli position.

Syria: The negotiations between Israel and Syria, especially over the Golan Heights, will undoubtedly be the toughest of all. In principle, Syria opposes territorial concessions to Israel in that region. Syria demands absolute sovereignty and is likely to demonstrate impatience while the negotiations with Egypt are going on. Strategically, the Golan Heights constitute Israel's weakest defense link. Thus the Israelis are not likely to abandon the Heights and once again leave their settlements in the Jordan Valley at the mercy of the Syrian generals. The future of the Israeli settlements in the Golan Heights is another stumbling block in addition to the fate of some twenty thousand Syrian farmers who left the region in the wake of the 1967 war.

No easy solution will be found to satisfy the demands of both the Israelis and the Syrians. However, Israel knows that additional territorial concessions on her part are essential in order to reach an agreement with Syria. Despite these obstacles, a Syrian-Israeli accord could follow an Egyptian-Israeli agreement if concessions could be made without Syrian loss of pride or Israeli loss of security.

Israel has already relinquished a stretch of land two to three miles wide along the Golan Heights which was beyond the 1967 cease-fire line as well as her control of Kuneitra and the strategic Mount Hermon. The Syrian government has been able so far to show "political and military gains" over the conditions that existed prior to the October, 1973 war. That is, although the Syrians lost additional territories in the October war, through negotiations (the disengagement accord of June 1974) they were able to regain not only this lost territory but also additional territory lost in the Six-Day War.

Based on the dire need of the Israelis for a total cessation of hostilities, it is possible that Israel would withdraw further from the Golan Heights and leave to Syria a three-to-five-mile stretch of land overlooking Israeli settlements in the Jordan Valley. Declaring its sovereignty over most of the Golan Heights would give Syria an additional boost to her national pride. On the other hand, the Syrians will have to allow limited Israeli forces to patrol the narrow stretch, while UN forces will be stationed in between.

The success of this plan is conditioned on the UN forces having an expanded authority to act as a military barrier and not merely as a symbolic one. Also, the presence of the UN forces should be based on a UN Security Council agreement, such that the veto power of the five permanent members can be exercised. Thus, neither the Israelis nor the Syrians will have any say as to the jurisdiction of the UN forces. Only those Israeli settlements on the Golan Heights that fall within the three to five mile stretch of land should remain; Syrian farmers should take possession of the others. This gesture of goodwill could enhance the prestige of Syrian President Assad and satisfy the "limited" presence of Israeli forces. One other important factor is that the entire buffer zone between the Israelis and the Syrians will have to be demilitarized. And the limitation of the Israeli and Syrian forces should be clearly spelled out, as well as the extent of manpower and the kinds of equipment each side is allowed to have in the area.

Both sides should be able to accept such an accord, to be implemented in stages so that a series of reciprocal acts by each side must always take place prior to the commencement of the next stage. As in the case of Egypt, explicit fulfillment of the Syrian-Israeli disengagement agreement of June, 1974 is especially important in demonstrating good will and a genuine desire to achieve peace.

Jordan: For all practical purposes, peace exists between Israel and Jordan. King Hussein committed himself immediately after the Six-Day War to seek a peaceful solution with Israel. The king's passive stance in the October, 1973 war and his refusal to open a third front against Israel were indicative of his sincerity. Yet Jordan as such cannot be considered an essential party to the Arab-Israeli crisis. The Jordanians have neither lost any of their own territory that was actually Jordan proper, nor have they by and large represented the Arab Palestinian cause, although Jordan has been the only Arab country that opened its doors to the Palestinian Arabs. Yet under the present conditions, many Arab Palestinians will not accept a solution that would link their fate with Jordan.

The separation of the interests of the Arab Palestinians from those of the Jordanians might turn out to be one of the most complicated issues standing in the way of total Arab-Israeli peace. Prior to the 1967 war, before substantial Israeli-Palestinian social and economic intercourse, it might have been conceivable to find a solution to the Arab-Israeli dispute while almost disregarding the Palestinians' immediate interests. However, since the Six-Day War several conditions have arisen that make that solution unacceptable today.

First, the civil war in Jordan in September, 1970 shattered any hope that the Arab Palestinians would view the Jordanian monarchy as their choice for a political and social future. The war made many Palestinians wonder whether their ultimate goal might not be served better by separating Jordanian interests from their own. In my numerous conversations with Arab Palestinians on the West Bank and in the Gaza Strip, I have come to the conclusion that indeed the consensus today among the Arab Palestinians is against the incorporation of their future with that of Jordan. "We are living in our own country," they say. "We have found better ways to make use of our relationship with Israel. Our economic situation has improved substantially since the Israeli occupation. We simply do not want to give that up. That is not to say," they cautioned, "that we prefer to be ruled by the Israelis, but we do not want to go back to Jordanian rule either; it is up to us to determine our future and we expect Israel to help us find this future."

Second, tens of thousands of Arab Palestinian laborers are working today in Israeli factories, institutions, and multi-million dollar projects. Most of these laborers dread the day when their source of livelihood will become unavailable due to certain political arrangements. The West Bank today cannot stand economically on its own. No matter what kind of political settlement is envisioned, I found hardly anybody who would deny the fact that future economic collaboration with Israel is a matter of continual survival.

Third, the conditions of the Arab Palestinians in the Gaza Strip are not much different from those of their counterparts on the West Bank. They, too, have found a new life, due to their ability to travel freely in Israel and the great demands for their skills. Thousands travel daily to Israeli industrial centers and/or agricultural projects and earn wages that they never dreamed of earning before. The Arab Palestinian in Gaza, however, has much less sympathy for Jordan; most of them flatly reject the idea of belonging to one Palestinian Jordanian entity.

Fourth, although the Fedayeen movement has had very little impact on the peace negotiations so far, still the recognition of the PLO by the UN and the Arab states as being the sole representatives of the Arab Palestinians may have separated the Jordanian interests in the West Bank from those of the Palestinian Arabs.

Fifth, over 55% of the Arab Palestinians live today either within Israel or in the occupied territories. The Palestinians have always wanted to remain within their own country. Events have, in effect, created a bi-national country, with social and economic interaction that has proven to be most successful. The only problem is that the Israelis cannot rule the occupied territories while maintaining the present status of the Arab Palestinians, nor can the Arab Palestinians remain under Israeli control indefinitely without having their own political rights. On the other hand, neither Israel nor the Arab Palestinians want to or could give up their present relationship; for the Israelis it is a matter of security tied to economic considerations. For the Arab Palestinians it is primarily a matter of economic livelihood and to a lesser degree, personal security, as they fear renewed hostilities by outside radical Arab groups.

A Palestinian Entity as a Natural Solution

In considering all of the above points, one inescapable conclusion must be drawn. The Jordanian-Israeli dispute is linked directly to the fate and future of the Arab Palestinians, Israel and Jordan have bery little to negotiate about. A solution to the linked problems of the Gaza Strip and the West Bank hinges on a formula that would (a) satisfy the Arab Palestinians, (b) give Israel a greater sense of security, and (c) satisfy the Jordanian government on moral, political, and legal grounds. Thus we find that the *ultimate* and probably the *only* solution to the Palestinian dilemma is a *Palestinian entity* with a political autonomy that would freely be established with the assistance of Israel and the UN, in the West Bank and the Gaza Strip. The participation of the PLO will have to be conditional upon their recognizing Israel's right to exist within secure borders.

It would probably be premature to draw up a specific constitution to which the new suggested Palestinian autonomy should subscribe. It is necessary, however, for the sake of stability, to allow the Arabs in the West Bank and the Gaza Strip to have their say regarding the kind of representatives they want. Therefore, establishing a certain number of constituencies from which representatives are freely elected is essential.

The representatives of the various constituencies could form an assembly, from which an interim executive committee could be elected with a governor at its head. The task of this assembly and committee would be to form the constitution of the new autonomous state, while a two-or-three-party system is developing. After a transition period of three to four years, a new election could be called, with candidates running for office on the basis of party affiliation.

This is, of course, only a general outline of how an autonomous government might eventually develop. The main consideration here is that through the period of transition, the Palestinian governing body should have the help and support of the UN in establishing political institutions free of external pressures.

Security: If this procedure is followed, Israel and the Arab Palestinians will be able to safeguard their interests. Israel should be able to keep most of its settlements in the West Bank and the Gaza Strip, although the Arab governments and particularly the Arab Palestinians might object to this condition.

There is an extremely strong sentiment among the Israelis regarding their settlements on the West Bank. The Orthodox faction as well as the Likud — second largest party — in Israel are not only committed to preserve the Israeli settlements but also to encourage further expansion there.

Yet an agreement on this issue may in the long run serve Arab economic and social objectives. In Israel today there are over 400,000 Arab Palestinians who are Israeli citizens. The presence of civilian Jewish settlements in the midst of an Arab entity will help create a closer relationship, hopefully, between the newly-born state and the state of Israel. The entire economic viability of the new state will largely depend on the degree of Israeli willingness to help support the Palestinians' economic needs. Only through mutual acceptance can economic viability be assured. In addition, the Jewish settlements will give Israel a sense of security that is crucial to her recognition of the national aspirations of the Arab Palestinians; to further enhance the Palestinian-Israeli social intercourse, dual citizenship could be granted the Palestinians living presently in Israel and the Israelis living in the West Bank. Arrangements could be worked out to ensure that the number of those who carry dual citizenship remain limited or proportionate.

Military: The West Bank and the Gaza Strip should be completely demilitarized. Israel should publicly declare her readiness to protect and preserve the new Palestinian state, so that the status quo will remain intact. Such an arrangement, once again, will work in favor of the new state, since it will not have to carry the burden of military expenditures. The fact that Israel's military might commit itself to preserving the territorial integrity of the new state will undoubtedly discourage outside factions from taking any irresponsible action inside or outside the Palestinian state that might affect the political status of the country. (There is also a possibility that the Jordanian government might join Israel in her efforts.)

Once the political situation is stabilized and the region starts to flourish economically, the formation of some sort of confederation between Israel, the Palestinian entity, and Jordan cannot be ruled out. There is no better safeguard to security than mutual need. After ten to fifteen years of cooperation, the Palestinians should be allowed to build up their own limited military forces primarily for internal policing purposes and for the sake of national pride and prestige. Under no circumstances, however, should the new Palestinian entity be allowed by the international community to unite with any Arab country that does not recognize Israel's sovereignty and territorial integrity. Nor would such unity result in a massive stationing of "foreign" military forces from any other Arab country in any form whatsoever.

Economy: The precarious economic condition of the West Bank and the Gaza Strip would compel the new state to continue its economictiese with Israel. The situation today allows thousands of tons of produce and other products to pass over the Allenby Bridge to Jordan. Here again, the Jordanian government must be assured of the continuous supply of food, for unless this is guaranteed, the Jordanians will be very hard pressed on the issue of a Palestinian state.

In due course, Jordan and the Palestinian state may express a desire to freely *unite*. Israel should not stop or discourage such a merger, provided that all the provisions mentioned above remain in force. Palestinian or Jordanian laborers should be welcomed to find work in Israel, yet with the provision that, like in any other country, the Israeli citizen has the priority; only the excess jobs available should be given to the Arabs from the neighboring states.

Secure borders: The establishment of a Palestinian state under similar provisions will undoubtedly make the border adjustments between Israel and the West Bank minimal. Once the Arab Palestinians adhere to the principle of an Israeli presence patrolling the west side of the Jordan River, and accept the presence of some Israeli settlements on the West Bank, the only major part that will remain under Israeli sovereignty will be the Old City of Jerusalem. As indicated before, that aspect of the Arab-Israeli dispute is most likely not negotiable. However, it is certain that major concessions will be made by Israel to insure that the Arabs have complete control over their holy shrines, leaving the door open to the democratic participation of the Israeli-Arab citizen in the administration of a united Jerusalem.

Self-determination: Many factions in Israel and Jordan which have objected to the idea of a Palestinian entity seem to be slowly changing their position. The idea has also been gaining momentum among scores of noted Palestinians and the Arab Palestinian populace at large. Many of them commented to me during a recent visit to the region in April 1975, "The Arab Palestinians are not a commodity to be traded and no Arab state or Israel can determine our fate arbitrarily. We feel that all the Arab states cannot compel Israel to accept any solution, whether of peace or war. We feel that the Arab states have been plotting against us and our future. Therefore, the only solution left to us is a Palestinian state."

Now the Palestinian Arabs are asking to become independent. Their voices are heard in Israel and in Jordan. Neither side can ignore them and decide against the wishes of the people who want to live their own lives after twenty-seven years of anxiety, fear, harassment, and persecution as refugees. Israel will not sacrifice her survival in order to appear humane in the eyes of the international community. Thus, many great concessions will have to be made by *both* sides if peace is to be accomplished. The Arabs and the Israelis are now put to the test.

The fate of the Palestinian refugees in the Arab states: Within this framework of peace, many Palestinian refugees may decide to return home. However, for the next five to ten years, neither the West Bank nor the Gaza Strip can accommodate an uncontrolled influx of immigrants. Yet the whole prospect of Arab-Israeli peace and the rehabilitation of the Palestinian refugees will depend largely on the kind of economic relationship established between the Arab states at large and Israel.

Iraq, Kuwait, and Saudi Arabia will have to apply more flexible policies regarding the admission of Palestinian laborers to their countries. Any serious influx of Palestinian refugees from the Arab countries back to the West Bank or the Gaza Strip is unlikely unless they are assured a source of livelihood. Resettlement of tens of thousands of Palestinian refugees in the Arab states will have to be an integral part of the peace formula. Syria and Egypt as well as Jordan should absorb additional numbers of refugees and encourage other Arab states, particularly the oil-producing ones, to do likewise.

Furthermore, the Arab states, the UN, and Israel should set up a specific program to deal with the resettlement and compensation of thousands of refugees who will most likely choose to settle permanently in the Arab countries. Israel's contribution in this instance should be in terms of technical aid and assistance. Israel's economic situation does not allow her to assume new and vast financial obligations. The Arab states and the Arab Palestinians will have to understand that the principal objective is to solve the problem of the refugees honorably and adequately. Therefore, inflated financial demands from Israel (i.e., on the grounds that the more than 600,000 Jews who left the various Arab countries were forced to leave behind almost all of their tangible assets) cannot be met either. Thus, some give-and-take between both sides would have to be the natural course of negotiations on this issue.

From a political and economic point of view, the aforementioned proposed solution to the Arab Palestinian dilemma might turn out to be extremely beneficial to all three major parties directly concerned — Israel, the Arab Palestinians, and Jordan. Generally, the global need for national identity has been on the rise for decades. Most recently, in Northern Ireland, Cyprus, Bangladesh and Iraq, the internal clashes arose from the desire either to have a separate country or to establish a national identity recognized by the other side. From this perspective, neither Israel nor Jordan would be able to absorb the Arab Palestinians without creating intolerable sociopolitical conditions that might become explosive in a short time. The concentration of Arab Palestinians in Jordan already provides the basis for them to assume control after the eventual departure of King Hussein. Israel, too, must rule out the possibility of absorbing the Palestinian Arabs into her society both for fear of losing her Jewish identiy and for reasons of security. A Palestinian entity, however, would from the beginning set the tone for Palestinian national identity.

Lebanon: The moment Egypt signs a peace treaty with Israel, the Lebanese will very likely follow suit. The only possible issue with Lebanon might be a demand to improve conditions of the Palestinian refugees within her borders. This is precisely why an Israeli-Lebanese peace treaty should be left to the end, for the Palestinian refugee problem is an integral part of every negotiation with all the Arab countries. A peace treaty between Israel and each independent Arab state should include a certain provision on the Palestinian refugees living in the Arab state in question. For only total cooperation between all the Arab states and the Arab Palestinians themselves would make it possible to achieve a resolution acceptable to Lebanon. The only difference in the case of Lebanon, however, is that constitutionally the country is ruled by Arab Moslems and Arab Christians. There is a sort of equilibrium between the two which, despite periodic outbreaks of antagonism has been working fairly well. If the Palestinians living there were granted citizenship they would undoubtedly tilt the social balance in favor of the Moslems, an objectionable possibility to the Christian Arabs. Therefore, a large number of the Palestinian refugees in Lebanon will have to be resettled. Otherwise, the recent mini "Civil War" in Lebanon might turn out to be only the prelude for a major confrontation between the Christians and the Moselms in the near future.

A Word of Caution

The above stated peace formula is not presented in the belief it will be automatically drafted by either the Arabs or Israel, but depends on a high degree of rationality being displayed on all sides for it to be implemented. Unfortunately, rationality does not always prevail in the Middle East, and both Arabs and Israelis may once again fall victim to their unwillingness to compromise. Emotions and prejudice play an influential role, nevertheless, under the present conditions, both sides have grown weary of constant tension, bloodshed, exploitation, fear, and disillusionment.

The Arabs and Jews have long histories of which they are equally proud. In many ways, it influences their present behavior. They possess a formidable degree of drive, vigor, and energy. What is needed today is a period of tranquility and mutual trust, so that these energies may be put to more productive use.

It should be told to the Arabs from the Israeli point of view, that unless they approach the Israeli issue with subtlety and sincerity, and fully relinquish the futile hopes of destroying Israel, the Arabs will be responsible for unleashing the engines of war again. Yet, even if the Arab states could succeed in eliminating every Israeli man, woman, and child, they would still have to face the hundreds of thousands of Jews from all over the world who would devote everything they have, their lives included, to terrorize the Arabs everywhere in the world on such a scale that would make the Fedayeen movement look like child's play. Thus, it is time to become sober, see the political realities as they are, and face them with dignity rather than challenge them on an emotional basis, which would only lead to repeating the cycle of senseless waste and destruction.

To the Israelis, it should be told from the Arab point of view that the mere fact of accepting Israel's existence is extremely painful. The Arab states may not want to reconcile all of their differences with Israel, but they are willing to co-exist with her. Israel can defeat the Arab states on the battlefield a hundred times, but Israel knows and the Arab states realize that in the long-run, the odds are against Israel. Therefore Israel should understand that, especially for the Arab people, pride, honor, and national dignity stand above life itself — they cannot be abdicated, because it is like abdicating life. Although the Arab states say that they will not give up one inch of their territory captured in June, 1967, what they really mean is, they don't want to give up the vast majority of it, but are willing to make some kind of border adjustments. They simply want to make sure that the Israelis don't have or harbor a plan of "Zionist territorial expansionism." So once the Israelis declare the sovereignty of the Arab states over most of the occupied territories, the rest will be negotiable. The Arab states understand the Israeli position on Jerusalem and their concern over the Golan Heights. Even to these complicated issues there must be a satisfactory solution. The Arab states have practically unlimited sources of manpower and finances. They can afford unlimited hardship.

Neither the Arab states nor Israel may be publicly stating these sentiments, but they say them over and over again to themselves, and to visiting foreign political observers. Both sides believe that the only solution that will insure their safety and prosperity is peace, but peace at a price. It is time to start the bargaining. The need for regional cohesiveness and cooperation will eventually open the door for a peaceful dialogue between Israel and most, if not all, of the Arab world.

In conclusion, one cannot rule out the possibility of renewed hostilities. But I would maintain that these will not have any *substantially* different effect on the ultimate peace between the Arab states and Israel. What might drastically change the present condition is a sharp shift either in policy or in intention on the part of the U.S. or the USSR in relation to their clients. The Arabs and the Israelis, however, still have options open and can exercise a certain degree of freedom in their search for a peaceful solution.

Arab and Israeli leadership will have to understand that in the final analysis a sense of a new direction must be instilled among Jews and Arabs alike. A new direction where reason prevails, and where courage is not confused with arrogance, and vigor is not mistaken for audacity. Realistic concessions on the part of each side will not reflect weakness, but courage, farsightedness and vision. This is the task of leadership.

Index

Abn Abi Tarik, Ali, 72
Action Organization for the Liberation of Palestine, 119f
Aflag, Michael, 75f, 76, 81
Al Amari, Fakri, 121
Al Buitar, Salah, 76
Al-Din, Salaeh, 72
Al Fatah, 95, 119, 119f, 120, 121, 122, 123, 126, 129, 138, 140, 140f, 142
Al-Qadhafi, Colonel Mu'ammer, xi, 187
Al Saika, 119, 120, 121, 122, 123
Alami, Mussa, 36, 37
Algiers Summit Meeting, 91
Ali, Anwar, 59
Ali, Rashid, 10
Aliyah, 54
Antonius, George, 12
Arafat, Yasir, 92, 120, 126, 127, 130, 133, 140, 143, 144, 146
Arab League, The, 37, 96
Arab Liberation Front, 119f, 141, 180
Arab Socialist Union, The, 84
Arieli, Yehoshua, 107
Ashkinazi, 45, 46, 47, 48, 49, 54
Assad, Hafez, xxvii, 186, 187, 196, 197, 208

Badeau, John S., 69f, 78f, 80f, 150f, 152f, 153f, 155f, 163f, 175f
Baghdad Pact, 166f
Balfour Declaration, 5, 12
Bar-Lev, General, 137f
Ben-Gurion, David, 12, 36, 93, 94
Black September, 119, 120, 127, 130, 131, 132, 138
Bourguiba, President of Tunisia, 25, 115f
Brezhnev, Leonid, 159, 182
British House of Lords, 10
Burdett, Winston, 18f, 22, 23, 70f, 83f, 86f

Carnegie Endowment for International Peace, The, 101, 102f, 103
Childers, Erskine, 98
Cuban Missle Crisis, 28

Dablan, Colonel Taher, 120

Diaspora, 13, 34
Dulles, John Foster, 163, 165

Eban, Abba, 25, 97, 97f, 98f, 103, 106
Eisenhower, 163, 165, 166, 166f
Elizur, Yuval, 26, 30, 31f
Elon Amos, 4f, 11f, 13f, 17f, 36f, 46f, 49f
Eshkol, Levi, 27

Fedayeen, xxiv, 30, 95, 112, 113, 118-146, 180, 210, 216
Ford, Gerald, ix, 161, 162, 207
Front for the Liberation of Palestine, 119f
Fulbright, William, 185

Ghorbiya, Bahjat Abu, 119f
Ghoury, Emil, 97
Ginsberg, Asher [See *Ahad Ha-am*]
Gorbal, Ashraf, 57, 91
Graubard, Stephen R., 66f
Gromyko, 161

Ha-am, Ahad (Asher Ginsberg), 8
Habash, George, 120, 122f, 124, 138
Hadithi, General Mashur, 129
Hakim, George, 97
Hamady, Sania, 19, 69f
Hammoudia, Yahya, 141f
Hawatmeh, Nayef, 119f
Haydar, Zaid, 119f
Haykal, Hassanein, 23, 25, 29, 92, 132
Herzl, Theodor, 5, 11
Higher Arab Committee, 12, 97
Hourani, Cecil, 25, 40, 41f, 56f, 73f, 77, 78f, 108
Hussein, King, xxvii, 24, 25, 87, 93, 110, 128, 130, 143, 144, 145, 187, 195, 208, 214

International Monetary Fund, 60

Jabotinsky, Vladimir Ze'ev, 10
Jackson, Senator Henry, 175
Jarring, 91
Jewish National Fund, 33, 34, 63
Jibreel, Ahmed, 119f

Johnson, Lyndon, 162, 167
Johnston, Eric, 64f

Kassem, General (also General Qasim), 83, 85, 166f
Kennedy, John F., 28, 162
Kerr, Malcolm, 77f, 80f, 85f, 89f, 101f, 157f
Kibbutz [See Kibbutznik]
Kibbutznik, 44, 124
Kissinger, Henry A., ix, xi, xxiv, 31, 66, 71f, 72f, 143, 151, 151f, 159, 160, 161, 168, 169, 169f, 170, 170f, 171, 172, 175, 176, 177, 182f, 185, 190f, 191, 193f, 205, 207
Knesset, 46, 50
Kosygin, Premier, 167
Krushchev, Premier Nikita, 28

Laffin, 110f, 112f, 121,f, 122f, 131, 131f, 134f, 135f, 136f, 137f
Laird, Melvin, 172
Lewis, Bernard, 15
Likud, 51, 211

Mapai, 50, 51
Marshall, General George, 24
Meir, Golda, 93, 189
Mills, Arthur, 35f
Mohsen, Zahair, 122

Narkiss, General, 136
Nasser, Gamal Abdel, xxviii, 18, 22, 72, 73, 77, 80, 81, 85, 86, 87, 88, 89, 93, 94, 115, 126, 139, 141f, 147, 151, 153, 154, 157f, 166, 167
Nazi Holocaust, 3
Nixon, Richard, 159, 162, 178
North Atlantic Treaty Organization (NATO), xxvi, 150

October War of 1973 [See Yom Kippur War]
OPEC Group, 58, 59

Palestine Arab Organization, 119f
Palestinian Armed Struggle Command (ASC), 123
Palestine Commission of Inquiry, 12
Palestine Liberation Organization (PLO), xxv, 92, 110, 111, 112, 113, 116, 118, 121, 125, 129, 132, 141, 142, 143, 144, 145, 210, 211

Peel, Earl, 12
Polk, William, 42f
Popular Front for the Liberation of Palestine (PFLP) 95, 119, 119f, 122, 123, 124, 126, 130, 131, 138, 140, 180
Popular Liberation Front, 119f
Popular Struggle Front, 119f
Proclamation of Independence, 4, 5, 24, 25
Provisional State Council, 4
Pryce-Jones, David, 96f, 97f, 104f, 105, 105f, 109f, 111f, 113f, 136f

Qasim, General (also General Kassem), 83, 85, 166f

Rabin, 51, 187f, 207
Rees, Dr. Elfan, 102f
Rejwin, Nessim, 76f
Richardson, Dr. Channing B., 102
Rifai Government, 129
Rockefeller, David, 59f
Rogers, William, 27, 168

Sadat, Anwarel, xxviii, 30, 32, 82, 90, 91, 93, 115, 130, 153, 154, 157, 157f, 158, 161, 181, 187, 189, 195, 204, 206
Sakharov, Andrei, 174
Salpeter, Eliahu, 26, 30, 31f
SALT Conference, 172, 176, 178
Sarabi, Hisham, 73
Sartawi, Issam, 119f
Saudi Monetary Agency, 59
Sayle, Murray, 129f
Sephardic, 46, 47, 48, 49, 50, 51, 54, 55, 56, 106
Shukairy, Ahmed, 98, 101, 101f, 141f
Sinai Campaign of 1956, 44, 87
Sirhan Sirhan, 131
Six-Day War of 1967, xxii, xxvii, 3, 26, 30, 31, 89, 90, 92, 108, 112, 114, 115-116, 128, 133 153, 154, 156, 164, 166, 167, 186, 188, 208, 209
Snow, Peter, 125f, 128, 128f
Solzhenitzin, Alexander, 174
Swemer, S. M., 17
Sykes, Christopher, 98
Syrian Ba'ath Party, 75, 76, 119f

Tell, Wasfi, 37, 121, 130

220

Teng Hsiao-Ping, Vice-Premier, 179, 179f
Truman, Harry, 162
Truman Doctrine, 164
Turki Fawaz, 102, 104, 104f, 116f

United Nations Relief and Works Administration (UNRWA), 96f, 102f, 105, 111, 114

Vickers, Ray, 19f, 47f, 59f, 60f

War of Independence, 16

Yazid, Mohammed, 138
Yom Kippur War, xxii, 26, 31, 114, 115, 142, 153, 158, 167, 181, 188, 203, 204-205
Yordim, 53
Young Turks' Revolution, 11
Yost, Charles, 72f, 154f